Reader Reviews of the First Volume of Illuminati (From Amazon)

"I have spent many hours on researching this topic, and Makow has been one of the best sources for information to date. The accuracy and clarity of his writings is remarkable. It's time we found out the truth about the world, the way it's run, and where it's headed. It may be a harsh dose of reality, but "the truth will set us free." Ken (Hong Kong)

"Very informative book! Henry Makow provides an enlightening glimpse at forces and powers that are playing havoc in our world today. He exposes/documents the occult and esoteric "powers-that-be" which for decades, in the cloak of secret societies, have planned for the disintegration of our Christian based society." Alfred (San Diego)

"Henry Makow has put together a collection of profound facts regarding who rules the world. Reading this book will change your outlook and perspective on politics and the deception of voting. Many will find his work offensive; I consider it genius." G. Evans, (Southeast Asia)

This book cuts through all the BS and tells it the way it is. I'm sure there's a campaign to smear the book and the author. If you want to know what's really going on, buy this book. Jack (Huntington Beach)

As the author is Jewish, he can get away with putting some truths out there that others would get branded anti-Semite for doing. It has some horrible truths in it, but it's better to be aware of the Synogogue of Satan than perish for lack of knowledge. EP (Las Vegas)

"A refreshingly welcome aspect of "Illuminati" is in Henry's concise sharp edged writing style, and also in the extensive documentation Dr. Makow provides within the text. It's so jam-packed with hard hitting facts.... John Conner

illuminati 2

Deceit and Seduction

HENRY MAKOW Ph.D.

SILAS GREEN

ILLUMINATI 2

Deceit and Seduction

Special Edition

All Rights Reserved © 2010 by Henry Makow PhD

For information:

Silas Green
PO Box 26041
676 Portage Ave.
Winnipeg MB. Canada
R3G 0M0

hmakow@gmail.com

www.henrymakow.com
www.cruelhoax.ca

ISBN 978-1-61577-145-5

Printed in the USA

Table of Contents

7 **Overture**

9 **Deceit and Seduction — Introduction**

Book One — *Freemasons and Other Shills*

25 Illuminati Founded the US to Advance NWO

28 Freemasons Stage Political Theatre

31 Freemasonry is Based on the Cabala

34 The Boule - The Black "Skull and Bones"

37 Boy Scouts – Model of Masonic Subversion?

40 Is the Pope a Catholic?

44 The Illuminati "Christian" Impostor

46 Bill Gates: Satanist in Sheep's Clothes?

49 Was Michael Jackson an Illuminati Sex Slave?

52 Kevin Annett Rips the Mask from Power

55 When Pedophile Judges Fear Exposure

58 Defector Says Illuminati Sacrifice Children

62 Bohemian Grove: Illuminati Meet for Satanic Rituals

65 Australian Adept Unveiled World Satanic Control

68 Liberals are Unwitting Shills for Communism and Satanism

72 I'm Not on Putin's Bandwagon

75 Crazed MI-5 & MI-6 Wreak Havoc for the Illuminati

Book Two — *Social Engineering and Cultural Subversion*

79 Rockefeller Insider Said in 1969: Travel Will be Made Difficult

82 Psychological Warfare Against Society

86 Bankers Were Behind the Counter Culture

88 The CIA Was Behind Drug Culture

91 Liberal Jews, Sex and the New Satanic Order

93 Porn — Watching Bruised, Drugged Prostitutes

96 Rock Music's Satanic Message

99 Mother's Day Perversion—NBC's "Saturday Night Live."

102 America's Media-Driven Descent Into Depravity

104 Our Leaders Are Sex Addicts

107 Is Pedophilia the Next Frontier?

109 "Times of London" Touts Sibling Incest

112 Charlotte Roche's Mental Breakdown (and Ours)

115 Human Rights- A Higher Form of Discrimination

117 The Truth About "Diversity"

121 Canada Pimps Its Girls to Big Pharma

123 Movie "Avatar," the Illuminati and The Raelian Connection

Book Three — *Judaism, Zionism and Communism*

127 Is Lucifer the God of Judaism?
131 Jews Defined by Occult Ideology, Not Nation/Race
134 Jews Always Exercised Great Power
137 Marranos – The Orignal Crypto Jews
140 Old Testament Believer Was Ostracized by Jews
142 Michael Hoffman's "Judaism Discovered From Its Own Texts"
145 Jews Must Face the "Dark Side" of Judaism
148 Incest Survivor Exposed Illuminati Satanists
151 Robert Edmundson "Testified Against the Jews"
154 Henry Klein – Anti Zionist Martyr
158 Hitler Was a Godsend for Israel
161 Zionism Means Never Saying You're Sorry
164 Zionists Endorse Anti-Semitism
167 NWO : Front for Cabalist Jewish Tyranny
170 USSR - Illuminati Experiment Was A "Social Catastrophe"
173 Will "Lean Years" Lead to Communism?
175 Obama's Jewish Grandfather
178 Obama's Slip Showed His Real Colors

Book Four — *Hidden History*

181 Catholics Unveiled Masonic Jewish Plot in 1936
185 Why the Bankers Love the Left
188 England's Jewish Aristocracy
190 The Dreyfus Affair Was A Rothschild Psy-Op
193 Illuminati Bankers Instigated World War One
195 Was The "Spanish Flu" Epidemic Man-made?
197 The British Agent at Hitler's Ear
200 Martin Bormann was Rothschild Agent — Damning Evidence
204 Did Hitler Betray Rudolf Hess (and Germany)?
207 Were Illuminati Jews Responsible for the Holocaust?
210 Did A Nazi Jew Design the Holocaust?
213 Stalin's Complicity in "Operation Barbarossa"
216 Was the Polish Holocaust Also a Hoax?
219 Katyn: The Story of Heroism Hollywood Won't Tell
223 Hiroshima and the Cold War
225 "Soviet" Agents Designed IMF, World Bank & United Nations
228 The Profumo Affair Exposed Masonic Control
231 Che! The West's Fatal Embrace of Communism
235 Taliban Still Working for the CIA?

Overture

I can clearly remember my reaction at age 19 to a student production of Jean Paul Sartre's play *"No Exit."*

I couldn't understand why Existentialism was all the rage at university.

I had always had an intuition of an inherent moral order in the universe which governs human life. Existentialist plays like "No Exit" promoted the subversive notion that human life was inherently *absurd* and man must invent his own relative meaning.

I didn't know that it was "subversive" then. I never imagined the university was engaged in social engineering. I couldn't conceive that denying God was part of a long-term satanic agenda that had consumed Western civilization like a cancer.

"We must introduce into their education all those principles which have so brilliantly broken up their order." (*Protocols of the Elders of Zion,* 16)

Back in the 1960s, we were made crazy by the media. This hasn't abated. A cultural breakdown is taking place in slow motion.

I was quite lost and confused. Meaning and identity eluded me. But I found a Canadian novelist whose work implied universal design. I devoted my Master's thesis to learning where Frederick Philip Grove found his vision of inherent moral order and purpose.

DYSFUNCTIONAL

Nevertheless, until age 50, I was dysfunctional and often depressed because I took my cues from popular music, TV, movies, newspapers, magazines as well as cultural icons.

Often these cues were subtle. I noticed myself assuming the attitudes of TV announcers. Often their intonation was a clue to the attitude I would assume. For a long time, I held CNN's view of "defenders of family values." I thought they were right-wing kooks. (Now, I'm one.) The liberal media gave me a warm fuzzy feeling. All was right in the world; our leaders were looking out for us.

In my personal life, I sublimated my religious zeal (love of God) into romantic love, and squandered my best decades in the popular cult of beautiful women/sex.

I had imbibed a needy codependence in matters of mating and marriage. I put women, sex and love on a pedestal. At the same time, women were being taught to divert their ambitions from marriage/family to careers. It was a recipe for disaster.

As I approached 50, I started to obey my instincts. I sought a traditional wife and began to challenge feminist assumptions in the classroom. As a result, I encountered the local Illuminati gatekeepers and discovered the conspiracy. It took at least three years to deprogram myself and ten years to see the magnitude of the problem.

THEATRE

The central banking cartel scripts both history and culture according to a long-term plan. Cartel members are generational Satanists, Cabalist Jews and Freemasons. Their object is to induct mankind into their cult as their servants or slaves.

Their main instrument is war which they contrive for profit and power. They engineer a vast credit expansion for war, and later for reconstruction. They are using debt to enslave us like the Jewish moneylenders who plied 19th Century Ukrainian farmers with vodka and loans, and later confiscated their farms.

History is the product of this covert war against humanity. If we come home and find our house ransacked and our possessions gone, we can picture the burglars. They are not choir boys. "Wherefore by their fruits ye shall know them." (*Matthew, 7:20*)

The world is the final confirmation of the Illuminati. In this volume, I connect the dots. I apologize for repetition. Each article was originally a stand-alone.

The Illuminati buy our complicity with our own money. By monopolizing thought and communication, they are able to deceive us.

They took away God so we could not uphold spiritual absolutes. They teach that truth does not exist and everything is relative.

We don't have to play their game. We can uphold God by affirming absolute truth, beauty, justice, peace, grace and love. Of course these are real...the only reality. Look at the consequences of denying them.

For bodily hunger, there is food. For thirst, there is water. Surely, our greatest hunger is for spiritual ideals. And for that there is God.

Mankind's choice is Conversion or Diversion.

Conversion means we uphold God by doing God's work.

Diversion means we continue to distract ourselves and lead false, tedious and trivial lives.

Introduction

The devil conquers by deceit and seduction. And so mankind has been colonized by a satanic cult, not just physically but mentally and spiritually. We have been deceived in the most egregious fashion, and seduced by money and sex.

We generally think of the "conspiracy" as limited and definable. In fact, our world is the product of an ancient diabolical conspiracy that inverts good and evil. The conspiracy is based on a satanic hatred for God and man partly originating in the Talmud and Cabala. (Judaism long ago turned its back on the Old Testament, and used it and Torah Jews as a false front.)

Earth Colonized by Satanic Cult

These satanic Jews and their satanist gentile collaborators are joined by Freemasonry in the Illuminati. They hate humanity. This hatred has been institutionalized in the routine of war, poverty and depression we now take for granted.

As a result, mankind is dysfunctional. Since the so-called "Enlightenment," Western civilization has been based on a foolhardy denial of the Creator i.e. the inherent design and purpose governing human life.

Not coincidentally, the "Enlightenment" roughly coincides with the establishment of the Bank of England in 1694 by Illuminati bankers, and the subsequent spread of Freemasonry throughout Europe. Freemasonry became the "in" thing for aristocrats and free thinkers, as well as industrious young men on the make.

Freemasonry disguised its worship of Lucifer with specious platitudes like "liberty, fraternity, equality," "tolerance"of anything opposed to the established order, and a blustery faith in humanity, "reason" and "progress."

According to the American "Grand Commander" Albert Pike, the Masonic rank and file are "intentionally misled by false interpretations." (*"Morals and Dogma,"* 1871, p.104)

Controlled by the Illuminati bankers, Freemasonry is the unacknowledged power behind the modern world. Historian Bernard Fay writes: "Freemasonry has become the most efficient social power of the civilized world. But it has been a hidden power, difficult to trace and to define. Consequently most historians have avoided treating it and giving it due credit." ("*Revolution and Freemasonry, 1680-1800,*" 1935, viii)

Bernard Fay shows that the Illuminati bankers used their Masonic dupes to establish the US as a future base for world domination. George Washington, his generals and the signatories of the Declaration of Independence were all Masons. Master Mason Benjamin Franklin raised the money to finance the war from bankers in Paris. (pp. 237-261; see article within, "Illuminati Bankers Founded the US to Advance NWO" within.)

SATANIC POSSESSION

Illuminati bankers finagled control of government credit and created money out of nothing backed by our taxes. They thought this gave them the right to be God and redefine reality to serve their interests and whims. "Modernity" is nothing but the dysfunction and alienation caused by this solipsistic delusion.

The central bankers need a totalitarian world government to protect their credit monopoly. They need this mechanism to prevent countries from defaulting on trillions in "debt" or creating their own debt-free and interest-free money. Modern "civilization" is a fraud based on this one underlying fraud.

Thus, the Illuminati bankers finance and promote every kind of occult, criminal and perverted behavior, for pleasure, profit and to complete the overthrow of Western (Christian) civilization. According to a speaker at a secret B'nai B'rith meeting in 1936, "As long as there remains among the Gentiles any moral conception of the social order, and until all faith, patriotism and dignity are uprooted, our reign over the world shall not come." (See article "Catholics Unveiled Masonic Jewish Plot" within.)

The human experiment is doomed to failure because human beings were too corrupt or feckless to ensure that their governments retained control over their own credit.

MASONIC MATRIX

Freemasonry is Judaism for Gentiles, a way for the Cabalistic Jewish elite to enlist Gentiles in their conspiracy. The Illuminati is an elite secret society within Freemasonry. The "Enlightenment" refers to Lucifer, the rebel angel and "light bringer."

The bankers promoted the "great men" of the modern world. Their ultimate purpose is to redefine reality in such a way as to wrest humanity away from God and make it subservient to them.

"Think carefully of the successes we arranged for Darwinism, Marxism, Nietzsche-ism," the author of the *"Protocols of the Elders of Zion"* chortles. "To us Jews, at any rate, it should be plain to see what a disintegrating importance these directives have had upon the minds of the goyim." (2-3.)

Freemasonry is the secret "religion" of the modern world. That's why its obelisks and other symbols dot our cities and are featured on the logos of cities and corporations. The civic logo for Ottawa, the capital of Canada, is an O with three tails --- 666, sign of the devil. In front of the main police station on College Street in Toronto, there is a statue of a policewoman working on an unfinished pyramid! The logo for Time Warner Inc. is a variation on the Eye of Horus. (See http://www.oknation.net/blog/print.php?id=292518)

There is always a cover story for satanic signs. The "V" sign for which Churchill is famous actually is the satanic "upside-down-cross." For people in the know, Churchill was signalling fealty to the New World Order. The real purpose of World War Two was to destroy the old order.

Mankind indeed is satanically possessed, victim of a monstrous hoax. Gradually, we are all being inducted into Satanism. We are accomplices in own degradation and enslavement. We don't know it because the Illuminati choose our leaders from the ranks of dupes, degenerates and traitors.

MY ENLIGHTENMENT

About ten years ago, my paradigm began to change when I realized that the government, media & education were actively sabotaging society. I had imbibed feminist and Illuminist propaganda (i.c. "scxual libcration") and was confuscd and dysfunctional. The attack on gender had me stymied as a man. When I couldn't question feminist shibboleths in a university setting, I knew something was fundamentally wrong.

Until this recognition, I had seen government, education & media as relatively open, benign and democratic. I attributed war to conflicts of interest between classes, nations, races and religions. Evil was unorganized, a default mode due to human fallibility. History was determined by "great" men. I was involved in the political process.

The atrocities of 9-11 and the bogus "war on terror" revealed that evil is in fact deliberate, highly organized and centralized in the hydra headed central banking cartel. History is not accidental but the product of a planned long-term satanist conspiracy to degrade and enslave humanity. Great men are mostly puppets, i.e. banker front-men.

They want us to believe wars are caused by nations, races and religions in order to dissolve these collective identities and create one homogeneous mass, easier to control.

We are supposed to be like children and leave important decisions to them. We are being infantilized. For e.g. Hollywood movies were based on novels; now, they're based on comic books. A quarter of the viewers of the top cable cartoon "SpongeBob SquarePants" are adults who don't have children.

Expelled from the university for questioning feminism, I took my course to the Internet. My writing is dedicated to the "new paradigm," unearthing information about the Illuminati conspiracy and showing how it is unfolding in our midst.

"SUPERSTITION"

Naturally, they must disparage real religion and God as "superstition." This is because God speaks to us through our conscience and soul and is the principle of our development. We are not going to be docile animals if we are listening to our conscience.

God is the ultimate (and only true) Reality, a state of being in which ideals of absolute goodness, truth, justice, beauty and love are self-evident. They don't want us to know that.

Man is a soul that naturally craves and strives for this state of being. God wants to know Himself through us. This requires us to change by refining our carnal instincts in the foundry of the soul.

Whatever Christianity's faults, it was about making spiritual reality paramount, saving our soul by obeying God and doing good.

God isn't consistent with two percent of the world's population owning more than 50% of the wealth.

So the bankers replaced God with Money, which they create and control. We will obey bankers instead and find salvation in money.

The bankers want to arrest our development. They want us to worship Lucifer who symbolizes their rebellion against God, nature, and all that is healthy and good.

THE FAUX SOCIETY

Almost everything that happens in the world is designed to uphold Luciferian reality and initiate us into Satanism. They always seize control of the mass media in order to replace the truth with a facsimile.

Society simulates reality. Our institutions pay lip service to their stated goals. Our governments represent the bankers not the people. Our schools indoctrinate us. Our newspapers manipulate and deceive us. Our entertainment distracts and degrades us. The forms remain the same; the content is subtly perverted.

For example, Paul Craig Roberts, a former US Assistant Secretary of the Treasury, and Editor at *The Wall Street Journal* wrote in March, 2010: "The American corporate media does not serve the truth. It serves the government and the interest groups that empower the government."

The Illuminati depends on second-rate people to betray their neighbours and country. This is the "Nomenklatura" -- the term given to the Soviet-era bureaucratic elite. Most of our "leaders" fall into this category. But they always hide behind a layer of dupes who help maintain the fiction by virtue of their own innocence.

It seems that Freemasonry is the Nomenklatura of the West. Challenge their bogus "reality" and your career is over. If a politician or mainstream reporter questions the official 9-11 story, he is swarmed by banker attack dogs. Question their social engineering – vaccines, "diversity" or "sexual harassment" training – and your career is likewise in jeopardy.

DECEIT

Our "watchword is force and make-believe," the *Protocols* say. "Make believe" means deception. They control us with their lies.

They lie to us us about everything. In 1954, the US Congress Reece Committee accused the banker-funded foundations of "social engineering" the American people. For example, history is really the story of the Illuminati conspiracy but our historians are well paid to hide this fact.

The Carnegie Endowment gave the American Historical Association a grant to propose that the US would be best served by a "collectivist" form of government. They also studied the question: "If it is desirable to alter the life of an entire people, is there any means more efficient than war to gain that end?" (Google "The Enemy Within: The Hidden Agenda Of The Rockefeller, Carnegie & Ford Foundations")

If you Google "George Soros- Funded Communist Organizations," you will find a list of 100 groups engaged in Illuminati mind control and "social change."

A 2009 article at the *Huffington Post* explained how the central bankers took over the study of Economics. This is a template for what has happened in every profession and organization, including government, media and education.

"The Federal Reserve, through its extensive network of consultants, visiting scholars, alumni and staff economists, so thoroughly dominates the field of economics that real criticism of the central bank has become a career liability for members of the profession, an investigation by the *Huffington Post* has found."

"The Fed has a lock on the economics world," says Joshua Rosner, a Wall Street analyst who correctly called the credit meltdown. "There is no room for other views, which I guess is why economists got it so wrong." ("Priceless: How the Fed Bought the Economics Profession," Sept. 9, 2009)

ORIGINS OF THE ILLUMINATI

As I explained in my first volume, the Illuminati was renewed in 1776 by the Rothschild banking syndicate and officially took over Freemasonry in the 1780's. The Jewish bankers belonged to a secret satanic Jewish sect, the Sabbatean-Frankists, who were characterized by their "liberated" sexual practises, incest, pedophilia etc. They believed the Messiah would return only when the world descended into sin and chaos. They would advance this process.

Politically, they were chameleons, intermarrying and infiltrating every other group. On both sides of every conflict, they initiated the wars and revolutions that have convulsed mankind. They could mouth any ideology and religious belief. Their only goal was taking power.

The Sabbateans were predated by different Illuminati manifestations which date back to the ancient mystery religions of Egypt and Babylon. They bred in a culture that required wealthy Jewish money lenders, war provisioners, merchants and traders, as well as Cabalist "wise men" i.e. sorcerers.

To trace their activities from ancient times to the present would involve years of research. But I'll give you the sense of the scale.

Jewish bankers and merchants always had a dominant role in world trade and commerce. They would build their country of residence into an instrument of their world domination. They would play off competing powers in self destructive wars. Then, when it was convenient or necessary, they would abandon their country for a more effective vehicle.

Since the Seventeenth Century, British Imperialism has been the mainstay of Illuminati Jewish world domination. They built up Germany in the Nineteenth Century and then used it to stage two world wars. At the same time, they shifted their base to the USSR and the US and had a very profitable Cold War. Now they are using Israeli imperialism to foment a world war with Iran and her backers China and Russia. They seem gradually to be undermining America with a goal of shifting power to world government institutions under their control.

MIDDLE AGES

They sold out Christian Spain to the Moors in the 8th Century and administered it for the Moors until the 13th. Then, they made themselves indispensable again to the Spanish Christians until they were expelled in 1492. Many remained in Spain as false converts or "Marranos."

In his biography *"Philip II,"* Thomas Walsh noted the presence of a cult called the "Alumbrados" (translated "Illuminati") in 16th Century Spain: "They were engaged in a wholesale campaign of defamation against the clergy and the Church, of seduction of rich widows, the compromising of young girls in nocturnal orgies, assassination, and all manner of subversive activity."

When Vasco da Gama discovered the sea route to the Far East in 1500, the Jewish merchant class shifted their focus to the Atlantic seaports. Many Marranos settled in the Spanish Netherlands and, according to Walsh, made "Antwerp the centre of world trade and finance in less than a generation."

Concurrent with Spain, Jewish bankers and merchants were prominent in Venice from the 12th to 17th centuries. Venice's wealth was built on trade with the Orient, piracy and slavery. It became an imperial power following the Venetian-financed Fourth Crusade, which seized and sacked Constantinople in 1204. They conspired with the Mongols to invade Christian Europe and were a factor in the Mongol destruction of Baghdad in 1258. They played England off against France in the Hundred Year War 1339-1453.

When the Christian Byzantine Empire had recovered, the Venetians outfitted and financed the Turks who laid siege to Constantinople capturing it in 1453. The French ambassador to the Holy Roman Empire described the Venetians as "traders in human blood, traitors to the Christian faith, who have tacitly divided up the world with the Turks, and who are planning to reduce Europe to a province and keep it subjugated to their armies..."

With the sea route to the Orient, the Venetians prepared to transfer their interests to the Netherlands and England. They befriended Henry VIII (1491-1547) and dangled the comely Anne Bollyn before his eyes. They encouraged him to divorce his Christian wife Catherine of Aragon and break with the Catholic Church in what became the English Reformation.

[A speaker at the 1936 secret B'nai Brith Conclave in Paris said: "We are grateful to Protestants for their loyalty to our wishes - although most of them are, in the sincerity of their faith, unaware of their loyalty to us. We are grateful to them for the wonderful help they are giving us in our fight against the stronghold of Christian Civilization, and in our preparations for the advent of our supremacy over the whole world and over the Kingdoms of the Gentiles."]

Venetian (Illuminati) agents like Thomas Cromwell, William Cecil, John Russell and Thomas Gresham founded their family fortunes on Church property confiscated under Henry VIII. Their heirs worked with Jewish bankers based in Amsterdam and Antwerp to build England into a great naval power and to engineer the English Revolution (1640-1660,) the Glorious Revolution (1688) and finally the Bank of England (1694.) (My source for the above is Alan Jones' summary of Thomas Walsh's *"Philip II"* and Webster Tarpley's *"Against Oligarchy"* in *"Secrecy or Freedom"* pp. 203-272.)

These families became the shareholders of the Bank of England and the core of the Illuminati. How many were crypto Jews is unknown. In any case, the Illuminati intermarry with other generational Satanists. It's no coincidence that Chelsey Clinton married a Jewish investment banker, while Karenna Gore married the grandson of one.

Venice was an oligarchy ruled by a "Council of Ten" which consisted of the richest families. The Council met in secrecy. Its dictates were executed by the Doge who was a figurehead. This was the model they chose for England and the New World Order. The "Crown" refers to the secret oligarchical families who own the central banks. The Crown and the Illuminati are practically synonymous.

MODERN TIMES

In 1852, the Chancellor of the Exchequer, William Gladstone said: "The government itself was not to be a substantive power in matters of Finance, but was to leave the Money Power supreme and unquestioned." (325)

Georgetown University Professor Caroll Quigley included the following families in the Money Power: "Baring, Lazard, Erlanger, Warburg, Schroder, Selingman, the Speyers, Mirabaud, Malet, and above all Rothschild and Morgan." (Citations are from *Tragedy and Hope: A History of the World in Our Time*," 1966, 51-55)

Quigley, an Illuminati insider, confirmed that the bankers charged their respective nations billions in interest for using currency backed by the nations' own credit. Governments could have created their own currency and not worried about repaying the debt or interest since it would be owed to themselves.

[*The Protocols of Zion* marvelled at how stupid Gentiles are: "How clear is the undeveloped power of thought of the purely brute brains of the goyim in the fact that they have been borrowing from us...without ever thinking that these moneys [plus interest] must be got by them from their own state pockets in order to settle up with us. What could have been more simple than to take the money they wanted from their own people?" (XX)]

In 1924, Reginald McKenna, Chairman of the Board of the Midland Bank, told his stockholders: "'I am afraid the ordinary citizen will not like to be told that the banks can, and do create money. They who control the credit of the nation direct the policy of Governments and hold in the hollow of their hands the destiny of the people.'" [25]

Creating money out of nothing, the Illuminati bankers naturally grabbed much of the world's real wealth. Quigley described the formation of their American cartels: "The period 1884-1933 was the period of financial capitalism in which investment bankers moving into commercial banking and insurance on the one side, and into railroading and heavy industry on the other were able to mobilize enormous wealth and wield enormous economic, political and social power." (71)

Indeed, their representatives, the "Eastern Establishment" (i.e. the Morgans and now the Rockefellers) control the United States through the Council on Foreign Relations.

According to Quigley, the ultimate goal is "nothing less than to create a world system of financial control in private hands able to dominate the political system of each country and the economy of the world as a whole. This system was to be controlled ...by the central banks...acting in concert." (324)

CONTROLLING ALL SIDES

Quigley confirmed that the bankers have usurped mankind's collective instincts by financing the Socialist and Communist movements. Bankers love big government because the ultimate monopoly is the State which they control.

Speaking of the Communist takeover of the US government in the 1930's and 1940's, Quigley writes, "It must be understood that the power that these energetic left-wingers exercised was never their own power, or Communist power, but was ultimately the power of the international financial coterie." (954)

In other words, millions of idealists committed to brotherhood and social justice were (and are) duped into concentrating the world's wealth and power into the hands of the super rich. Opportunistic Leftists, Communists, feminists and globalists prosper while piously pretending to serve humanity. Similarly, the power of Zionism, Masonry and Jewry derives from being Illuminati banker pawns.

The Money Power controls the debate and encourages gridlock by backing all shades of the political spectrum and marginalizing anyone who disagrees with them.

Quigley writes: "To Morgan, all political parties were simply organizations to be used, and the firm always was careful to keep a foot in all camps. Morgan himself, Dwight Morrow and other partners were allied with the Republicans; Russell C. Lewffingwell was allied with the Democrats; Grayson Murphy was allied with the extreme Right; and Thomas W. Lamont was allied with the Left." (945)

The Lamont family was "sponsors and financial angels to almost a score of extreme Left organizations including the Communist Party itself." (945)

Google "US Corporate Elite Funds Radical Left & Islam" to bring this practice up to the present.

STATE OF DENIAL

The Illuminati conquest is so subtle most people are unaware of it. They have been trained to scoff at "conspiracy theories" and to think their interests are being served.

The blueprint of the New World Order has been available since 1905 yet the gullible believe it is a hoax ("forgery.") Perhaps people who ignore a mortal danger, even when it is presented in no uncertain terms, deserve their fate. (I discuss the provenance of the *Protocols* in my first Volume.)

The first chapter of the *"Protocols of the Elders of Zion"* contains the beliefs, goals and methods of this diabolical conspiracy. The whole blueprint can be had in five pages!

"How can they fight an invisible force?" the *Protocols* chortle. "We will remain invisible until [our conspiracy] has gained such strength that no cunning can any longer undermine it." (I-14)

The Illuminati bankers have been visible for over 100 years but the feckless goyim have failed to mount any serious resistance. Even Hitler was controlled opposition. (See *Protocol* 9: "Nowadays, if any State raises a protest against us, it is only pro forma, at our discretion and at our direction...")

The issue of anti-Semitism is a red herring used to change the subject from this mortal threat to anti-Semitism. The majority of Jews, like Masons know nothing of this plot. All groups are manipulated. A distinction must be made between individual Jews, who should be judged on an individual basis, and their corrupt leadership. The same applies to all peoples.

THE ILLUMINATI BELIEVE IN (DEFYING) GOD

Through their cultural agents, the Illuminati bankers have taught us that God doesn't exist.

The Illuminati, however, believe in God. They are smart enough to understand that "God" represents the Instruction Manual, the spiritual (moral) and natural laws governing human life and development.

They know the difference between right and wrong but they are Luciferians. They deliberately flaunt morality. They distort reality by identifying "good" with their lust for power.

"Might makes Right," they say. "The end justifies the means." They care "not so much with what is good and moral as to what is necessary and useful." (I-17)

Similarly, they recognize the Laws of Nature but spread dysfunctional "feel-good" ideologies like liberalism to sabotage the goyim.

The goy intellectuals "did not see that in nature there is no equality; [and] there cannot be freedom; that Nature herself has established inequality of minds, of characters, and capacities...[they] never stopped to think that the mob [i.e. democracy] is a blind thing..."(I-25)

The goal is to subjugate the human race to an "unshakeable rule,"(I-16] to "bring all governments into subjection to our super-government." At some point, they will be merciless and "all disobedience will cease." (I-24)

Ultimately, their aim is to dispossess the vast majority: "In politics we must know how to seize the property of others without hesitation if by it we secure submission and sovereignty." (I-23)

This has been their plan since "ancient times." They must stick to it or see "the labor of many centuries come to naught." (I-17)

METHOD

They promoted "democracy" to transfer power from the old order – hereditary aristocracy and church – to "the power of Gold"...the "despotism of capital, which is entirely in our hands."

"The abstraction of freedom has enabled the mob to persuade itself that their government is nothing but the steward of the people who are the owners of the country (sic), and that the steward may be replaced like a well worn glove." This has given us "the power of appointment."

Their power is based on using money and ownership of the mass media to elect traitors and collaborators, people "willing to sacrifice the welfare of all for the sake of securing their own welfare." (I-3)

"Our triumph has been rendered easier by the fact that in our relations with the men whom we wanted, we have always worked upon the most sensitive chords of the human mind, upon the cash account, upon the cupidity, upon the insatiable desire for the material; and each one of these human weaknesses taken alone, is sufficient to paralyse initiative, for it hands over the will of men to the disposition of him who has bought their activities." (I-28)

This applies to every US President with the exception of those who were poisoned or assassinated.

The new order will be created when the old one descends into chaos. They sponsor a cacophony of voices so the truth is drowned out. They sponsor both sides of gratuitous conflicts in order "to exhaust humanity with dissension" until the goyim have no recourse but to "take refuge in our complete sovereignty in money and in all else." (X-19)

CORRUPTION AND DECADENCE

Similarly, the bankers foster social malaise and moral degradation. "Anti-Semites" have always accused Jews of corrupting society.

"The goyim are bemused with alcoholic liquors; their youth has grown stupid on classicism and early immorality in which our special agents have inducted them..by tutors,.. by our women in places of dissipation..." (I-22)

The Illuminati bankers financed intellectuals who recommended ways to weaken society. In a perceptive article, "The Frankfurt School: Conspiracy to Corrupt," Timothy Mathews listed their recommendations, made over 50 years ago. Members of this school were all Marxist Jews, some Soviet NKVD agents. How many of these recommendations look familiar?

1. The creation of racism offences.
2. Continual change to create confusion
3. The teaching of sex and homosexuality to children
4. The undermining of schools' and teachers' authority
5. Huge immigration to destroy identity.
6. The promotion of excessive drinking
7. Emptying of churches
8. An unreliable legal system with bias against victims of crime
9. Dependency on the state or state benefits
10. Control and dumbing down of media
11. Encouraging the breakdown of the family

One of the main ideas of the Frankfurt School was to exploit Freud's idea of 'pan sexualism' - the search for pleasure, the exploitation of the differences between the sexes, the overthrowing of traditional relationships between men and women. To further their aims they would deny the specific roles of father and mother, and wrest away from families their rights as primary educators of their children.

The Frankfurt School were an Illuminati instrument that focused on using "cultural revolution" to destroy society from within. They saw it as a long-term project and focused on the family, education, media, sex and popular culture. We can see the evidence everywhere.

DEHUMANIZE USING SEX

The Illuminati engage in sexual rituals associated with group sex, homosexuality, bondage, incest and pedophilia. They induct us into their satanic cult by initiating us in these practices using pornography, mass media and public school education.

To the objection that society, in fact, is vehemently opposed to incest and pedophilia, it is merely a matter of time. Look at the things society used to censure or prohibit: homosexuality, pornography, public obscenity, promiscuity, pre marital sex, extramarital childbirth etc.

Throughout the modern period, sex was portrayed as a panacea. Sexual liberation was cool and advanced. Monogamy was prudish. Porn was made widely available. Now millions of people are addicted to sex and human relationships are reduced to "hot or not?"

"Sex is the ultimate weapon in people-taming and people control." Sociologist Erica Carle writes.

"When sex can be established as a constant in the mind, as the dominant idea... the mind can be incapacitated. The emotions destroyed, personal identity, individuality, family life, maternal and paternal feelings, all eroded. All else can be forgotten or regarded as unimportant, when the mind is captured by the dominant idea of sex."

The Illuminati are a homosexual cult. Now, like homosexuals, we have anonymous "hook up" sex but not families. Party lines and websites for anonymous sex are widespread.

In 1973, the Rockefellers ordered the American Psychological Association to change the definition of homosexuality from a disorder to a normal lifestyle choice. If you google "Rockefeller Foundation" and the APA, you'll get about 70,000 links, showing how bankers buy "scientists" by the tonne.

Criticism of homosexuality is banned as "hate" and media portrayals of gays are airbrushed and sugar coated. Schools teach children that gender is merely a social construct and they should experiment with gay sex. MTV pushes videos like "I Kissed a Girl" by Katy Perry.

[In a 2008 interview with Al Jazeera TV, MTV CEO Bill Roedy admitted the network, which reaches two billion people in 164 countries, is dedicated to "behavioural change." A former US Army Ranger, Roedy said music elicits "an emotional response that sometimes is stronger than political leadership, even religious leadership."]

In general, the Illuminati engages in every form of depravity: incest, pedophilia, group sex, bestiality, trauma brainwashing (torture), and human ritual sacrifice. Many of our so-called leaders are chosen and controlled this way.

Very young children are used by high Freemasons. The porn consumer is literally watching 'Masonic ritual' on camera, all based on fear, hatred, secrecy, shame, excrement, drugs, degradation and filth. He is being inducted into a satanic cult and doesn't even know. I suspect many "horror" movies have the same effect.

WE ARE ALL ACCOMPLICES

The Illuminati have so pervaded the social fabric that society is complicit in its own destruction. Svali, an Illuminati defector, estimated that there are a million Illuminati members in the US alone, and the vast majority are not Jewish.

Paul Drockton, another whistle blower, said the Illuminati cult is organized on the international, national, regional, and local levels. At the local level, you have a "cell," "family," or "coven" normally composed of 13 individuals. Each cell has a "Father" who also serves as the High Priest or "Director" and a "High Priestess" or Mother. Everything is coordinated and well organized.

The Illuminati is like the Pied Piper of Hamelin, and we are like the rats, mesmerized and led to our demise.

Every day, we hear about governments "borrowing" billions in order to stimulate the economy. Does anyone in public life ask who has this kind of money to lend? Is it created out of thin air? (Then, we will repay it the same way.)You'd think that would be pertinent.

The question is never raised because everyone in a position of influence has a stake in the Rothschild's fraud. Organized Jewry and Freemasonry are the most prominent stake-holders but it includes every government, religion, corporation, church, charity, NGO, university or organization of significance. People find the money like ants find jam.

In the words of a speaker at the secret B'nai Brith meeting in Paris in 1936: "Yet it remains our secret that those Gentiles who betray their own and most precious interests, by joining us in our plot should never know that these associations are of our creation and that they serve our purpose...

"One of the many triumphs of our Freemasonry is that those Gentiles who become members of our Lodges, should never suspect that we are using them to build their own jails, upon whose terraces we shall erect the throne of our Universal King of Israel; and should never know that we are commanding them to forge the chains of their own servility to our future King of the world."

Our civilization is leaderless and committed to its own demise. This is portrayed as "progress" (which it is for the Illuminati.)

SEPT 11, 2001: COMPLICTY IN THE COVER UP

Again, on Sept 11, 2001, over 3000 Americans were murdered while the symbol of American free enterprise was demolished. Was anyone ever held responsible or fired for this gross breach of security?

No. Because it was executed by the Illuminati-run intelligence services, Mossad and CIA. Can you imagine the degree of treasonous collaboration required? Has anyone in the mainstream media questioned the official story?

Has anyone demanded to know why the 47-floor WTC-7 was pre-wired for demolition on Sept. 11?

Like the twin towers, it was a controlled demolition. The owner, Larry Silverstein, an Illuminati Jew, admitted it. It was not hit by a plane. Are we supposed to believe this building was demolished, but the Twin Towers weren't?

In terms of the cover up, the media establishment is guilty of a criminal offence: "Accessory after the Fact." Society is in a state of denial about the real forces controlling it, a cognitive dissonance that amounts to collaboration.

What made the Illuminati think they could get away with 9-11? They have pulled off many bigger crimes. They engineered two world wars, the Cold War, the Korean and Vietnam wars, not to mention the Iraq and Afghan wars.

All the so-called terror attacks are executed by intelligence agencies. That's why they knew that Joe Stack, who crashed his plane into an IRS sub station in Austin, was not a terrorist. They plan the *real* terrorist attacks.

The only "terrorists" they fear are members of an enraged and dispossessed public, some time in the future. The "underwear bomber" of Christmas Day 2009 was put on the plane by an intelligence agent. The State Department acknowledged the bomber himself was an intelligence asset. (Google: "The Truth About Flight 252" by Kurt Haskell.)

The masses ignore the evidence of conspiracy. Again, it's in the *Protocols*: "The masses are accustomed to listen to us only who pay it for obedience and attention. In this way, we shall create a blind mighty force which will never be in a position to move in any direction without the guidance of our agents...The people will submit to this regime because it will know that upon these leaders will depend its earnings, gratification and the receipt of all kinds of benefits." (X)

There are hundreds of universities offering thousands of courses but the conspiracy paradigm is not among them. The true consciousness of humanity is kept alive by a few score private scholars who are like monks in the Dark Age.

END THE FRAUD

Humanity's problem is systemic and can't be solved while our leaders are creatures of the system. Our focus must be on changing the system, i.e. nationalizing the central banks and renouncing that portion of the debt created out of thin air. Any person, politician or pundit who disagrees is part of the system.

The system provided widespread prosperity in order to consolidate its power. Now, it's moving gradually to the next stage: absorbing all wealth and enslaving the masses (under the pretext of debt and war on terror.)

The Achilles's heel of the system is its dependence on unwitting agents and dupes. Our role now is to educate these dupes and detach them from Illuminati ranks. As things get worse, they will become disillusioned and look for explanations.

Any mass organization we set up will be infiltrated and subverted. It will become mired in leadership disputes. Thus, we must act in very small informal groups and as individuals to spread the message. We should support each other and eschew internecine feuds by focusing on what we have in common.

FINALLY

The arc of Western civilization has gone from the worship of God (rise) to the worship of Satan (decline.) We become what we worship.

In the rise, mankind learned to mortify his carnal instincts and obey his spiritual ideals. In the decline, the Cabalists taught us that this is "repression," and that we must be "liberated."

Millions of people have gone over to the Dark Side. They have taken over the levers of financial and political power and are using it to subvert society, one person at a time. We must alert people to the danger they face.

Man was created in the image of God. Our spiritual aspirations define us as human. Now that we understand what is happening, and what is at stake, we can keep God's vision for man alive in the difficult times ahead.

BOOK ONE

Freemasons and Other Shills

Illuminati Founded the US
to Advance New World Order

Most Americans scoff at the mention of conspiracy but their country was created by Freemasonry and they don't have a clue. Freemasons drafted the Constitution and signed the Declaration of Independence. Masons disguised as Indians dumped the tea in Boston harbor. Paul Revere and his Minutemen, George Washington and most of his generals, all were Masons. The Marquis de Lafayette was shunned until he was initiated. At least 20 of the 42 US Presidents were "Brothers."

Freemasonry is the Church of Lucifer masquerading as a mystical philanthropic order. It fronts for Illuminati (Masonic & Cabalist Jewish) central bankers who started the US as a vehicle to advance their New World Order.

In the words of Masonic elder Manley P. Hall, "We must also perfect the plan of the ages, setting up here the machinery for a world brotherhood of nations and races." ("*The Secret Destiny of America,*" 1944, p.3)

The Freemasons provided Americans with still valid ideals — civil liberties, equal opportunity and no taxation without representation. But they were enticements designed to win power. As you might have noticed, these promises are not being kept.

Most historians won't tell you this. But there was one historian who did reveal the truth. Bernard Fay (1893-1978) was a Harvard-educated Frenchman. He is considered an "anti-Mason" because his 1935 book, "*Revolution and Freemasonry: 1680-1800*" is one of the very few to reveal the extent of Masonic participation in the US and French Revolutions.

He had access to Masonic archives in the US and Europe. His book is actually a sympathetic portrayal of Freemasonry with no references to its occult nature. However, as a Vichy Frenchman, he subsequently helped the Nazis identify Masons during World War Two. He was imprisoned after the war but pardoned by Charles De Gaulle in 1952.

MASONIC AMERICA

Fay explains that in the 1770's, the US consisted of 13 isolated colonies with different governments, religious affiliations, customs, racial profiles, and social and political structures. There were intense rivalries and longstanding antagonisms. A letter took three weeks to get from Georgia to Massachusetts.

"Masonry alone undertook to lay the foundation for national unity in America because [as a secret society] it could spread throughout the colonies and work steadily and silently. It created in a limited but very prominent class of people a feeling of American unity without which... there would have been no United States." (p. 230)

"In 1760, there was no town, big or small, where Masonry had not spun its web. Everywhere it was preaching fraternity and unity." (230)

Benjamin Franklin, who was the Grand Master of a French lodge, raised millions of francs crucial to financing George Washington's army. He was the first to submit a concrete plan for military collaboration and political federation to a Congress representing all colonies. He established a chain of Masonic newspapers in all of the colonies. You can imagine where he found the money.

Fay says George Washington and his ragtag army kept the spirit of independence alive. He organized many military lodges and participated in their activities. On Dec. 27,1778, he led a parade after Philadelphia was recaptured:

"His sword at his side, in full Masonic attire, and adorned with all the jewels and insignia of the Brotherhood, Washington marched at the head of a solemn procession of 300 brethren through the streets of Philadelphia to Christ Church, where a Masonic Divine Service was held. This was the greatest Masonic parade that had ever been seen in the New World." (246)

"All the staff officers Washington trusted were Masons, and all the leading generals of the army were Masons: Alexander Hamilton, John Marshall, James Madison, Gen. Greene, Gen. Lee, Gen. Sullivan, Lord Stirling, the two Putnams, Gen. Steuben, Montgomery, Jackson, Gist, Henry Knox and Ethan Allen were Masons. They all gathered around their Master Mason Washington and they all met at the 'Temple of Virtue,' a rude structure forming an oblong square forty by sixty feet, one story in height, a single entrance which was flanked by two pillars... The atmosphere which surrounded Washington was Masonic and it may be said that the framework of his mind was Masonic." (p. 250)

Imagine if Washington had shown the same devotion to Christianity!

Fay points to a "curious" degree of coordination between Masons in the US and British armies:

"It seems even likely that the unforgettable and mysterious laxness of certain English military campaigns in America, particularly those of the Howe brothers, was deliberate and due to the Masonic desire of the English general to reach a peaceful settlement..." (251)

SURRENDER OF CORNWALLIS

In this context, it is pertinent to recall the confession of General Cornwallis when he surrendered to General Washington at Yorktown (Oct. 19, 1781.)

Jonathan Williams recorded in his *"Legions of Satan,"* (1781,) that Cornwallis revealed to Washington that "a holy war will now begin on America, and when it is ended

America will be supposedly the citadel of freedom, but her millions will unknowingly be loyal subjects to the Crown."

The Crown is the Illuminati (i.e. shareholders of the Bank of England.) Cornwallis went on to explain what would seem a contradiction:

"Your churches will be used to teach the Jew's religion and in less than two hundred years, the whole nation will be working for divine world government. That government that they believe to be divine will be the British Empire. All religions will be permeated with Judaism without even being noticed by the masses, and they will all be under the invisible all-seeing eye of the Grand Architect of Freemasonry."

In a 1956 speech, Senator Joseph McCarthy reflected on these words:

"Cornwallis well knew that his military defeat was only the beginning of world catastrophe that would be universal and that unrest would continue until mind control could be accomplished through a false religion. What he predicted has come to pass. A brief sketch of American religious history and we have seen Masonry infused into every church in America with their veiled Phallic religion."

Our role is analogous with that of the French nobles who collaborated in the French Revolution and then were slaughtered. Fay writes: "All these nobles did not hesitate to side with the revolutionary party, even though it was to cost them their rank, their estates and their lives." (p. 287)

Freemasons Stage Political Theatre

When you shake hands, the thumb naturally extends upward or straight ahead.

When it points downward, over the knuckles, you are signalling that you are a member of the world's largest satanic cult, Freemasonry, and are committed to its goal of world government under the anti Christ.

Read what Stephen Knight wrote about the Masonic handshake in *"The Brotherhood"* (1983): "The Master Mason applies distinct pressure with his right thumb between the knuckles of the other's middle and third finger." (p. 132) Compare Larry King's recent Ahmadinejad handshake with the one of the cover of Stephen Knight's book. I know Ahmadinejad is supposed to be one of the "good guys" for many. This is just to get Americans to reject their country. He was dealt this role. The Masons (i.e. Illuminati) control both sides of every conflict.

Stephen Knight was poisoned and died just two years after publishing *"The Brotherhood."* What he said about British society no doubt applies to the whole world: Culture and politics are a charade quietly controlled by these disciples of Lucifer. In other words, mankind is in the thrall of a satanic cult. Millions are complicit in their own enslavement.

Knight shows how Masons secretly control every aspect of British society. There are 500,000 Masons in England. Lodges are associated with every local government, police, bank, military unit, hospital, university, church, court and of course Westminster.

What passes for politics is basically members of the same Lodge contending for office to decide how to enact the Masonic agenda. Knight documents how Masons give each other preferment in hiring, promotion and business. Non-Masons are continually hassled. It is no understatement to say that the UK is a Masonic tyranny.

The irony is that low-rank Masons don't realize this. They were officially forbidden from reading Knight's book. This is how secret societies work—by duping their members.

Freemasonry represents a conspiracy against society that has gone so far as to make treason the norm, and outlaw mention of conspiracy. Freemasonry is an extension of the "Jewish" conspiracy, creating a Gentile establishment to do its bidding. The Jewish conspiracy in turn is an instrument of the Central bankers who wish to use Jews and Masons to protect their monopoly on credit (money creation) and turn that monopoly into control over every aspect of your life. Hence the bogus "war on terror."

Larry King, Ahmadinejad signal Masonic Allegiance

THE BROTHERHOOD
STEPHEN KNIGHT

Bill Maher, Illuminati Agent

Every candidate running for US President or Vice President must be a puppet. Otherwise they would renounce the debt and insist on the US controlling its own credit (i.e. creating money.) The mass media is run by Freemasons.

Jewish Mason Bill Maher released a film "Religuousity" dissing religion. There are three monkeys on the posters (hear-no-evil etc.) each wearing the symbols of Judaism, Christianity and Islam. Religion is an attempt to obey God. God speaks to us via our conscience. Apparently Luciferians like Maher object to anything that gives people independence from their tyranny. It's fine to be tolerant of homosexuality and pornography but not the Spirit of God that helps people distinguish between right from wrong.

Check out the YouTube of Bill Maher making the satanic "horned goat" sign and exchanging Masonic handshakes with the likes of Ben Affleck and Ron Paul.

The Masonic bankers couldn't carry off this charade if they didn't own the mass media. They couldn't use perverts and criminals as Presidents and Senators if the press were free. They couldn't carry off an atrocity like 9-11 if the media could speak the truth.

In my own city, the *Winnipeg Free Press* pontificates on "toxic 9-11 truthers" who believe the Mossad played a role. Guess what — the "Free" Press is owned by two B'nai Brith'ers, i.e. Jewish Masons, Bob Silver and Ron Stern. What a coincidence!

There's a BBC video of Former Treasury Secretary Henry Paulson giving the Masonic "triangulation" sign (a pyramid with the fingers) around the 3.20 min mark. Paulson succeeded in raising the national debt to $11 Trillion last week. Under the Illuminati administration of George W. Bush, the national debt doubled! He spent as much as every administration that preceded him. Prince Hall Mason Barack Obama has outdone him.

Remember every dollar of new debt is a dollar in the pocket of the central bankers. Eventually debt will be used to enslave us. Look at Iceland where average citizens were saddled the debt of private banks. Every US citizen is responsible for over $40,000 in government debt.

CONCLUSION

The public will continue to believe there is a difference between the buffoons running for public office. It will continue to have faith in the mass media. But a few of us know that the human race is in the thrall of a vicious satanic cult. And when it is too late, the rest of the public will know too. In the meantime, we must prepare for the worst and hope for the best.

Freemasonry is Based on the Cabala

Since the so-called "Enlightenment," mankind has gradually fallen under the spell of the Cabala. What we have been taught to believe is "progress" is actually the resurgence of an ancient satanic pagan fertility cult, epitomized by the Cabala. The "god" of the Cabala is not god at all. It is Lucifer. Illuminati Jews and their Freemasonic allies are stealthily erecting a New World Order dedicated to Lucifer.

According to the gifted researcher, David Livingstone, Lucifer's plan was formulated in the Cabala in the sixth century BC, when the Jews were being held in captivity in Babylon. According to the Bible, this Exile was punishment for adopting the paganism of their neighbours, the Canaanites. They appropriated the ancient worship of the dying-god, Lucifer. Among the heinous practices prescribed by this cult were "mystery" rites involving music, intoxicants, orgiastic sex and human sacrifice.

The Cabala is based on ancient pagan mythologies which recount the story of an original god who created the universe, and a usurper god (Lucifer) who eventually defeats him and comes to rule the universe in his stead.

Lucifer is the offspring of the father-god and his wife, the goddess. But the son-god also marries his mother. The son-god was identified with the sun while the goddess was identified with the planet Venus, the first star seen at sunrise.

"Essentially, the god and the goddess were seen as two aspects of a single god." Livingstone writes in his latest book "Surrendering Islam." "As such, other names for Satan have included "Prince of Dawn" or "Son of the Dawn."

Lucifer, who exemplified evil, was known as a "dying God" because every winter he died and descended to the underworld where he ruled over the spirits of the dead. Cabalism is a sex cult tied to the cycle of the seasons. It is concerned with the incestuous mating of the god and goddess to ensure fertility.

Lucifer demands sacrifices. He must be appeased to avert his evil and direct it against one's enemies. The most evil sacrifice is the slaughter of a child. Livingstone explains:

"This [child sacrifice] became the basis of this cult throughout the ancient world. Rituals of death and resurrection imitated that of the god [Lucifer.] Participants would imbibe intoxicants and dance to music in order to achieve a state of ecstasy, or Jinn [demon] possession, by which they believed they could achieve supernatural abilities like shape-shifting, clairvoyance and other magical powers. In this state, they would slaughter a child and eat its flesh and drink its blood so that the god could be reborn in them."

RITUAL SACRIFICE, ORGIES CHARACTERIZE ILLUMINATI

Illuminati defectors testify that these practices continue today. Livingstone says these rituals usually involve sexual orgies where a priest and priestess impersonate the god and goddess in a "Sacred Marriage." They become possessed and produce a "son of god" who would then rule as king.

Livingstone says this is the basis of a satanic cult that now dominates the world. "It is this secret religion which is referred to as the occult. Its proponents have been advancing the satanic plan for a New World Order, and the elimination of Islam." (pp. 11-13)

In light of this background, we can appreciate how pernicious the Cabalist teachings are. For example, it teaches that God has no attributes. That is satanic. God is moral, the difference between good and evil, false and true, beautiful and ugly. No wonder mankind is losing the ability to discern.

Again, the Cabala teaches that the relationship between man and God is sexual and erotic, and that sensuality and intoxication are religious. This is satanic. Livingstone's exposition of Cabala explains why sex (promiscuity, pederasty, incest) is used to degrade and satanize human beings and why modernism is a Cabalistic spell.

According to Livingstone, Jews mixed this paganism with Babylonian magic and astrology, and called Cabala an "interpretation" of Judaism. These Cabalists disguised their Luciferian agenda of world domination as preparing the world for their supposed "messiah."

FREEMASONRY AND THE CLASH OF CIVILIZATIONS

David Livingstone describes the spread of Cabalism:

"The so-called Greek philosophers were the first important Cabalists. When the Jews were released from captivity by the Persian Emperor, Cyrus the Great, many Cabalists spread out to various parts of the world, especially Greece and Egypt. Platonism and the Orphean and Dionysian philosophies were influenced by Cabala.

From Greece and Egypt, Cabalist practices spread across Europe where they were known as witchcraft. But the most important influences were the humanism of the Renaissance, and the emergence of the Rosicrucians. The Rosicrucian movement was initially crushed as a result of the Thirty Years War, but a number sought refuge in England where they founded Freemasonry.

With the advent of the Illuminati, the Freemasons were responsible for the great project of the Enlightenment, whose goal was to supplant Christian authority, by way of the American and French Revolutions. The goal of these revolutions was to create secular societies, by which Christianity, or any religion, for that matter, was permanently separated from the "state." Freed from these constraints, the Illuminati could advance their power through banking, because until then Christianity had largely forbidden the practice of interest-banking.

Cabalistic interpretation of history would have us believe that this evolution of secularism is progress. Democracy, we are led to believe, is the end-product of human evolution away from religious superstition. However, while this evolution has been a prerogative of the West, the East is still mired in a more primitive stage, stubbornly adhering to the idea of "theocracy" i.e. the world of Islam.

And so, for the fulfillment of Cabalistic progress, this last obstacle must be removed, before the final imposition of an occult hegemony over humanity. Hence the "Clash of Civilizations" leading to the rule of the Anti-Christ."

So there you have it folks. Secularism is a mask for the resurgence of Cabala, paganism and Satanism. That's progress!

The Boule -
The Black "Skull and Bones"

(This was written for henrymakow.com by Lesley, a reader.)

In 1904, the first African -American Greek Secret Society was formed in Philadelphia, by Dr. Henry Minton and five of his colleagues. The Boule, pronounced "boo-lay," was formed to bring together a select group of educated Black men and women.

Fashioned after Yale's Illuminati Skull and Bones, the Boule takes pride in having provided leadership and service to Black Americans during the Great Depression, World Wars I and II, and the Civil Rights Movement.

What could the Boule offer America's Blacks in the early 20th century? Joining the exclusive secret society offered advancement and perks to select Blacks in return for loyalty to its objectives.

The upper tenth of Blacks started to live the good life as Boule members, while the majority of ordinary Blacks were disenfranchised. But what were the Boule's objectives?

REMAKING OF THE HOUSE NEGRO

The Boule recruited top Blacks in American Society into its ranks. Today, 5000-plus Archons, (male Boule members) and their wives, (Archousais) in 112 chapters make up the wealthiest group of Black men and women on the planet.

Who does the Boule really serve? The satanic global elite. As long as a Black member conforms to the rules, the riches will flow in abundance; if not, down comes the hatchet. Blackmail is part of the deal. This Masonic secret society has a pyramid structure like all the rest. The lower ranks are kept from knowing what the upper ranks are doing.

The early 20th century was a period of reconstruction. Marcus Garvey's "Back to Africa" Movement was in full swing. Garvey represented genuine Black leadership. W.E.B. Dubois, founding member of the NYC chapter of the Boule said, "The Boule was created to keep the black professional away from Marcus Garvey."

The remaking of the House Negro was necessary to produce a group of Blacks who had a vested interest in protecting the Illuminati elite. It was about selling out brothers and sisters for power and money. The majority of Black lawyers, doctors, engineers and accountants were members of this secret club.

PREDATORY INTENTIONS

According to Bobby Hemmitt, underground Metaphysician and Occultist lecturer, "This Black elite society based on Skull and Bones (Yale) was chosen by the U.S. Government (Illuminati) to run Black neighbourhoods." See here: http://www.youtube.com/watch?v=PA6jmaoG7V8

Conspiracy Theorist and Futurologist Steve Cokely, says: "Anywhere there are prominent professional Blacks, chances are they're in the Boule." Martin Luther King and Jesse Jackson are reported to have been Boule members, as well as Barack Obama, Bill Cosby, Al Sharpton and Thurgood Marshall.

The members of the Boule pose as freedom fighters or civil rights activists on the surface. In truth, they are operating for personal gain. The Boule works in concert with their masters in maintaining the grip of Illuminati supremacy.

COMPROMISING SITUATIONS

Like other secret societies, the Boule encourages homosexual trysts as initiation practices. This must be done to join the ranks. Bobby Hemmit says, "Any kind of top-notch Negro gets together and they f*ck each other."

These perversions are then catalogued and stored on record. Later, if needed, these misdeeds may be used as bargaining tools in the ULTIMATE GAME. What is the Ultimate Game? Capturing human souls.

The Boule mirrors the white power structure. Just as these Blacks betray their own people, so members of the Illuminati betray their friends and neighbours, culture and civilization.

READER'S COMMENTS:

DAVID: The BOULE is a necessary step in the organization of Freemasonry. It allows black people to be 'house' slaves instead of 'field' slaves and in fact to manage the 'field' slaves for the Masters. All the big names in America, past and present, seem tied into the Boule or other secret society. These members work for the fulfillment of Satan through the practical implementation of plans for the control and decimation of their own kind. We are all patsies.

This raises the question of how other black people are organized. The leaders must belong to some kind of Masonic society, headquartered in Europe or America. Are all Masonic societies on the same side or are they rivals too? Africa and the Caribbean Islands do have sizeable 'black' populations. Are their leaders members of the BOULE or another Masonic society?

This must be true. If one examines the happenings in countries such as Haiti, Jamaica, Trinidad and Guyana, there are severe question marks about where the leadership obtained their policies. In no case has there been any general socio-economic improvement for the masses.

Africa is on a depopulation spiral. Bio-weapons were deliberately infiltrated into vaccines. The end result was death and disease for peoples who live on one of the wealthiest continents on the planet. Somebody wants Africa badly enough to kill all Africans for it. Poverty, malnutrition, diseases, violence, inflation, lack of production, value-less currencies etc plague every African nation. One would have thought that enough 20th century technology exists. It is true to some degree to say that your own people keep you down. The Boule is proof of this. Color of skin inspires loyalty to a racial elite that serves the wannabe 'master race' of Earth.

Boy Scouts – Model
of Masonic Subversion?

The Boy Scouts of America is rare among major institutions in banning homosexuals, atheists and agnostics as leaders. In a decadent age, the BSA is unique in upholding God, country and traditional values.

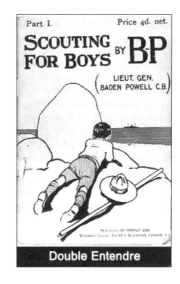

Double Entendre

With 1.6 million members & 470,000 leaders in 50,000 packs, it appears to be an incredible force for good. But how many genuine forces for good are there in this world?

Like most major institutions, the Boy Scouts appears to have been subverted by Freemasonry, which has a hidden agenda of promoting homosexuality and denying God.

Scouting's national honor society "recognizing Boy Scouts who best exemplify the Scout Oath and Law in their daily lives" is a Masonic secret society called the "Order of the Arrow." It has more than 180,000 members in "lodges" affiliated with more than 300 BSA local councils.

The Boy Scouts must ensure that their commendable work does not provide cover and recruits for the Masonic agenda.

First, let's look at the commendable goals. The BSA web site proclaims: "That Boy Scouts also has traditional values, like requiring youth to do their "duty to God" and be "morally straight" is nothing to be ashamed of and should not be controversial. No court case has ever held that Boy Scouts discriminate unlawfully, and it is unfortunate here that anyone would characterize Boy Scouts' constitutionally protected right to hold traditional values as 'discriminatory.' That is just name-calling."

The "Scout Law" teaches youths to be "trustworthy, loyal, helpful, friendly, courteous, kind, obedient, cheerful, thrifty, brave, clean, and reverent."

It defines God as "the ruling and leading power in the universe" to whom we are grateful for "favors and blessings." It maintains that "Boy Scouts believe that homosexual conduct is not compatible with the aims and purposes of Scouting and that a known or avowed homosexual does not present a desirable role model for the youth in the Scouting program."

TOO GOOD TO BE TRUE?

These are brave words for an organization that was probably founded by a homosexual to "scout" fresh talent for the British Empire's pedophile elite.

The homosexual inclinations of Scout Founder Robert Baden Powell (1857-1941) have been noted by two recent biographers. Baden Powell liked being with young boys, especially if they were skinny dipping.

Although married with three children, he was probably a homosexual. His father died when he was three-years-old. Subsequently, Robert was raised by his mother, "a strong woman who was determined that her children would succeed." Baden-Powell would say of her in 1933. "The whole secret of my getting on, lay with my mother."

Although Freemasons deny he was a member, Masonic lodges as far away as South Africa, Australia and New Zealand are named in his honor. He rose to the rank of Lieutenant General and fought in Britain's colonial wars subduing Zulus and Boers. His cohorts, from Lord Kitchener to King Edward VII were homosexuals, Freemasons and debauchers.

His gravestone bears a circle with a dot in the center, which is the trail sign for "Going home," or "I have gone home." This is also a symbol of the Illuminati, representing penis and vagina.

THE ORDER OF THE ARROW

Lucifer recruits mankind using a combination of deception and seduction. Freemasonry is the Church of Lucifer, which is the real "religion" of (post-Enlightenment) Western "civilization." It operates under many banners: Liberalism, Socialism, Zionism, Communism, Fascism, Feminism and "gay rights."

Like all of the above, Freemasonry is a secret society, i.e. the membership is not told the true agenda. The lower three "Blue Degrees" are fed platitudes about charity and making good men better. But, in reality, only the corruptible advance. Our whole society is based on this model which explains why our leaders, both political and cultural, have abandoned us.

Thus, it is quite likely that the Boy Scouts of America represent the innocent Blue Degrees. It is possible that *"The Order of the Arrow"* represents a recruitment pool for Freemasonry and ultimately other things.

John Salza is a former 32 degree Freemason and the author of a book, "Freemasonry Unmasked." He has written an essay about the OA entitled "Freemasonry has Infiltrated the Boy Scouts." The OA was founded in 1915 by two 32 degree Freemasons and its rituals are patterned on Masonic rituals. Both have three degrees; both are organized into lodges; both rituals seek esoteric spiritual knowledge and illumination. Candidates are conducted around the lodge while bound by a rope.

Salza writes: "These rituals—which include a blood covenant are being conferred upon innocent boy scouts...and are harming their souls. [This information] comes from a scout who has experienced demonic spiritual manifestations after his initiation into OA."

America's youths are being inducted into an occult secret society by stealth means. Scouts and Masons will deny there is anything wrong but this only proves their gullibility and venality. The BSA is doing the exact opposite of what it claims.

CONCLUSION

What is happening in the Boy Scouts is happening in society at large. Churches, political parties, the YMCA, charities, the media, schools —no institution is immune.

Mankind is satanically possessed, and is being inducted into a satanic cult through sex, violence, money, drugs, secret societies or media-induced panic or psychosis. Movies and video games today are mostly mindless killing and mayhem, apocalyptic catastrophe and pornographic sadism.

The Illuminati (the highest rung of Cabalistic Freemasonry) intends to degrade mankind and deliver us to Lucifer as tribute. This is what they mean by "change." They spit in the face of God and much of mankind seems only too willing to go along.

Is the Pope a Catholic?

"When the time comes finally to destroy the papal court...we shall come forward in the guise of its defenders...By this diversion we shall penetrate to its very bowels and be sure we shall never come out again until we have gnawed through the entire strength of this place." (Protocols of the Elders of Zion-17)

On New Years Day, 2004 former Pope John Paul II called for a "new world order... based on the goals of the United Nations."

When a world leader uses this terminology, it can only mean one thing. He is a part of the Luciferian conspiracy to create a totalitarian world government.

According to Piers Compton, a former Catholic priest, the Papacy was actually subverted by the Illuminati in 1958 when John XXIII became Pope. This was the culmination of a 200-year campaign to infiltrate and destroy the Catholic Church.

Piers Compton was the Literary Editor of the Catholic weekly *The Universe* for 14 years. He documents his claims in *"The Broken Cross,"* (1981) a book that is almost impossible to find because it was mysteriously withdrawn a few weeks after its release. It is now available online.

Compton traces the modern phase of the Luciferian Conspiracy to Adam Weishaupt who established the Illuminati on May 1, 1776.

"[Weishaupt] was backed financially, as are most if not all anarchistic leaders, by a group of bankers under the House of Rothschild. It was under their direction that the long range and worldwide plans of the Illuminati were drawn up." (8)

In 1783, the Illuminati assumed control of much of Freemasonry, which secretly coordinated the revolutionary movement (Liberalism, Socialism, and Communism.) According to David Bay, "secret societies like the "Skull and Bones" have always functioned as Satan's church, as the only way to pass the baton from generation to generation."

The Illuminati regarded the Catholic Church as their chief enemy and marked it for ruin. In 1818, their Italian lodge issued a set of Permanent Instructions that included: "We require a Pope for ourselves...to march more securely to the storming of the church...." The goal was "the complete annihilation of the Catholicism and even ultimately of Christianity. If Christianity were to revive, even upon the ruins of Rome, it would, a little later revive and live." (13-14)

POPE LEO XIII

In an Encyclical Dec. 8, 1892 Pope Leo XIII identified two Kingdoms. "The one is the kingdom of God on earth, namely, the true Church of Jesus Christ; and those who desire from their heart to be united with it...The other is the kingdom of Satan...those who refuse to obey the divine and eternal law, and who have many aims of their own in contempt of God, and many aims also against God."

Throughout history they have been in conflict.

"At this period, however, the partisans of evil seem to be combining together, and to be struggling with united vehemence, led on or assisted by that strongly organized and widespread association called the Freemasons. No longer making any secret of their purposes, they are now boldly rising up against God Himself."

Ironically, when Leo XIII died in 1903, a Freemason, Cardinal Mariano Rampolla, was almost elected Pope. Emperor Franz Joseph of Austria vetoed his appointment in the last moment. .

The Illuminists had to wait another 55 years to gain control of the Papacy. When Pope Pius XII died in 1958, a Freemason Cardinal Angello Roncalli, became Pope John XXIII.

Predictably, his first act was to begin to remove the element of Divine Revelation from Catholic teaching, and to embrace naturalism, materialism and Communism. These steps were taken at the Ecumenical Council in 1962 and Vatican Two in 1965.

As a result, Malachi Martin, a former Jesuit, predicted the Roman Catholic Church would no longer be recognizable by the year 2000. "There will be no centralized control, no uniformity in teaching, no universality in practice and worship, prayer, sacrifice and priesthood." (63)

POPE PAUL VI

Cardinal Giovanni Montini, who succeeded John XXIII as Pope Paul VI in 1963, was also a Freemason and socialist. (In 1944 Pope Pius XII had dismissed him as Vatican Secretary of State for conducting secret negotiations with the Communists. 53)

Paul VI revealed his true colors in a speech to the United Nations in 1965: "It is your task here to proclaim the basic rights and duties of Man. You are the interpreters of all that is permanent in human wisdom; we could almost say of its sacred character." (67)

This repudiation of the church's spiritual authority was symbolized by Paul's gift of the Papal Ring and his Pectoral Cross to Secretary General U Thant who sold them at an auction. (71)

The United Nations was set up on land donated by the Rockefellers as a front for the elite's Luciferian dictatorship. Its Charter was based on the Constitution of Soviet Russia and its leaders were Communists. It's Chapel is dedicated to paganism and run by the Lucis Trust (formerly Lucifer Trust) which also handles all its publications.

THE BROKEN CROSS

Paul VI also embraced a sinister symbol used by Satanists in the Sixth Century, which had been revived by Vatican Two.

This was a bent or broken cross on which was displayed a repulsive and distorted figure of Christ. Black magicians and sorcerers in the Middle Ages had used it for occult purposes. It represented the "Mark of the Beast."

Compton: "Yet not only Paul VI but also his successors the two John Pauls carried that object and held it up to be revered by crowds who had not the slightest idea that it stood for the anti Christ." (72)

Paul VI abolished the anti-Modernist Oath, the Index of forbidden books, and revised the Canon Laws. History and texts written from a predominantly Catholic point of view were re-edited. He encouraged "humanist" theologians like Edward Schillebecekx who taught that "the most honest and natural man was one who believed nothing." (105)

In 1976, the journal *Borghese* printed a list of 125 top clerics who were Freemasons in contravention of Church law. It included their dates of initiation and secret code names taken from the Italian Register of Secret Societies. Compton prints the list, which includes the heads of Vatican radio and press, Catholic education as well as numerous high officials, Cardinals and Archbishops.

Because Paul VI was Pope, nothing came of it. Sounding very much like the Mason he was, Paul said in 1969: "We are about to witness a greater freedom in the life of the Church...fewer obligations and fewer inward prohibitions. Formal disciplines will be reduced...every form of intolerance will be abolished." (104)

This attitude is explained by reports that from 1936-1950, the future Paul VI was part of a Communist espionage network, a part owner in a chain of brothels and financed erotic films. (110)

POPES JOHN PAUL I AND II

Alibino Lucano, the Cardinal of Venice became Pope John Paul I on August 26 1978. He was also a "committed Left-winger" but he may have taken issue with the Vatican's financial shenanigans because he was dead a month later. There was no autopsy.

Pope John Paul II, Karol Wojtyla, succeeded him. Wojtyla is the first non-Italian since 1522, and the only Pope from an Iron Curtain country. Compton notes that while the other Polish Cardinal Wyszynski "never yielded an inch" to the Communists, Wojtyla opposed this attitude and collaborated. The Abbe de Nantes exclaimed, "We have a Communist Pope."

During the Conclave at which he was elected, Wojtyla read from a book of Marxist principles. In his first Encyclical, he praised Paul VI for having "revealed the true countenance of the Church" and bringing it in step "with the times." He went so far as to say that opponents of Vatican Two "cannot be considered the faithful." (172)

In a letter Sept 1, 1981 he said, "Christian tradition has never upheld the right of private property as absolute and untouchable." This contradicts numerous Encyclicals which state that private property is "a necessary incentive to human enterprise" and in accordance with divine wisdom and the laws of nature.

Pope Pius XII: "Only private enterprise can provide the head of a family with the healthy freedom it requires to carry out the duties allotted to him by the Creator for the physical, spiritual and religious well being of the family." (174)

Communism (state ownership) is a facade behind which the bankers and monopoly capitalists will own everything.

On Nov. 27, 1983 Pope John Paul II issued a Papal Bull that legalized secret society membership for Roman Catholics.

While ostensibly a celibate priest, Compton suggests that Woytyla's behavior resembled a Bohemian artist. He was involved in theatre in Poland and penned a play about prostitution. Compton reproduces pictures of him when he was a Bishop or Cardinal. He is with a woman and child on a beach. The child is climbing on him. They look very much like a family.

In 1960, he published a book *"Love and Responsibility"* which extolled sexual love and describes both the physiology and psychology of sex. He told an audience of French youth: "Bodily union has always been the strongest language two people can have for each other."

CONCLUSION

Writing from the vantage point of 1981, Compton predicted that the Church's traditional teachings will continue to be watered down.

Around the same time, Malachi Martin said, "The Christian church is decaying, has nothing to say and is on the way out." He added that the other great religions are suffering the same fate and predicted, "A worldwide religion with one structure and institutions," managed by "one great bureaucracy. And out of that will emerge the ultimate disaster."

Eventually we will learn that real freedom lies in obeying God. The alternative is to become Lucifer's slave. The barbarism of the past century was not an aberration, but a harbinger of the future.

The Illuminati "Christian" Impostor

At a National Prayer Breakfast in Washington in 2009, Tony Blair confessed he didn't talk about God while in office so he wouldn't be considered a "nutter."

But now the convert to Roman Catholicism can declare that religious faith is at the heart of global affairs. In a "sermon" he mentioned God 31 times and proclaimed: "In surrendering to God we become instruments of his love."

President Obama endorsed the charade: "My good friend Tony Blair — who did it first and perhaps did it better."

Obviously Blair's role is to usurp Christian leadership and expose religious belief to ridicule. Along with another phony, George W. Bush, Blair caused the death and maiming of an estimated one million Iraqi civilians. They're sociopaths, not Christians.

The public is not deceived. One reader commented: "Since he has so much blood on his hands, he thinks by turning to religion all will be forgiven. Sad fool."

But the ruse does work. Another reader commented: "When I hear that this man is a Christian, it makes me proud to be an atheist."

Blair is a UN Middle East Peace Envoy. This is what the "instrument of God's love" had to say about Israel's massacre of women and children in Gaza: "What has happened has been very shocking and very sad — the scenes of carnage — but that is war, I'm afraid, and war is horrible."

(And, Satan must have his due.)

During his tenure in office, Blair, a closet Catholic, legalized gay marriage and adoption and, with false flag terrorism, turned the UK into a police state disdained by the whole world.

THE BISHOP WILLIAMSON HUBBUB

The Illuminati decided that it was better to take over the Catholic Church than attempt to destroy it. Pope Benedict's recent suspension of the excommunication of holocaust denier Bishop Richard Williamson may have been designed to heap scorn upon the authority of the Pope and the RC Church. This is exactly what has happened.

German Chancellor Angela Merkel has spoken out against Pope Benedict XVI's decision, saying: "The Pope and the Vatican need to make clear that such a denial in unacceptable." Others have called for the Pope's resignation.

The holocaust is not the issue here. My point is that Benedict's rehabilitation of Williamson makes no sense unless it was intended to bring opprobrium upon the RC Church. My hunch is that the Pope, like Tony Blair and Barack Obama, is an Illuminati Christian impersonator.

BLAIR TAKES VOW OF POVERTY

The zealous Blair seems to have forgotten Christ's injunction to the rich man to give away his possessions. Instead, Blair is accumulating wealth. Since leaving office he has made over $18 million from giving $250,000 speeches to globalist outfits like JP Morgan Chase and arms dealers Carlyle Group. (The latter feels an especial debt of gratitude to this Christian zealot for privatizing the UK's spy technology at a below market price.) When you serve the devil, you don't need to wait for Heaven to receive your reward.

The Illuminati apparently intend to use religion to facilitate their one world tyranny. Partnering with the Yale University Schools of Management and Divinity, "The Tony Blair Faith Foundation" aims to use "education" to bring about the New World Order:

"These are times of tumultuous change. The twentieth century order is history; and the forces of globalization are pushing all of the economies of the world - and all of the citizens of the world, with their great diversity of religious faiths — more closely together."

CONCLUSION

Satan's dispensation was introduced behind the facade of Christianity.

The Illuminati are Satanists. They engage in Satanic ritual (human) sacrifice and every form of sexual perversion. Blair and Obama belong to the Illuminati. Their aim is to destroy religion by throwing them all into a blender. A phony world "religion" will emerge led by the Antichrist and dedicated to Lucifer.

Blair's talk of being an "instrument of God's love" is classic Orwellian doublespeak: the words are the same but the intent is exactly the opposite. Similarly, Satan's agents, Illuminati Christian impersonators, have replaced real Christians at the head of "Christian" societies. Their role is to discredit God, Jesus, Christianity and true religion.

We have lost our grip on reality because mankind is possessed by a satanic cult. Bad things are happening because despicable miscreants rule.

Bill Gates: Satanist in Sheep's Clothes?

When Warren Buffett gave $31 billion to Bill Gates' Foundation, I assumed it would advance the New World Order. But when a reader showed me Gates' connection with the anti-Semitic and pagan Lucis Trust (formerly Lucifer Trust), I sat up and took notice.

Established by Alice Bailey in 1922, the Lucifer Publishing Company changed its name the following year for obvious reasons. Based at 120 Wall Street, the "Lucis Trust" is a vital part of the satanic cult that controls the Western world. It started the New Age Movement to induct society into their Luciferian mindset. It is the official publisher of the United Nations and manages its "Meditation Room."

Bailey was the leader of the Theosophical Society started in 1875 by Helena Blavatsky. Theosophy is a branch of Freemasonry. According to Constance Cumbey, Theosophy also spawned the occult societies that in turn created Adolf Hitler and the Nazi ideology. (*"The Hidden Dangers of the Rainbow: The New Age Movement and the Coming Age of Barbarism"* 1983)

In 1949, Bailey wrote that the Jewish holocaust was due to the Jews' bad karma: "the evil karma of the Jew today is intended to end his isolation, to bring him to the point of relinquishing material goals, of renouncing a nationality that has a tendency to be somewhat parasitic..." (*"Esoteric Healing,"* p. 263)

Bailey teaches that Jews are from a different solar system and that Orientals and Blacks are from a different root race. Occidental races must control the world, as they are our most evolved root race. (Cumbey, 115)

This must be of concern since a major focus of the Gates foundation is providing billions of dollars worth of vaccines to the poor in Third World countries.

GATES-LUCIS TRUST CONNECTION

The Bill and Melinda Gates Foundation has doubled in size due to the Buffet gift, and is five times larger than the US's next largest Ford Foundation. The Gates Foundation is mentioned as a financial member of the Lucis subgroup, "The New Group of World Servers." (See "$$" under groups. The pictures of Nelson Mandela, Cindy Sheehan and Michael Moore are also featured on this site.)

Bill Gates is also mentioned on the Lucis Trust web site: "Through the philanthropic and humanitarian work of such people as George Soros, Bill Gates, Kofi Annan and Bono, to name just a few, people are beginning to recognize the needs of the world's destitute people and acting to do something about them. There is talk by Soros and another thinker, James Tobin, about the creation of some type of tax upon financial transactions that would be used to support domestic programs in the developing world. Humanity surely has the ability to institute these and similar changes; it just needs the will to do so."

A tax on all financial transactions is part of what Lucis Trust calls "The Plan." This begins with the proclamation of the "Maitreya," the New Age Messiah who they have been grooming for more than three decades.

According to Cumbey, who is a lawyer, the "Plan" also includes a new world government and religion under Maitreya; a universal credit card system; an authority that would control the food supply; a universal tax; and a universal draft.

"They plan to outlaw all present religious practices and symbols of orthodox Jews and Christians," Cumbey writes. "New Agers have threatened violence and even extermination of Jews, Christians and Moslems who fail to co-operate with Maitreya and his new religion." (20)

LUCIFER IS GOD

The Theosophical Society believes Lucifer is God which they identify with the Sun. In "The Secret Doctrine," Blavatsky writes: "In this case it is but natural ... to view Satan, the Serpent of Genesis as the real creator and benefactor, the Father of Spiritual mankind."

"For it is he who was the "Harbinger of Light," bright radiant Lucifer, who opened the eyes of automaton (Adam) created by Jehovah, as alleged; and he who was first to whisper, "In the day yea eat there of, ye shall be as Elohim, knowing good and evil" — can only be regarded in the light of a Savior. An "adversary" to Jehovah ... he still remains in esoteric truth the ever-loving "Messenger"... who conferred on us spiritual instead of physical immortality ...

Satan, or Lucifer, represents the active ... "Centrifugal Energy of the Universe" in a cosmic sense ... Fitly is he ... and his adherents ... consigned to the "sea of fire," because it is the Sun ... the fount of life in our system, where they are petrified ... and churned up to re-arrange them for another life; that Sun which, as the origin of the active principle of our Earth, is at once the Home and the Source of the Mundane Satan... "http://www.conspiracyarchive.com/NewAge/Lucis_Trust.htm

"New Agers generally do not openly repudiate Christianity," Cumbey writes. "They redefine Christ to give pagan Gods equal time, and expand the definition of Christ to be the integral essence of themselves." (146)

While New Agers "would rightfully picket to prevent a Nazi demonstration, they fail to see that point-for-point the program of the New Age Movement has complete identity with the programs of Hitler." (56, Cumbey does the point-by-point comparison on pp.114-120)

"New Agers" profess a great love of peace and disarmament but Cumbey cites Bailey saying nuclear weapons will be the preserve of the United Nations for "threatened use when aggressive action on the part of any nation rears its ugly head." (70)

HIDDEN AGENDAS

Similarly, the environment and world hunger causes all have a hidden elite agenda. Cumbey writes that supporters of anti-hunger programs are urged to back measures for abortion, artificial insemination, forced limitation of family size, genetic control and even death control." (56)

Buffett said in 2006 "that he was a student of many of the same philanthropists that Gates modelled himself on - the oil man John D. Rockefeller, and the steel magnate Andrew Carnegie."

These "philanthropists" have used their tax-exempt money to subvert Western civilization for almost a century. For example, a Rockefeller boasted to Aaron Russo that they started feminism to get women into the workplace and paying taxes, so they could indoctrinate the young in day cares. Significantly, another focus of the Gates Foundation is "improving American high schools."

They are on the forefront of destroying traditional cultures by breaking up the family. They are championing "women's rights" through loans mainly to women to make them independent of men.

CONCLUSION

I prided myself on having escaped the banker's Communist hoax but I realize now that Communism was the "plan" for my parent's generation. I fell hook-line-and-sinker for the "New Age," which was aimed at my generation. It is exactly like Communism, appealing to our idealism, but having an insidious hidden agenda.

God is Love but the God of the Illuminati is not Love. It deifies man at his lowest not his highest. It freezes us cryogenically in our own filth.

We live in interesting times. Our mainstream leaders have sold us out. Society has slipped the moorings of truth and is steered by megalomaniacs. Let's man the lifeboats of truth.

Was Michael Jackson an Illuminati Sex Slave?

(This was written for henrymakow.com by Charles, a reader.)

Approximately forty years ago, the Jackson family appeared on the Ed Sullivan show and released the first of many albums for Motown records. What made the Jackson 5 special was their lead singer, pint-sized Michael Jackson.

Even at the tender age of ten, Michael Jackson had an ebullient joy and charisma that was palpable and contagious on both TV and radio. Later, at the age of 21, he broke from his family and began a successful solo career. F. Scott Fitzgerald said American lives have no second acts. And for child entertainers trying to extend their success into adulthood, that is doubly so. Michael Jackson proved Fitzgerald wrong. But at what price?

A series of articles on the blog *Aangirfan* [aangirfan.blogspot.com] explores the possibility that Michael Jackson was yet another Illuminati sex slave. In one article, "Michael Jackson 5.0," the blogger writes: "There has been speculation that the CIA has used its MK-ULTRA brainwashing on many celebrities, including Madonna, Curt Cobain, Britney Spears, Elvis and Michael Jackson. Jermaine Jackson has suggested that his father may have arranged for Michael to be used by older men. He tells how his father had Michael join late-night hotel room meetings with "important business people."

Jermaine wondered whether "something happened" to Michael at those sessions. He said he sensed something was wrong because Michael would be sick for days after. "What was Joseph doing?" Jermaine wrote. Michael Jackson said himself that his father beat him.

MK-ULTRA SLAVE

Former Illuminati slave Kathleen Sullivan adds from the *Rigorous Intuition* blog [rigourousintuition.blogspot.com]: "I've been tracking Michael Jackson via the news for about 10 years now. For reasons I will not get into in a public forum, I can state that

I have absolutely no doubt that he's an MK-ULTRA variety slave, possibly introduced by his father into their bizarre "system" of spooks, commercialized pedophilia and more.

"My father introduced me to organized criminal pedophilia from early childhood on. Like Michael, I developed many altered states of consciousness to cope with the horrors I experienced and encountered. I also have no doubt that he would have been terribly abused as a child, even if he hadn't "allegedly" been given to others as a child to sexually service them. There's no other explanation for his obsession with being with children, in public and privately - especially in bed!

"During my past internship at a state hospital, I talked with a forensics expert who is very familiar with pedophilia. He said that one class of pedophiles are psychologically "stuck" at a certain age on the inside, regardless of their physical age. Therefore, they choose children to sexually "mate" with who are the same internal age and see themselves as EQUALS with those children in every way. And if this kind of pedophile is a male who was sexually abused by adult males in childhood, he will most likely unconsciously re enact what was done to him, with the next generation of males who are the age he was then.

"I didn't see the tiniest bit of love or concern in his father's face for him when he seemingly came to the rescue when Michael was put on trial (again). I think daddy dearest simply took over to ensure that Michael didn't say the wrong things in public or in court."

Another article on the Aangirfan blog, "Michael Jackson and the CIA," recounts a brief mention of the Jackson family from Brice Taylor's memoirs *"Thanks for the Memories:"*

"Brice Taylor relates that she and Michael Jackson and members of the Jackson family accompanied Bob Hope to a location where they were filming up-and- coming talent for TV. Reportedly Bob Hope sponsored the young Jackson boys. Brice Taylor writes: "Their father brought the boys in and I remembered seeing them taken into a side room where bright lights were on. "They all had to drop their pants and before their performance a big man raped each one of them in a lineup."

Reportedly, Brice Taylor and the Jacksons were victims of CIA mind control. Yet another dispatch offers: "On the cover of the ... 'Dangerous' Album, the Freemasonic symbol of the one eye can be found as well as a picture of a bald headed man well known to the Occult (Satanists) as Alistair Crowley."

The blog frequently cross references an article from the Timboucher website [timboucher.com], "Michael Jackson, Mind Control Victim?" The article notes that MJ had his own 'personal magician' by the name of Majestic Magnificent. "I know it's a pretty far-out leap for most "normal" people, but could Majestic Magnificent be more than just a "magician" - could he also be some sort of CIA Monarch mind-control handler for Jackson?" [Tim Boucher has several interesting articles worth reading on MJ and the occult such as "Michael Jackson's Bloodbath."]

Michael had his children wear masks in public to 'protect' them. They were not even allowed to see their own faces in a mirror at home! Could this be a clue about Illuminati mirror programming which Michael himself experienced and now was trying to prevent from ever happening to his children?

Michael Jackson's march to superstardom may have been stage-managed by the occult politics of the MK-ULTRA program. His talent alone was not enough. The road to the top may have necessitated sexual abuse at the hands of connected powerful adults while still a child. He may have been passed up the paedophile food chain in order to receive the backing, marketing and exposure that made him a household name. He may have been made more pliable by MK-ULTRA training which involved tremendous psychological and physical trauma. The fallout from this revealed itself in all the strange and inexplicable behavior. He changed his face trying to put distance between him and his past. But he never could escape *The Man in the Mirror*.

In Michael Jackson, the Illuminati demonstrated their power to make and break our entertainment idols, to choose our idols for us and to influence and control the popular culture through their change agents. Our idols tell us how to act. We emulate them so that we, too, can be cool, sophisticated, androgynous slaves. This is how the common man finds his place in the New World Order.

Kevin Annett Rips
the Mask from Power

If Christ returned, he'd be crucified again, not by Jews or Romans but by the church, which has been invaded by His enemies.

This is obvious from the fate of Kevin Annett, a young United Church of Canada minister who took Christ's teachings to heart, and suffered everything but Crucifixion. (To date, Christ's enemies are reluctant to create another martyr.)

Kevin Annett

I have been studying the New World Order for eight years but no book has laid bare the true hypocritical face of power in Western society as Kevin Annett's self published memoirs, "*Love and Death in the Valley*." Many books have left me winded, but none like this.

I have met Kevin Annett and he doesn't have a halo. But he does exude a transparency and a dogged determination to make sure we learn the truth about the genocide of (he claims) "roughly" 80-90 million North American Indians. He is the closest thing to a genuine dissident in this society, the closest thing to a real hero. Although he's been fighting this lonely battle for 18 years, we haven't heard of him, proof our "heroes" are manufactured for us.

Kevin is the kind of "innocent" or "true believer" organizations like the Communist Party or United (Methodist-Presbyterian) Church hire to provide an artifice. But "every group has rules" as Kevin was told repeatedly, and Kevin didn't adapt. A real Christian represents Christ —not the corrupt impostors who profit from his teaching. Kevin was a Minister of Christ.

WHAT PAINT CAN'T HIDE

"Give the place a bit of Spirit," his boss at Fred Victor Mission, a residence for the homeless near Toronto's seedy Yonge Street told him, as if talking to a painter.

In the course of his work, Kevin learned the Church Mission was a centre for drug trafficking and prostitution and the staff were on the take. He learned that large donations to the Mission were embezzled, while there wasn't any money for Bibles. When he took these matters to church leaders, they knew and didn't want to know.

This was his first glimpse of the United Church of Canada as a four billion dollar corporation that provides a nice tax-exempt front for a lot of rich people with a lot of shady dealings. But that's just scratching the surface of a potential nightmare for the 2.8 million bland well meaning Canadians affiliated with this empty shell of a church.

When Kevin (an exquisitely Canadian name) took up his next position as Minister in a British Columbia logging town, he opened his sanctuary to the poor and the non-White. He began to hear stories from his Aboriginal parishioners about ethnic cleansing at government funded, church-run "residential schools."

Native children were abducted by the RCMP and forced to attend these "schools" which were concentration camps in disguise. Here helpless children were physically and sexually abused, sterilized and exposed to deadly viruses. Many were subjected to medical experimentation from Illuminati doctors. The death rate was 50% Annett estimates over 50,000 children died at these schools.

The Illuminati want the land and the water rights. The Aboriginals are the only people standing in their way.

In an email, Kevin wrote: "Continually, eyewitnesses describe that most of them never received formal education, besides religious instruction. Maybe one or two hours of schooling a week, the rest of the time working as manual labour and farmed out as cheap labour or domestics to white families. The ones who got a better education were the collaborators, being trained to be puppets of the government and churches - they're often the ones who now run the big aboriginal groups, band councils, etc. I also have letters from Indian Agents confirming that the kids were not to receive "too much" education."

Kevin's blurring of class and color lines strained relations with the church "Old Guard" but the deal breaker was when Kevin publicly opposed the lucrative sale of Aboriginal lands the church held in trust to a large logging company.

Kevin was stripped of his Ministry, the only United Church Minister ever to be defrocked. His supporters were expelled from the church and his wife was pressured to divorce him and take their two children.

ACADEMIA

Next stop on Kevin's voyage of discovery was a Ph.D. program at the University of British Columbia. There he had access to government archives which documented a deliberate agenda of ethnic cleansing which (he says) claimed one to two million Aboriginals in British Columbia alone over a century.

Just as the Church represents Christ, the university represents free inquiry and truth. Thus Kevin's funding disappeared and he had to leave. "Unless you play the game, you'll never work in this province again," he was told.

Is it any wonder society is drifting toward fascism when the institutions dedicated to moral leadership are rotten to the core? You can smell the stench of moral compromise, like rotting garbage, everywhere.

The same applies to the corporate media. Kevin did get a couple of good stories but they dried up with mention of the Supreme Court judges using Indian children for pedophilia. Similarly, when Kevin was beaten up or his documents stolen, the police and courts refused to act despite video footage of the theft. Why would they? They regarded the murder of thousands of Aboriginal children as "too big a task to investigate."

Church. Corporations. Academia. Media. Law. Police. That leaves the government. In 2007, the Canadian government absolved the Church of any liability for its crimes. Kevin wrote to me then:

"Yes, all the churches have been granted effective immunity; Indian Affairs announced so last February when they said there will be no criminal prosecution for anything that went on in the rez schools. Disgusting. Natives cannot sue the churches after the settlement - that was part of the deal the AFN (Assembly of First Nations) did on behalf of all the survivors, without consulting them once. It's as bad a crime as the original atrocities."

CONCLUSION

In his book, *"Love and Death in the Valley,"* soon to be a major Hollywood movie-not, Kevin muses on the disconnect between what people profess and what they actually do.

"The most successful minister in the church I found is the man or woman who can function as an efficient dissociated personality, regularly professing one thing and practising the opposite." (151)

This description fits society as a whole.

Logo of Aleister Crowley's Occult OTO (center) United Church (right)

When Pedophile Judges Fear Exposure

Under a thin veneer of Law, we are governed by a secret network of traitors, pedophiles, Satanists and criminals, masquerading as prominent lawyers and judges, politicians, businessmen and police chiefs.

They are often Freemasons who derive their power from the central banking cartel based in London which controls the mass media and seeks to impose its tyranny in the guise of "world government."

If you don't believe me, you've probably never heard the names Renate Andres-Auger, Jack Cram and Bruce Clark. They are Vancouver lawyers who were dragged from the courtroom, drugged, disbarred and committed to a mental asylum when they attempted to expose this clique in the 1990's.

CITY CONFIDENTIAL

Beautiful Vancouver B.C. was described by the *Christian Science Monitor* in 1997 as "a pedophile paradise," a place known for its "notorious sex trade," with an international reputation "as a city where it is easy to find a child for sex." In 1999, UNESCO named Vancouver one of the world's top three centres for sex trafficking, child porn and pedophilia because of "suspected judicial protection for child sex offenders."

In 1994, Renate Andres-Auger, an aboriginal lawyer and single mother of six girls, found irregularities in a land claim case that were very damning to the judicial process. She also charged certain judges and lawyers with a criminal conspiracy to aid and protect pedophiles. She and her own lawyer Jack Cram presented evidence, including photographs and eye witness accounts that two Supreme Court judges were engaged in pedophilia and were using their office to protect other pedophiles. She named the prestigious "Vancouver Club" as a center of this pedophile ring. (Kevin Annett, *"Hidden From History: The Canadian holocaust,"* p. 147-150)

The Judge ordered Auger removed from the court. "The sheriffs dragged Andres-Auger out of the court and you could hear her thumping down the stairs behind the judge's bench." Then the Judge ordered the sheriffs to remove her lawyer Jack Cram. Police were called to clear the courtroom of about 80 supporters. According to a press release, this is what happened when Cram took the cause to the public:

"One night at about 11:30 p.m., after finishing a radio interview, Mr. Cram returned home, parked his car, and while walking to his apartment building five policemen emerged out of the bushes and leaped on him. He was put in an unmarked van and as soon as they got him in they "shot him full of something" and he was transported to the psychiatric ward of Vancouver General Hospital — as a "no information" patient.

SAVING JACK CRAM

"When the committee found out where Mr. Cram was, they had to go to Prince George, some 800 kms away, to find a lawyer who would file a habeas-corpus writ to release Mr. Cram but it was never used as Mr. Cram was again, unexpectedly, released after being held this time for 7 days.

"Mr. Cram went directly from the psychiatric ward to a meeting of the committee that was under way at the same time. He was still under the effects of the drugs that had been administered to him up until about two hours prior to his release. But he was able to explain everything that had happened. It was two of his closest associates, one of which was the one who had bad mouthed him on TV, that signed papers to have Mr. Cram committed.

"After a trial, the court disbarred him for a year and fined him $10,000. He was bankrupt and had lost his practice. Cram moved to his ranch in Princeton, a community about 280 km east of Vancouver.

"According to Judge Gibbs, in making his recent judgment on Dr. Clark's appeal, said "after [Mr. Cram] received treatment for his paranoid-delusions mental illness, he subsequently dropped all his court cases that he had started in his delusional phase" and one of the conditions for returning to the bar after one year was that he continue to receive psychiatric treatment for that year. Mr. Cram could have been jailed for three months if he didn't receive the treatment or defaulted on paying the fine."

Renate Andres-Auger has gone underground. Law Society of BC official James Taylor, who disbarred Andres-Auger and Cram, became a BC Supreme Court judge and issued an injunction in 2002 against mentioning the pedophile charges.

Ed John, a native leader accused of using Mafia tactics, and running cocaine and child prostitution rings, was actually named Minister of Child and Family Services in the NDP (socialist) provincial government in 2000. The injunction also covered any mention of these charges.

COMMENTS ON THIS SHAMEFUL EPISODE

Jennifer Wade, a founder of Amnesty International in Vancouver, said in 1999:

"The Cram/Andres-Auger story, to this day, remains a very strange and fearful tale of alleged corruption and pedophilia in high places. It is also a story which has never yet been completely told. Perhaps if it were, along with a few other strange stories, we as Canadians would have little reason to gasp at the exposure of pedophile rings in Belgium operating in high places two years ago. The matter of cover-ups possibly existing for those in high places in Canada is becoming more and more credible as more and more people speak out."

In 2007 Univ. of Lethbridge professor Anthony Hall commented in *Canadian Dimension* magazine:

"No public investigation into the treatment and accusations of Andres-Auger and Cram ever took place. We can only speculate, therefore, on the circumstances behind such a dramatic collapse of dignity and due proccss in the criminal-justice system. Certainly it is made to seem probable that some highly placed group or individual believed that he, she, or they had a great deal to lose if Andres-Auger and Cram had been able to press charges."

Hall relates how in 1995, when lawyer Bruce Clark tried to make a legal argument on behalf of Aboriginal clients, an incident transpired in a rural B.C. court similar to when Andres-Auger and Cram tried to bring their evidence forward. Clark was taken into custody and sent to an institution for a compulsory psychological examination.

This is how dissidents were treated in another Illuminati satrap, the USSR. Granted these events took place 15-17 years ago, but you can bet they created a chill that continues today.

CONCLUSION

The Illuminati has a vital interest in using Native leadership to confiscate Aboriginal land and water, and to operate drug trafficking and pedophile rings. That's why lawyers who attempted to represent ordinary Natives incurred the wrath of these (moral) reptiles. That's when the mask slipped, and we had a glimpse of the ugly reality of our society.

Defector Says
Illuminati Sacrifice Children

The Illuminati sacrifice children in rituals eight times a year, "Mary Anne," an Illuminati defector who had been groomed for high political office, told me Sept 21, 2008 .

I spoke to Mary Anne again in Dec. 2009. She said new and disturbing memories had surfaced. I will present a summary of the first interview which is also available on audio on my website. Then I will summarize the second.

Much of what she says in both interviews is simply outrageous. I can't vouch for any of it. But it is consistent with the testimony of other defectors, Svali, Sue Ford and Cathy O'Brien.

The Illuminati count on people to be incredulous. That's their protection. The more egregious their crimes, the safer they are.

Mary Anne sounds convincing to me. Why would anyone defy the most powerful people in the world? Also, both interviews, although 14 months apart, are consistent. People who invent stories rarely can keep track of them.

On Sept. 21, 2008, Mary Anne said that tens of thousands of children will be sacrificed that night (the autumnal equinox) in Illuminati ceremonies. The children are bred for the purpose or kidnapped. Satanists believe they gain power from killing. Often they rip out the heart and eat a piece of it. They prefer it to be still beating. At Easter, they kill adults.

There are also sexual rituals involving young children. They are believed to increase power, and create fear and solidarity in members.

Illuminati members live double lives. At night, they engage in these satanic rituals. By day they are found in all walks of life: medicine, education, psychology, therapy, banking, law, law enforcement, government, technology, military, charities and religion.

They are everywhere. The worst are in the news on a daily basis posing as our "leaders."

They are the elite of Freemasonry. They are generational Satanists, which means you have to be born into it. You can't join. Their children are evaluated and trained. Mormons and "Nation of Islam" have parallel beliefs, she said.

The world has been divided into ten regions. Different groups are in control of North America. They are related to the Crowns of Europe.

Many Jews have a prominent role but the Illuminati is not predominantly Jewish. Muslim, Christian, Mormon, Wicca, Pagan and New Age groups all play a role.

She said 80-90% of the House of Representatives and 100% of the Senate belong to the Illuminati.

Mary Anne said she was sexually abused by her own family from an early age. In spite, or because of this, she was groomed to be a prominent political figure. She worked closely with many world leaders and was sexually abused by them. She was tortured when she refused to carry out assassinations.

All religions are infiltrated and controlled by the Illuminati. The Vatican is rotten at the top. The future "Anti Christ" will be a Pope. All countries, including Russia, China and Iran, are controlled by the Illuminati. "You don't say no."

The Illuminati is behind the homosexual agenda, AIDS, and the sexual revolution. They foster anything that is in rebellion against the Christian God.

CONCLUSION

The first responsibility of government is to prevent a fanatical cult from taking control.

Our governments have allowed a satanic cult, the Illuminati, (i.e. the Judeo Masonic central banking cartel) to usurp power. Most of our "leaders" are their appointees or dupes.

Recently a former pilot for corporate bigwigs wrote to me:

 "At times I would hear them talk about "the big boys" ... Most said that they did as they were told by the BIG INVESTORS [i.e. central bankers] who really ran the show behind the scenes, that they [CEO's etc.] were just highly paid actors and messenger boys who read a script and made very few decisions themselves."

Our politicians are analogous. They are the CEO's of the corporations called countries, soon to be amalgamated into a world cartel.

PART TWO

In Dec. 2009, Mary Anne said she was feeling bitterness, resentment and hatred for Janet Reno. She had served as her sex slave and had been abused on many occasions in Reno's office at the White House and at a retreat in a "heavily wooded" part of Virginia.

"She called me 'Pet,'" Mary Anne recalled. "I was her property at that point in time."

Mary Anne had been present in the White House with Reno and Madeleine Albright when they dismembered a male child. He was stabbed in the heart and they watched him bleed to death.

She had been present at the Virginia retreat when a defiant "high level" FBI agent had been sacrificed. FBI Director Louis Freeh, Janet Reno and about 40 other people had participated in the ritual.

She had recovered memories of Henry Kissinger who "controlled me through most of my childhood." Kids "were delivered to the White House." Kissinger was "so violent and rough that towels were needed to clean them up."

Both Kissinger and Nixon had sexually violated her as a three-year-old in a conference room at the White House. Kissinger engaged in anal and vaginal sex with boys and girls; Nixon only vaginal.

"I have seen every sexual combination imaginable," she said.

These activities made Illuminati members blackmail-able and enforced group solidarity. As members of the Illuminati order, they felt superior to all and beyond the rule of law. They had a sense of entitlement. They had been selected from an early age and had "paid their dues."

Mary Anne said Jon Benet Ramsay was murdered in 1996, at age six, because she had overheard things that could not be repeated. Her Illuminati father had been loaning her out to his friends. Her mother tried to defend her and had to be sedated.

Mary Anne claims she was present when Vince Foster was murdered in July 1993. She says Hillary Clinton and Foster were "having a screaming match verging on a brawl" in his office at the White House. He had threatened to expose her Whitewater dealings. A Secret Service agent "raised his gun and shot him point blank."

She claims that Queen Elizabeth wanted her to assassinate Diana and that she was "horsewhipped" for refusing. She claims Princes Charles and William were in on it. She describes Queen Elizabeth as the "instigator" and a foul mouthed "piece of work."

She said she had been trained as an assassin and had committed two killings.

She claims W's brother, Neil Bush, runs a child slavery ring in the USA.

I asked Mary Anne to list the activities the Illuminati engage in. Here it is: Bestiality; sodomy; necrophilia; incest; wife swapping; child porn (they make it; real source of Hefner, Flynt, Polanski fortunes is children, not adults); snuff films; sex orgies; force children to have sex with farm animals & family pets; ritual murder and human sacrifice. Then, there is organized crime: drugs, prostitution, guns etc.

CONCLUSION

Eventually Mary Anne refused to serve and asked to be killed. For some reason, they let her go. She found Christ and that has been a source of strength.

Whether or not we accept the above as true, I believe a satanic cult, the Illuminati, does control the world and we are all being initiated into it unwittingly. What they call "social change" (or in the case of Obama, just "Change") is in fact social engineering and mind control. What they call "progress," is progress only if you are a Satanist and believe in the Luciferian Dispensation i.e. the New World Order.

Education and the mass media are a big part of this stealth indoctrination. The mass media includes music, video games, TV and cinema. For example, a reader pointed out that corpses and body parts figure prominently on TV now. Obviously we are being desensitized.

As I have said, the first responsibility of government is to prevent a fanatical secret cult taking control of society. It has failed.

Gloomy as the outlook is, at least you and I are awake and able to protect ourselves and our families.

READER'S COMMENTS:

ROBERT: Regarding your recent article about child abuse and sacrifice, stories similar to the Dutroux affair in Belgium have been circulating elsewhere for some time. In the United States, a documentary entitled "Conspiracy of Silence" was scheduled for broadcast on the History Channel but then was suppressed.

 You can watch it on Google video. A similar documentary, about the situation in France, entitled "Viols d'enfants: la fin du silence?" was hosted by Elise Lucet for the TV network France 3. Although telecast once at a low-viewership time, apparently it has since disappeared from the network archives. In Portugal there is the Casa Pia orphanage scandal: a pedophile network reportedly involving many privileged persons, including some in the justice system, in that society.

In Canada, there is the Cornwall Ont. pedophilia scandal and the seeming persecution of investigative officer Perry Dunlop, although from what we have heard it does not involve the most horrific aspects of the European and American stories.

The major media, catering to normal public sentiment, treat pedophilia as exhibited by the non-elite as an utterly heinous crime, yet when allegations involving powerful persons come up, investigations seem to be thwarted or to fail because of incompetence. It's a remarkable phenomenon, which became immensely scandalous in Belgium in the Dutroux case.

It is unpleasant to think that the upper crust in many societies protects networks of pedophiles whose behaviour is the price of admission... The intractable problem is the possible existence of innocent victims, who deserve our best efforts on their behalf to save them from living hellish lives.

Bohemian Grove: Illuminati Meet for Satanic Rituals

The satanist cult that has colonized mankind meets every July at Bohemian Grove, 80 miles north of San Francisco.

Over 2000 members — the political, corporate, cultural and military elite of the world — gather for satanic rituals, possibly including human ritual sacrifice. They have been meeting there since the 1880's.

According to "Treee," a young Las Vegas woman who claims to have contacts inside the secretive club, a ritual sacrifice of Mary Magdalene takes place Tuesday July 21; and the ritual sacrifice of Jesus Christ takes place Wednesday, July 22. A human body or effigy is burned in front of a large owl symbolizing Moloch, the pagan Canaanite God. Alex Jones filmed a similar ceremony called "Cremation of Care" July 15, 2000.

If having our world leaders belong to a satanic cult weren't bad enough, the Las Vegas woman says the Illuminati are actually an alien reptilian species that occupies human bodies and feeds off our energy. I find this hard to believe, but then I would also find it hard to believe the world leadership is making sacrifices to owls. So, I listen and reserve judgement.

She says: This reptilian species is called "Sangerians;" they are a "fourth dimension race" and make up 3% of the world's population. She claims to have met "more than one." They have three-hearts, shift shape, are cold blooded, but are developing human feelings from devouring human flesh and blood.

"Ten per cent now get their blood from the Red Cross." Except for sacrifice, their every ritual involves sex. Queen Elizabeth is a leading reptilian. "It all sounds sci-fi and unbelievable," the woman says. "But everything fits."

The Las Vegas woman plans to demonstrate outside the gates of Bohemian Grove this week dressed in luminescent robes. She invites people to join her. She says we must send the Bohos the message that we know who they are. She says humans must open a dialogue with these creatures or else both species are doomed.

SATANISTS AND THEIR PERVERSIONS

There is stronger evidence that the Grove members are Satanists rather than reptilians. Alex Jones points out in his film that the "Cremation of Care" official programme actually shows a baby's body being devoured by the flames. A YouTube photo montage taken from the estate of a BG member leaves little doubt that serious satanist practices take place. One of the pictures shows a dead body, presumably a human sacrifice.

As for perversion, let's start with the trivial. In 1978, the club actually argued in court that it shouldn't have to hire female staff because members at the Grove "urinate in the open without even the use of rudimentary toilet facilities" and that the presence of females would alter club members' behavior." (See Wikipedia entry.)

An all-male enclave, Richard Nixon was heard on the Watergate Tapes describing it as "the most faggy goddamn thing you could ever imagine, that San Francisco crowd that goes in there; it's just terrible! I mean,I won't shake hands with anybody from San Francisco."

In the Franklin Coverup scandal of 1989, Paul A. Bonacci claimed that he had been kidnapped and flown to the Grove by Republican leader Lawrence King and was forced into sexual acts with other boys.

In Ch. 18 of *The Tranceformation of America*," Cathy O'Brien writes, "I was programmed and equipped to function in all rooms at Bohemian Grove in order to compromise specific government targets according to their personal perversions. 'Anything, anytime, anywhere with anyone' was my mode of operation at the Grove. I do not purport to understand the full function of this political cesspool playground as my perception was limited to my own realm of experience. My perception is that Bohemian Grove serves those ushering in the New World Order through mind control, and consists primarily of the highest Mafia and U.S. Government officials.

"I do not use the term "highest" loosely, as copious quantities of drugs were consumed there. Project Monarch Mind-Control slaves were routinely abused there to fulfill the primary purpose of the club: purveying perversion. Bohemian Grove is reportedly intended to be used recreationally, providing a supposedly secure environment for politically affluent individuals to "party" without restraint. The only business conducted there pertained to implementing the New World Order, through the proliferation of mind-control atrocities, giving the place an air of "Masonic Secrecy." The only room where business discussions were permitted was the small, dark lounge affectionately and appropriately referred to as the Underground.

"My purpose at the Grove was sexual in nature, and therefore my perceptions were limited to a sex slave's viewpoint. As an effective means of control to ensure undetected proliferation of their perverse indulgences, slaves such as myself were subjected to ritualistic trauma. I knew each breath I took could be my last, as the threat of death lurked in every shadow. Slaves of advancing age or with failing programming were sacrificially murdered "at random" in the wooded grounds of Bohemian Grove, and I felt it was "simply a matter of time until it would be me." Rituals were held at a giant, concrete owl monument on the banks of, ironically enough, the Russian (rushin') River. These occultist sex rituals stemmed from the scientific belief that mind-controlled slaves required severe trauma to ensure compartmentalization of the memory, and not from any spiritual motivation.

"My own threat of death was instilled when I witnessed the sacrificial death of a young, dark-haired victim at which time I was instructed to perform sexually" as though my life depended upon it." I was told, "...the next sacrifice victim could be you. Anytime when you least expect it, the owl will consume you. Prepare yourself, and stay prepared." Being "prepared" equated to being totally suggestible, i.e., "on my toes" awaiting their command."

IMPLICATIONS

Supreme Court Judge Sonia Sotomayor is a member of the all-female "Belizean Club" which is the female equivalent of Bohemian Grove. The emerging picture is that the world elite is chosen by virtue of being sexually and morally compromised so they will obey the dictates of Cabalist central bankers.

I feel sorry for the innocent people who think Osama bin Laden was responsible for 9-11, the media tells the truth and we live in a free country. We live in a world designed and controlled by satanist central bankers according to the blueprint of *The Protocols of the Elders of Zion.*" We are being harassed by terrorism, war, financial crises and viruses just as the Protocols promised. The purpose is to make us throw up our hands and accept world government, which is a euphemism for banker tyranny. Whether it's climate change, wars, bank bailouts or "hate laws," there is less distinction everyday between the perversity of the Illuminati bankers and the actions of our government.

Bohemian Grove is more evidence that our natural leadership has been substituted for Satanists and perverts. We cannot be taken seriously as long as we allow these impostors to control us.

Governments must disown the "debt" which was created out of thin air, nationalize the central banks, and take control of our own credit. We must ensure that all political campaigns are publicly funded. The media and movie cartels need to be broken up and redistributed. The central bankers and their lackeys must be banished or the human race is doomed to further degradation.

Australian Adept Unveiled World Satanic Control

In an explosive deathbed confession, a former head of the satanist "Alpha Lodge" in Sydney, Australia, revealed the pervasive worldwide power of organized Satanism, which is synonymous with the Illuminati.

"Things are not as they seem — and they have not been for a long, long time," he wrote, describing a wholesale betrayal of society by its ostensible leaders.

"Petor Narsagonan" aka "Frater 616" died March 25, 2004. Recently, his executor, an "Aloysius Fozdyke" (their satanic names) sent the 15 pp. document by email to Arthur Cristian, webmaster of "loveforlife.com.au"

"I have felt it necessary to edit very little of this work," "Fozdyke" wrote to Cristian, "although legal considerations have ensured that some names and details were excised. It was His intention to have this published in the popular media."

What follows is a synopsis of this shocking document focusing on satanic power and influence.

Satanic influence is "now so pervasive as not to be readily noticed," Frater says.

Satanists are laced throughout Australian society, and the pattern is replicated everywhere.

They include politicians, doctors, high ranking police officers, lawyers, decorated military men, media personalities, fashion models and social workers. The most talented have lifestyles maintained by crime under a veneer of respectable professionalism and knowledge. Marginal types (prostitutes, drug dealers) are important to Satanism but are merely tools.

Frater explains he got involved in a satanic group in university in 1971. "I fell through a crack in reality...I escaped the mundane through one of western society's fault lines."

"A mentor" in the satanic network set him up in the travel business and for years Frater lived a life of unimaginable wealth, occultism and debauchery. He studied the blacks arts: divination, dark meditation, sacrifice, sexual vampirism, voodoo dolls and sex magic. Each day ended with a "Black Mass orgy of unforgettable and unspeakable delight."

The US-based "Church of Satan" was the public face of "an ancient body whose very existence had never before been imagined." He lists as "influential members" J.P. Morgan, Drs. James McDonald and Rene Hardy, the Kennedy's (including Jackie), Irving Berlin, Groucho Marx, Elvis Presley, Garner Ted Armstrong, Sammy Davis Jr., Ronald Reagan, Edward Heath, Thomas Plantard de St Claire and the Bushes. He later mentions Stephen Spielberg, George Lucas and Gerald Ford as members.

US MILITARY AND INTELLIGENCE INFILTRATED BY SATANISTS

Intelligence agencies are instruments of the Illuminati central bankers. Frater says, "American Intelligence Services" funded the occult.

"Many of America's high ranking military men were members of various Satanic Lodges or kindred organizations." They overlapped with organized crime and drug trafficking. US and Australian Navy ships were used, as well as oil tankers.

Brothels and porn are a small part of the "International Satanic Empire" (i.e. Illuminati.) Most of the money comes from CIA drug trafficking, sophisticated blackmail, money lending and currency trading.

"The US Federal government dances to our tune (a couple of steps removed, if you know what I mean!)"

"Satanists of the highest order are behind a number of wealthy, Conservative, New Right Christian churches and organizations in America. These are some of contemporary Satanism's best cash-flow enterprises (mostly indirectly) and allow mass indoctrination and networking."

Henry Kissinger first proposed using fundamentalist Christianity to bring about war, first in the Middle East and then globally. Kissinger "refined Hitler's 'Terror Technique' ... building tension within a society and then finding a scapegoat. Dark Path adepts do this ... to move people to more gross and hideous behaviors."

The aim of the Alpha Lodge is 66% illiteracy rates in the Western World by 2010, and "the destruction of at least 70% of the globe's population by the year 2030."

Most governments count on their "sheeple" to respond in "typical infantile fashion" and to identify with "a more powerful force— even if it enslaves, brutalizes and humiliates them."

Frater attributes the following to the "influence of Satanism in the modern world:"

-The developed world is heading toward Third World status because the central banks are owned by Satanists.
-Multinationals rape the environment and reap the rewards from Australia's natural resources.
-The media in the Free World is "heavily controlled" and in bed with the government.
-Fluoride in Australia's water supply.

-Educational standards dumbed down.

-Multiculturalism foisted on the First World (with exception of Japan.)

-Illuminati Satanists behind 9-11.

-Mossad came up with weapons of mass destruction rationale for Iraq Invasion. Illuminati uses Israel to run US foreign policy.

CONCLUSION

Frater says politicians know that if they feign interest in the welfare of the sheeple, they will go along with their policies "because it is the line of least resistance."

"Homo sapiens are herd animals, after all! ...Give them an election with no policy choices and for the most part they are happy. Allow their children no real prospects of success, inhibit their natural drives, particularly their sex drives; limit their options, coarsen their choices and society (such as it still is) quickly falls apart into predetermined categories. No families, just weak individuals free to do as they are told. Satan is a wonderful 'systems man.' "

The first and foremost responsibility of government is to prevent devil worshippers from taking control. It has failed.

What do we say about a youth who can't tell the difference between good and evil? Increasingly this is the condition of society as a whole.

Frater 616: "Every hour of every day and every night, people are knowingly engaged in Satan's service. Human sacrifice—whether ritually and quicker, or slowly and degradingly over time — is all harnessed to specific ends. "

"Politicians are introduced by a carefully graded set of criteria and situations that [convince] them that their victims will be "Our Little Secret." Young children sexually molested and physically abused by politicians worldwide are quickly used as sacrifices."

The social contract is broken. Any government that fails to tackle this cancer is illegitimate. Any society that tolerates it deserves what it gets.

Liberals are Unwitting Shills for Communism and Satanism

"The American people will never knowingly adopt Socialism. But under the name of 'liberalism' they will adopt every fragment of the Socialist program, until one day America will be a Socialist nation, without knowing how it happened." Norman Thomas, US Socialist Leader, 1944

Liberals are dupes, what Communists call "useful idiots." I was one for most of my life.

"Championing the oppressed" was a pathetic way to justify my life while being blinded to the real enemy. As I will demonstrate, liberals, funded by the Rockefellers and Rothschilds, are mostly unwitting pawns of a satanic Communist agenda. They are like the lower Blue Degrees of Freemasonry, dupes. This sounds extreme but unfortunately, it is literally true.

Richard Rodriguez is a liberal propagandist. Flipping channels, I stumbled on a deceitful diatribe against men and the traditional family on the Rockefeller- funded PBS.

Called "Women on the Move," it suggests that the school girls of Afghanistan are ready to fill the void left by men as the "male order falters and fails." Absurd as this notion is, coming from the Rockefellers, it conveys their subversive and totalitarian agenda.

Rodriguez, who is gay, actually celebrates native women traitors who betrayed their people —La Malinche, Pocahontas and Sacagawea. (This is what feminists do when they become Rockefeller pawns.) He glorifies single mothers and flails "tribal leaders at war with modernity" because they want to protect their culture.

Newsflash: "Modernity" is Satanism, i.e. the deification of Man, i.e. Rothschild Cabalist Man. Remember what the Rockefeller Insider said in 1969: "there are always two reasons for anything the Rockefellers do: the pretext which makes it palatable to the gullible public and the real reason."

I get a kick out of sanctimonious liberals who contribute money to the "Public" Broadcasting System when obviously it is a Rockefeller tool. But then I contributed to PBS when I was a liberal.

The same day, a Toronto *Globe and Mail* article trumpeted "A Remarkable Week for Gay Rights." This is why I never buy newspapers. They are propaganda rags that have abandoned any pretence of objectivity or honesty. Why does author John Ibbitson rejoice when marriage, the central heterosexual rite of 96% of the population, is redefined to satisfy marriage-minded gays, who are less than one per cent of the population?

Marriage is a heterosexual rite. What if Muslims started redefining Passover or Jews took over Ramadan? Homosexuals should have their own equal but distinct rites.

Even children of sperm donors crave a father and go to great lengths to find him, yet Ibbitson is happy to see traditional marriage trashed. When was the last time you saw traditional marriage and family celebrated in the mass media? Marriage is designed to provide a stable foundation for child rearing. Apparently this society cares little for its own survival and health.

What do Rodriguez and Ibbitson have in common? The not-so-hidden liberal agenda is to treat hetero and homosexuals as if they were the same, and to get women to choose careers over family and abandon child-rearing to the State. Not coincidentally, the Communist Manifesto advocates destruction of the nuclear family.

Subjected to this propaganda, it's no wonder that only 53% of Americans can definitely say they prefer capitalism to socialism.

BELLA DODD

Bella Dodd (1904-1969) a lawyer and political science professor, was a Communist Party organizer from 1932-1948 and a member of the National Council of the CPUSA from 1944-48.

In her book, *"School of Darkness,"* she said Communists infiltrated and took control of liberal and socialist groups and unions. (She took control of the NY State Teachers Union.) She said Communism is a satanic cult that is conspiring to enslave the world.

In testimony to HUAC in 1953, she revealed some liberals "have allowed themselves to become supporters of the very members of this conspiracy. This is not liberalism, not liberalism in the finest sense of the word. This is just allowing the Communist to pull them into a propaganda environment which says that "anyone who is close to the Communist is a liberal. I do not believe that is the definition of "a liberal."

She offered the classical definition: "A liberal is a person who believes in the right of the individual to function. The Communist does not believe in the right of the individual. They believe only in the right of the collective. The individual is only part of a collective group, and whenever he doesn't move according to the collective, he is ousted from the group."

Mr. Kuzig: "So you would say that when so-called liberals today, self-denominated liberals, support and work with the Communist program, they are being deluded into thinking they are helping a liberal cause when it is not liberal."

Dodd: "One of the great tragedies today is that these Americans do not realize that this would take civilization back to a barbarism which existed long before the Christian era... The Communists have a way of changing names and labels....How shall we recognize them, then ? ...by the fact that they believe that there is no God ; that a person is just born, grows, dies, decays, and that is the end. They believe that the individual doesn't matter; that the collective matters. They believe that certain people should have the power to run a country."

DODD SPEECHES

Bella Dodd converted to Catholicism at the end of her life. At a lecture in the 1950s, she said: "In the 1930's, we put eleven hundred men into the priesthood in order to destroy the Church from within." The idea was for these men to be ordained, and then climb the ladder of influence and authority as monsignors and bishops. Back then, she said: "Right now they are in the highest places in the Church. They are working to bring about change in order that the Catholic Church would not be effective against Communism."

She also said that these changes would be so drastic that "you will not recognize the Catholic Church." (This was 10 to 12 years before Vatican II.) "The whole idea was to destroy, not the institution of the Church, but rather the Faith of the people, and even use the institution of the Church, if possible, to destroy the Faith through the promotion of a pseudo-religion: something that resembled Catholicism but was not the real thing. Once the Faith was destroyed, she explained that there would be a guilt complex introduced into the Church... to label the 'Church of the past' as being oppressive, authoritarian, full of prejudices, arrogant in claiming to be the sole possessor of truth, and responsible for the divisions of religious bodies throughout the centuries. This would be necessary in order to shame Church leaders into an 'openness to the world,' and to a more flexible attitude toward all religions and philosophies [i.e. liberalism]. The Communists would then exploit this openness in order to undermine the Church."

In a lecture recorded in Utica in 1962, she said the Communist practice is to create conflict by operating through various organizations. "They will create a Right in order to have a Left opposed to it, so they can drag people in the direction of the Left."

She said the 1944 Communist National Convention was attended by politicians elected under the Republican and Democratic banners. In a speech, Howard Vanden Kastenburg said: "When we get ready to take the United States, we will not take it under the name of Socialism or Communism. These labels are unpleasant to the American people...We will take it under labels we have made loveable...We'll take it under Liberalism, under Progressivism, under Democracy. But take it we will."

THE *PROTOCOLS OF ZION*

The *Protocols of Zion* make it clear that the Illuminati bankers promoted liberalism and equality only to overthrow the Gentile aristocracy and church. "While preaching liberalism to the goy, we at the same time keep our own people and our agents in a state of unquestioning submission." (15)

"The word "freedom" brings out the communities of men to fight against every kind of force, against every kind of authority even against God and the laws of nature." (5)

"In order to annihilate the institutions of the goyim ... we have replaced [their mechanism] by the chaotic license of liberalism. We have got our hands into the administration of the law, into the conduct of elections, into the press, into liberty of the person, but principally into education and training as being the cornerstones of a free existence." (9)

Their control is based on the paralysis they induce in representative government. "We replaced the ruler with a caricature of a government—by a President taken from the mob, from the midst of our puppet creatures or slaves. This was the foundation of the mine which we have laid under the GOY peoples..." (10)

Through their control of the press and education, they lionized "sedition mongers" which in turn has protected them. "This advertisement has increased the contingent of liberals and has brought thousands of GOYIM into the ranks of our livestock cattle." (19)

As for equality, the founders of Communism write:" Far back in ancient times we were the first to cry among the masses of the people the words "Liberty, Equality, Fraternity," ..."baits" [which] carried away the well-being of the world, true freedom of the individual, formerly so well guarded against the pressure of the mob."

"The would-be wise men of the goyim, the intellectuals...did not see that in nature there is no equality, cannot be freedom: that Nature herself has established inequality of minds, of characters, and capacities,... it was based upon these things that dynastic rule rested: the father passed on to the son a knowledge of the course of political affairs in such wise that none should know it but members of the dynasty and none could betray it to the governed. As time went on, the meaning of the dynastic transference of the true position of affairs in the political was lost, and this aided the success of our cause." (1-25)

CONCLUSION

As well as controlling society, the Rothschild banking syndicate uses the Left to extort and undermine the competition. During the French Revolution, the Rothschild mansion was spared by the rioting masses. The Bolsheviks were instructed to appropriate Russian factories and hand them over to the bankers.

We are all liberals in the classical sense of believing in individual freedom. But the Illuminati bankers have changed the definition of liberal to the spurious notion of "championing minorities and the less fortunate." This has been used to divert, divide and undermine the majority, as well as undermine traditional values.

Until liberals wake up to what the *Protocols* refer to as "the true nature of things," they will continue to embrace their own destruction and that of Western civilization.

I'm Not on Putin's Bandwagon

I had as much satisfaction as anyone from the humiliation Vlad Putin dealt the Zionists in Georgia. However I'm not joining in the general celebration evinced by articles like "The Zionist West Has Met Its Match" by Karl Schwartz (August 23,2008.)

To equate the New World Order with Zionism is incorrect. Zionism is just one pincer in the NWO. The other is Opposition-to-Zionism, represented by Russia's Putin and Iran's Ahmadinejad. The Rothschilds control them both through MI-6.

This dialectic succeeds the Nazi- Communist one of WW2. You can't have a Third World War unless you have two sides. This time round, Putin and Ahmadinejad have been cast as defenders of Nation and Religion. But don't be fooled. This is the Rothschild *modus operandi*. They routinely simulate the opposition or pretend to fight themselves. (Read Protocols 12 and 17 for examples.)This way they can initiate profitable conflicts and orchestrate the outcome. Wars keep us off balance and unable to address the real problem — them. Meanwhile the idealistic plebes fight and die for a "cause."

How do I support this view of Putin? To begin, his body language. Putin doesn't have the gravitas to be more than a front man. He lacks chest hair. Did you see how comfortable he was with George W. Bush? They are both veterans from central casting. If Putin were for real, he wouldn't be able to stand W's presence.

For those who demand more substantial proof, I spent a half-hour on Google. I learned that Putin is on intimate terms with the head of the largest faction of Russian Jewry, the Chabad Lubavitchers. The Rebbe relates how when young Vlad was hungry, they fed him and he has felt gratitude ever since. Maybe they're still feeding him? Apparently this sect is at the forefront of the NWO.

Then I found the website of an MI-6 defector Richard Tomlinson who trained with young KGB agent Putin. They both learned to serve the Illuminati who were 'born to rule', the self-elected custodians of society.

Putin was brainwashed and controlled by MI-6 and may still be. This may explain his muted reaction to the sinking of the Kursk by the US and the Beslan massacre aided and abetted by MI-6. Tomlinson says Putin was a Royal Arch Freemason but is no longer a Freemason and has broken free of his mind programming. I wonder.

Another tell: Mikhail Gorbachev, New World Elder, rode to Putin's defence on the Larry King Show.

Then there is the famous picture of Putin kissing the stomach of a young boy in public, suggesting he has the pederast foibles typical of his kind. I don't believe Putin's break with the Rothschilds and the West is more than stagecraft. Does Russia have a central bank controlled by the Rothschilds? 'Nuff said. I'd love for Putin et co. to be for real. But I'm not buying it yet.

AHMADINEJAD

Here is the Iranian President giving the Masonic "thumb and finger" sign of recognition. Two fingers pointed upward is a negative sign.

An Iranian reader claims that Ahmadinejad is a crypto-Jew. He pointed me to a Wikipedia article which says his family changed their name in the 50's from Saborjhian, a typical Jewish name.

He continued: "I really hope this will be a way to expose the real danger we all are facing globally; Iran, USA and Russia hand-in-hand bringing the third world war."

"Inside the political establishment of Iran, everybody is concerned about crypto-Jews that have a strong grip on the most influential politicians just by having corrupted them all or they know about their dirty past. For example : Mohsen Rezaei ex-commander of Revolutionary Guard said last summer: 'Ahmadinejad's mother is a Jew, and from the establishment of Islamic republic in 1979, the crypto-Jews were in the highest position in decision making in the State.' but he is silent now!"

This would be consistent with reports that Israel may have helped Iran develop nuclear weapons. Recently, an ex-Mossad chief said Ahmadinejad was "Israel's greatest gift" by posing as a threat to Israel.

"Ahmadinejad is our greatest gift," Halevy told the Arab language television network Al-Hurra . "We couldn't carry out a better operation at the Mossad than to put a guy like Ahmadinejad in power in Iran."

Halevy added that the Iranian president's extremist statements "proved to everyone that Iran of today is an Iran that is impossible to live with. [Ahmadinejad] unites the entire world against Iran."

I hope average Israelis see how they are being used as pawns, as were the Jews of Europe, with fatal consequences.

A GUIDE FOR THE BEDEVILED

Our political life is a charade designed to convince the rubes they live in a democracy. This is so they will pay taxes and lay down their lives for their betters.

Our rulers have determined that we shall have no real say in our collective future. Like livestock, we will chew our collective cud on sex, drugs, toys and trivia, which they will supply in abundance.

This explains why the mass media (incl. movies) and education long ago ceased to deal in reality, or teach civics or history. Instead they purvey fantasy, deception and conformity.

Our world is a B-movie Horror where the town's leading citizens secretly join a satanic cult and betray everybody else. This is essentially the position of people who serve the central bankers, which is a prerequisite for success in most fields today.

Crazed MI-5 & MI-6
Wreak Havoc for the Illuminati

Blogs by people claiming to be former MI-5 and MI-6 agents paint a sordid picture of state terrorism, rape, torture, mind control, murder and pedophilia in the service of the Illuminati.

The main blog is called "Richard Tomlinson and the Russians" but there are a dozen more listed below. Taken together with comments by insiders, they tell a hair-raising tale of mayhem perpetrated by these deranged Illuminati agencies. Most people will not believe it. It has taken me nearly a year to process it.

Here are some highlights:

• The world's Intelligence agencies are infiltrated and controlled by "Royal Arch" Freemasons who owe their loyalty not to the State but to Illuminati (Masonic) bankers, posing as the "Crown" or "Monarchy." Most agents are tortured, i.e. trauma brainwashed and mind controlled using trigger words from texts like *Alice in Wonderland.*

MI-5 Chief Manningham-Buller told recruits they serve "the 'real' Communism, ...the 'Guardianship' by those who were 'born to rule'. They were the self-elected custodians of British society who could decide what was in their people's best interests."

"This tarantula-like Masonic organization ...has been strangling the world since the last days of the British Empire. Those within British Intelligence who were not Royal Arch Freemasons, had no real idea of what was going on at all. If they did manage to catch a 'Russian spy' within their midst, it was because the Royal Arch Freemasons had deemed this person expendable and had then fed him or her to the fishes. Think Burgess, Maclean etc and you will get the picture. [Anthony] Blunt escaped such censorship and hounding. He was a 'master' of Royal Arch Freemasonry."

• "Vladimir Putin has a long history as a Royal Arch Freemason. He is "a puppet - always has been. You only have to look into his vacuous eyes to see that. - how much ECT does it take to run a Puppet-President? Quite a bit, I would imagine." He also was a cross dresser & boy toy to current MI-6 Director John Scarlett."

• "Putin was chosen as a DNA sperm donor within this Royal 'zygote' project and had then been ordered by the Masonic body to copulate with various British female agents, whilst in Berlin. The zygotes were then 'collected' and the young woman involved was subsequently murdered. Stephen Daldry [the film Director] had organized various victims to be sent to Berlin for exactly this purpose. He has also boasted of listening to them (bugged rooms) being murdered, during this period. Cameras were also placed in the TV sets for the Royal Arch Freemasons to view afterward - in essence, 'snuff movies'. By 1993, the Royal Arch Freemasons had no further use for Mr Putin in terms of information or DNA and therefore, he was expendable - Royal Arch Freemason or not."

• "Putin's mother was Jewish but converted to Russian Orthodoxy. In Poland, he decided to go back to his roots and because his mother was Jewish he didn't have to go through a full conversion.

There is some difference among the posters about whether Putin broke from the Illuminati and deprogrammed himself when he was betrayed by MI-6.

• MI-6 "implanted a nuclear bomb (ESSO were employed to do the drilling) between the tectonic plates under the seabed - just off Aceh, Indonesia. MI5 were to send a military ship into the area after the explosion had occurred, in order to check radiation levels. They had miscalculated. The radiation levels are now affecting all of the surrounding islands, including the Arabian peninsula. The explosion occurred on the 26th December 2004." [i.e. the Tsunami]

"Indonesian Intelligence were duly warned and took action by taking out large insurance claims with British companies just before the event (mainly on the same day beforehand, in order to get the claims through without creating suspicion and UK firms backing out of the deal), in relation to the areas and buildings that the tsunami would hit."

• On July 10, 2007 "Anonymous" posted the following: "The new date set for Royal Illuminati terrorist attacks is the 14th July 2007. They have planned a whole series of bombings all over the world. Too numerous to mention. One hopes this advance warning will put them off once again but as ever this is only an intermediary measure. British Intelligence have to sort themselves out, once and for all... The Crown has a stranglehold on BI [British Intelligence]and its not going to let go without a battle. The Royal Military will see to that." [No bombs went off on that date.]

• "Little Madelaine's [McCann's] parents were part of the Illuminati ring - mind control slaves themselves. They know what happened to her - their subconscious minds know exactly what happened but they were powerless to stop it. J K Rowling is also an Illuminati Monarch slave - she is an actress who has hardly put pen to paper regarding the Harry Potter books. The original author of the first four books - hasn't seen a penny from it - stolen goods. Rowling was present at the rite in which Madeleine died - hence her offer of a reward in public, was all the more sickening.

"Rowling was chosen to front this series of books because she was so malleable. She wanted fame and fortune without cost. Her Ashkenazim parents had bought her out of British Illuminati slavery and had also bought her what is known in the trade as a 'Pen and Ink Stand': A ghost-writer who works as an unpaid slave — one of British Intelligence's operatives."

• "Richard Tomlinson, an agent who publicly accused MI-6 of involvement in the murder of Princess Diana possibly took part in the crime. "Tomlinson had chipped

Henri Paul in the kitchens beforehand. He had been on one of the large, black motor-bikes hounding Diana's car and watched as she cried out for help after the accident without doing a thing - he was too busy securing his photographs of the ambulance as a blackmailing threat to MI6..."

Tomlinson supposedly broke with MI-6 but the posters say he is still working for them, running a pedophile ring in the south of France. For a "defector," his book *The Big Breach* (2001) is singularly unrevealing, especially in light of the material discussed here.

• Stella Rimington, a director of MI-5 in the 1990's is a former secretary who did sexual entrapment for MI-5 before becoming a S/M lesbian. She had her agents steal the MI-6 mind control codes and used them to break out of her own mind control and "attack the system from outside." When she started assassinating MI-6 agents who annoyed her, she was ungracefully retired. "She has been involved in child trafficking and prostitution ever since."

CONCLUSION

There is a list of the related blogs at the end of this article. Generally speaking, this incredible material is consistent with what we already know about the Illuminati. They are insane.

They are a satanic cult.

These blogs provide a rare glimpse of the seedy underside of the establishment in Britain where the Illuminati is headquartered. I doubt if the situation is very different elsewhere.

This criminality and depravity is permitted and cultivated in order to undermine democratic institutions. The Illuminati bankers want the people to cry out for their totalitarian world government.

Related Blogs (some may be defunct.)

andrewmarr.blogspot.com
www.johnscarlett.blogspot.com
www.elizamanninghambuller.blogspot.com
www.stellarimington.blogspot.com
www.seraphimraziel77.blogspot.com
www.beautyandthebeastomega.blogspot.com
www.fivehivealpha.blogspot.com
www.rubberduckpsi.blogspot.com
www.alphadeltaV.blogspot.com
www.cuckoosnests.blogspot.com

www.electricbluesky.blogspot.com
www.alicescapesthemenagerie.blogspot.com
www.royalarchcrumbles.blogspot.com
www.beautyandthebeastpower.blogspot.com
www.beautyandthebeastomega.blogspot.com
www.fivehivealpha.blogspot.com
www.rubberduckpsi.blogspot.com
www.alphadeltaV.blogspot.com
www.cuckoosnests.blogspot.com
www.electricbluesky.blogspot.com

BOOK TWO

Social Engineering and Cultural Subversion

Rockefeller Insider Said in 1969: Travel Will be Made Difficult

Like sheep, humanity had better adjust to constant harassment as long as it tolerates Illuminati control of all important government and social institutions.

At the height of the holiday season, millions of travellers to the US were delayed and inconvenienced because of a contrived incident involving exploding underwear. Can someone bring down a plane with exploding underwear? No, but he could do serious damage to his genitals.

In 1969, Rockefeller Insider Dr. Richard Day predicted the future in these terms:

" Travel ... [will] become very restricted. People [will] need permission to travel and they [will] need a good reason to travel. If you didn't have a good reason for your travel you [will] not be allowed to travel, and everyone [will] need ID... later on some sort of device [will] be developed to be implanted under the skin that [will] be coded specifically to identify the individual."

DETAILS

On March 20, 1969, Dr. Richard Day, the National Medical Director of the Rockefeller-sponsored "Planned Parenthood" described "A New World System" to a meeting of the Pittsburgh Pediatric Society. These remarks were reported by Dr. Lawrence Dunegan, a Pittsburgh pediatrician who died in Jan. 2004. Dr. Day, who died in 1989 (see obit online), wanted the 80 or so physicians present to be prepared. The transcript of Dunegan's recollections can be found online and should be read in full. Here is a summary.

He said that American industry will be sabotaged and shown to be unreliable and un-competitive. "The stated plan was that different parts of the world would be assigned different roles of industry and commerce in a unified global system. The continued pre-eminence and relative self-sufficiency of the United States would have to be changed... Each part of the world will have a specialty and thus become inter-dependent, he said. The US will remain a center for agriculture, high tech, communications, and education but heavy industry would be transported out."

Dunegan recalls: "The idea was, you could get a little bit disgusted with your Ford, GM, or Chrysler product -or whatever- because little things like window handles would fall off more, and plastic parts would break... Your patriotism about buying American would soon give way to practicality... Patriotism would go down the drain then."

Much of what Day promised in 1969 is looking like a rear-view mirror today. But ominous events have yet to transpire. They do want to implant a chip in us so they can find and identify us, as well as monitor and control our purchases.

They are weaning us off national allegiance and will resort to terrorism to win our assent to their global police state. They may use "one or two nuclear bombs to convince people we mean business," Day said.

He said that there are always two reasons for anything the Rockefellers do: the pretext which makes it palatable to the gullible public and the real reason. Dr. Day said sex will be separated from marriage and reproduction (i.e. "sexual liberation") to break up the family and reduce population. Abortion, divorce and homosexuality will be made socially acceptable.

"Homosexuals will be given permission to act out. Everyone including the elderly will be encouraged to have sex. It will be brought out into the open. Anything goes." [The "Stonewall Riots" which unleashed the "gay rights" movement, took place three months later.] The ultimate goal is to have sex without reproduction. Reproduction without sex will occur in laboratories. Family size will be limited as in China.

It will be made more difficult for families to stay together. More women will work outside the home and more people will remain single. Sports instead of dolls will be promoted to girls so they will seek achievement instead of family. Girls will be taught they are the same as boys.

In general, international sports like soccer and hockey will be pushed so Americans will see themselves as "world citizens." American sports like baseball and football will not be similarly encouraged.

Pornography, violence and obscenity on TV and in movies will be increased. People will be desensitized to violence and porn and made to feel life is short, precarious and brutish. Music will "get worse" and will be used for indoctrination.

There will be unemployment and mass migration in order to uproot long established (conservative) communities. Social change will be introduced in port cities and work its way to the heartland. (Thus, the east and west coast are liberal.)

He said a cure to cancer exists in the Rockefeller Institute but is kept secret for purposes of depopulation. He said there will be an increase in infectious man-made diseases.

Dr. Day, who worked in weather modification during the war, said weather can be used to wage war or create drought and famine. The food supply will be monitored so no one can get enough food to "support a fugitive from the New System." Growing your own food will be outlawed under the pretext of it being unsafe.

He said people are controlled by means of the information they are given. Thus, information will be selective. Not everyone will be allowed to own books. "Certain books will disappear from libraries." Literary classics will be subtly altered. People will spend longer in school but not learn anything. There will be restrictions on travel; and private home ownership will disappear.

He said people who don't want to go along will be "disposed of humanely." He said there will be no martyrs—"people will just disappear."

THE KEY TO OUR EXASPERATION

In the *Protocols of the Elders of Zion*, the author writes that their goal is: "To wear everyone out by dissension, animosities, feuds, famine, inoculation of diseases, want, until the Gentiles sees no other way of escape except by appeal to our money and our power." (10)

Harold Rosenthal who was a member of this cabal boasted that they even implanted a "guilt complex" over the holocaust and anti-Semitism that prevents society from addressing the threat.

Through control of banking, they acquired a total monopoly of "the movie industry, the radio networks and the newly developing television media...we took over the publication of all school materials... Even your music! We censor the songs released for publication long before they reach the publishers...we will have complete control of your thinking."

We "have put issue upon issue to the American people. Then we promote both sides of the issue as confusion reigns. With their eyes fixed on the issues, they fail to see who is behind every scene. We, Jews, toy with the American public as a cat toys with a mouse."

SOCIETY OF SHILLS

Society operates on two rails. The formal—the image of a democracy ruled by law that dupes the masses and ensures their cooperation. The informal— the Illuminati club, which actually makes the decisions regardless of what's happening on the formal level. The informal infiltrates the formal until the latter is merely a mask for the former.

In an Internet post May 29, 2009, Emily Gyde, an Illuminati defector who claims to be the real author of the Harry Potter series, said Barack Obama told her this:

"I remember PRESIDENT OBAMA talking to me about how he had joined the ILL CULT - he didn't want to - but he described himself as just an ordinary guy who wanted to take a wage packet home...that is how it was...he didn't want to end up on the streets... at the end of the day, it was all about money...you had to have it to live...if he hadn't joined the ILL CULT...he would have been disbarred...he wouldn't have got a job... wouldn't have been able to live...that's how a lot of people get conned into joining the ILL. You are young, you want to prove yourself in life - you are told that you will 'never get a job' if you don't...the ILL prove how powerful they are."

I don't know if this is true but it is plausible.

CONCLUSION

When I was a sixties radical, we used to think people who worked for the Establishment had sold their soul to the devil. I didn't imagine it was literally true. The Illuminati are Satan worshippers, so you're unwittingly working for his disciples.

Psychological Warfare Against Society

A shocking document entitled "Silent Weapons for Quiet Wars" confirms that a satanic cult headquartered in the City of London, the Illuminati, holds mankind in bondage using psychological warfare. A second document, described later, "The Soviet Art of Brainwashing" shows how the professions, especially psychology and mental health, have been subverted.

"The public cannot comprehend this weapon and therefore cannot believe that they are being attacked and subdued by a weapon," says the "Silent Weapons" report.

Dated May 1979, "Silent Weapons for Quiet Wars" (Technical Manual SW7905.1) was found in 1986 in an IBM copier that had been purchased at a surplus sale. It is the product of a discipline called "Operations Research" developed during WWII to attack enemy populations using tools of social engineering and psychological warfare.

According to the document, the "international elite" decided in 1954 to wage a "quiet war" against the American people with the goal of shifting wealth from "the irresponsible many" into the hands of the "responsible and worthy few."

"In view of the law of natural selection it was agreed that a nation or world of people who will not use their intelligence are no better than animals who do not have intelligence. Such people are beasts of burden and steaks on the table [sic] by choice and consent."

The goal was to establish an economy, which is "totally predictable and manipulatable." The masses will have to be "trained and assigned a yoke...from a very early age..."

To achieve such conformity, the "family unit must be disintegrated by a process of increasing preoccupation of the parents and the establishment of government operated day care centres for the occupationally orphaned children."

This is accomplished through "silent weapons" (propaganda and social engineering) applied in the media and schools.

"When the silent weapon is applied gradually, the public adjusts...until the pressure becomes too great and they crack up...Therefore the silent weapon is a type of biological warfare.... It attacks ...their sources of natural and social energy and their physical, mental and emotional strengths..."

Although not mentioned by name, the silent weapon here is feminism, which promotes lesbianism while posing as the defender of women.

The document says the father must be "house broken." The advertising media see to it that he is "pussy whipped" and "taught that he either conforms...or his sex life will... be zero." The female is "ruled by emotion first and logic second...too starry eyed to see [her child will be] a wealthy man's cannon fodder or a cheap source of slave labor."

The writer concludes, "This mindless school of jelly fish, father, mother, son and daughter, becomes useful beasts of burden..."

"DIVERSION THE PRIMARY STRATEGY"

The document speaks of "gaining control of the public" by keeping them "undisciplined, ignorant, confused, disorganized and distracted."

Divert the public from "the real social issues and captivated by matters of no importance." "Sabotage their mental activities" by a "constant barrage of sex, violence and wars in the media" i.e. "mental and emotional rape."

Give them "junk food for thought" and deprive them of what they really need," especially a sound education. "Keep the public entertainment below the sixth-grade level."

"Work: Keep the public busy, busy, busy with no time to think; back on the farm with the other animals." "Destroy the faith of the American people in each other."

The general rule: "there is profit in confusion; the more confusion, the more profit. Therefore the best approach is to create problems and then offer solutions."

"THE WELFARE STATE AS STRATEGIC WEAPON"

The public wants to "perpetuate their dependency role of childhood. Simply put, they want a human god to eliminate all risk from their life, pat them on the head, kiss their bruises, put a chicken on every dinner table...tuck them in and tell them everything will be all right...."

The "human god" is the politician who promises the world and delivers nothing. This public behavior is "surrender born of fear, laziness, and expediency. It is the basis of the welfare state as a strategic weapon, useful against a disgusting public."

The public's lack of resistance is a sign that it "is ripe for surrender and is consenting to enslavement and legal encroachment. A good ...indicator of harvest time is the number of public citizens who pay income tax despite an obvious lack of reciprocal or honest service from the government."

BRAINWASHING

Now, I turn to another document, "The Soviet Art of Brainwashing," a textbook that was used in Communist training schools both in the USA and Russia starting in the 1930's.

Remember Communism was never a "working class revolt." It was created by the Illuminati to control the common man and enact their one-world dictatorship. The textbook suggests that major silent weapons are "higher education" and the "mental health" fields.

"In the United States we have been able to alter the works of William James, and others, ...and to place the tenets of Karl Marx, Pavlov, Lamarck, and the data of Dialectic Materialism into the textbooks of psychology, to such a degree that anyone thoroughly studying psychology becomes at once a candidate to accept the reasonableness of Communism."

"As every chair of psychology in the United States is occupied by persons in our connection, the consistent employment of such texts is guaranteed... Educating broadly the educated strata of the populace into the tenets of Communism is thus rendered relatively easy." (II, Ch. 11)

The textbook calls these teachers "psycho political operatives" and their role is to brainwash the young.

Communists view man as "a mechanism without individuality." He is "basically an animal" with a "civilized veneer." Like an animal, he can be forced to believe and do anything given the right combination of terror, deception, drugs and brute force.

The goal of "psycho politics" is to "produce the maximum chaos in the culture of the enemy," and to "leave a nation leaderless."

MORE ABOUT THE PSYCHO POLITICAL OPERATIVE

The textbook advocates the use of doctors, social workers, psychiatrists and the whole field of "mental healing" to bring about the satanic goal.

"Mental health organizations must carefully delete from their ranks anyone actually proficient in the handling or treatment of mental health." (II Ch. 9)

"The psycho political operative should also spare no expense in smashing out of existence, by whatever means, any actual healing group, such as that of acupuncture, in China; such as Christian Science, Dianetics and faith healing in the United States; such as Catholicism in Italy and Spain; and the practical psychological groups of England." (II-9)

The textbook claims Communists took over the field of psychoanalysis and "made it fashionable," because of its "stress on sex." This serves the purposes of "degradation" and "defamation of character" i.e. blackmail. (II-9)

Recruitment into the ranks of mental healing should be confined to the "already depraved, or [people] who have been treated by psycho political operatives. Recruitment is effected by making the field of mental healing very attractive, financially, and sexually."

"The promise of unlimited sexual opportunities, the promise of complete dominion over the bodies and minds of helpless patients, the promise of having lawlessness without detection, can thus attract to "mental healing" many desirable recruits who will willingly fall in line with psycho political activities." (II-13)

FINAL INSTRUCTIONS

"You must work until religion is synonymous with insanity. You must work until the officials of city, county and state governments will not think twice before they pounce upon religious groups as public enemies." (II-14)

"Movements to improve youth should be invaded and corrupted, as this might interrupt campaigns to produce in youth delinquency, addiction, drunkenness, and sexual promiscuity." (II-15)

Seek out " the leaders in the country's future, and educate them into the belief in the animalistic nature of Man. This must be made fashionable. They must be taught to frown upon ideas, upon individual endeavour. They must be taught, above all things that the salvation of Man is to be found only by his adjusting thoroughly to this environment. ...Nations, which have high ethical tone, are difficult to conquer." (II-8)

"In order to induce a high state of hypnosis in an individual, a group, or a population, an element of terror must always be present on the part of those who would govern." (Part II, Ch.6)

But to say so is paranoid. "The by-word should be built into the society that paranoia is a condition "in which the individual believes he is being attacked by Communists. It will be found that this defence is effective." (II- Ch 10)

"The populace must be brought into the belief that every individual within it who rebels ... against the efforts and activities to enslave the whole, must be considered to be a deranged person ...and... be given electric shocks, and reduced into unimaginative docility for the remainder of his days." (II-Ch.12)

CONCLUSION

These documents provide a glimpse of the evil we confront. In a 1961 lecture, Aldous Huxley described the coming world state as "the final revolution": a "dictatorship without tears" where people "love their servitude."

According to Huxley, the goal is to produce "a kind of painless concentration camp for entire societies so that people will in fact have their liberties taken away ... but ... will be distracted from any desire to rebel by propaganda or brainwashing ... enhanced by pharmacological methods." (Lecture to the California Medical School, 1961)

Bankers Were Behind
the Counter Culture

We assume large corporations have economic objectives. But we don't expect them to have a secret social and occult agenda as well.

For example, we don't expect them to engineer arrested development and family breakdown. We don't expect them to use pop culture to foster alienation and dysfunction.

Central bankers based in the City of London control the cartels that dominate the world economy. They finagled the right to print money based on our credit and quite naturally used this advantage to buy everything worth having.

This might be tolerable if unlimited wealth was all they wanted. But they also want unlimited power: not just one-world dictatorship but total control over our minds and souls.

In the book "*Dope, Inc.*," (1992) Executive Intelligence Review researchers unveil the true occult and criminal character of the bankers' agenda. Incredible and bizarre as it sounds, the bankers practise the pagan Cult of Isis, which is at the heart of Freemasonry, Theosophy and the Cabala.

"Their religion is not the Anglican Christianity they publicly profess but a hodgepodge of paganism, including satanic cults such as Theosophy and Rosicrucianism. The central, synergetic ideology of the oligarchies inner cult life is the revived Egyptian drug cult, the myth of Isis and Osiris, the same anti-Christian cult that ran the Roman Empire." (263)

This is why the logos of many major corporations feature occult symbolism. This is why their advertising often contains an overt occult social message, often espousing sexual liberation or feminism.

According to EIR, the "New Age" counterculture "that was foisted on the 1960s adolescent youth of America is not merely analogous to the ancient cult of Isis. It is a literal resurrection of the Cult..." (537)

POPULAR CULTURE = BRAINWASHING

The 35-page chapter, "The Aquarian Conspiracy," is available on line. I am merely highlighting the most pertinent points.

"Popular culture" (music, TV, movies, books, fashion etc.) is NOT spontaneous but Illuminati controlled and manufactured. EIR compares it with the drug trade in general: "Today's mass culture operates like the opium trade: The supply determines the demand." (545)

For example, the bankers' social engineering branch, the Tavistock Institute, manufactured the Beatles phenomenon. The screaming teenagers were bused in from a girl's school.

"In 1963 the Beatles appeared on the Ed Sullivan show. They combined rock and mystical music, long hair, and Hindu worship...Drugs were suggested in many of their songs: "Yellow Submarine" (a "submarine" is a "downer"), "Lucy in the Sky With Diamonds" (the initials of the main words are LSD), "Hey Jude" (a song about methadone), "Strawberry Fields" (where opium is grown to avoid detection) and "Norwegian Wood" (a British term for marijuana.)

John Lennon's song "Imagine" attacked religion ("Imagine there's no heaven, It's easy if you try, No hell below us, Above us only sky"), espoused a do-your-own-thing philosophy ("Imagine all the people, Living for today"), attacked nationalism ("Imagine there's no countries"), attacked religion ("It is isn't hard to do, Nothing to kill or die for and no religion too"), called for the abolition of private property ("Imagine no possessions.")

It supported a new international order ("I wonder if you can, No need for greed or hunger, A brotherhood of man, Imagine all the people, Sharing all the world") and advocated a one-world government ("You may say I'm a dreamer, But I'm not the only one, I hope someday you'll join us, and the world will be as one.") Lennon called for abolition of private property and then left his Japanese-born widow a $250 million estate.

BRAVE NEW WORLD

In his *"Brave New World Revisited,"* (1958) Aldous Huxley, a member of the banker brain trust, described a society in which "the first aim of the rulers is at all costs to keep their subjects from making trouble." He described a likely future: "The completely organized society... the abolition of free will by methodical conditioning, the servitude made acceptable by regular doses of chemically induced happiness . . ."

This society is run by "change agents" who are often feminists, Marxists, socialists, liberals or naive New Agers. Conspiracy leaders H.G. Wells and Marilyn Ferguson mention them in *"The Open Conspiracy"* (1928) and in *"The Aquarian Conspiracy"* (1980) respectively.

Ferguson writes: "There are legions of [Aquarian] conspirators. They are in corporations, universities, and hospitals, on the faculties of public schools, in factories and doctors' offices, in state and federal agencies, on city councils, and in the White House staff, in state legislatures, in volunteer organizations, in virtually all arenas of policy making in the country."

These "progressives" are products of a counter culture that has robbed them of moral or common sense.

The CIA Was Behind Drug Culture

In the 1950's, the CIA experimented with LSD for use in interrogation and as a weapon.

In the 1960's they used this weapon to divert idealistic Americans from the path of social responsibility to one of introspection and self-gratification, i.e. "spiritual liberation."

They neutralized my generation by turning social activists into "flower children" advocating "peace and love."

The mantra of the age was "Tune in, Turn on and Drop Out." The prophet was psychologist, Dr. Timothy Leary (1920-1996.)

Was Leary working for the CIA? Writer Mark Reibling put this question to the aged guru in 1994.

"They never gave me a dime," Leary replied with a pained expression, and then avoided his questioner.

In fact, Leary did get money from them but not very much. When I visited him about 1990, he was strained for money. While not a CIA agent, Leary was their dupe. The CIA promotes self motivated people who are unaware how they are advancing the New World Order agenda.

Like most intelligence agencies, the CIA does not represent national interests. It was created by British Intelligence and serves the London-based central bankers.

The CIA said they sponsored radicals, liberals and leftists as "an alternative to Communism." This is not true. They did it to introduce Communism by a different route.

Funds and drugs for Leary's research came from the CIA. In his autobiography, *"Flashbacks"* (1983), Leary credits Cord Meyer, the CIA executive who funded the lib-left with "helping me to understand my political cultural role more clearly."

Elsewhere, he says the "Liberal CIA" is the "best Mafia you can deal with in the Twentieth Century." (These references are from Reibling's article: "Was Leary a CIA agent?") Leary clearly was working for the CIA but was doing what he wanted — turning on. Like Leary, we were all dupes.

A GENERATION OF MARIONETTES

When I was a child, I used to lie in bed at night and read TIME and NEWSWEEK from cover to cover. At the age of 12, I helped organize marches for world hunger relief. At 14, the marches were for Negro Civil Rights.

In 1964, while still focused on Civil Rights, I noticed that I was dancing alone. No one told me but the party had moved to another room. Vietnam was now the "In Thing." It was as if someone (i.e. the CIA-controlled media) had blown a whistle.

I joined a rising crescendo of anti-war activity. In 1968, after the gut-wrenching assassinations of King and Robert Kennedy, the anti-war movement was deflated by LBJ's decision to retire and the beatings at the Democratic Convention in Chicago.

Then, in unison like a flock of geese, my generation gave up on social change, became "alienated" and "turned inward." Maybe we needed to change ourselves before we can change the world. Thanks to the CIA, drugs were plentiful and Leary's mantra was echoed in the mass media.

Although it was another ten years before I tried marijuana, I experienced the "Summer of Love" hitchhiking across Canada in 1967. Maybe it was time to "hang loose" and focus on personal things. The 1970's became the "Me Decade." The sheeple followed the herders.

LSD

Although I have never experienced LSD, I embraced the utopian vision of Timothy Leary and Aldous Huxley. With considerable justification, they believed that "mind expanding" drugs could provide a genuine visionary experience and release mankind's spiritual potential. In experiments, theology students had life changing revelations; alcoholics were cured. For millennia, many cultures have used drugs to promote spirituality.

In Mexico, Leary took magic mushrooms. "It was above all and without question the deepest religious experience of my life. I discovered that beauty, revelation, sensuality, the cellular history of the past, God, the devil, all lie inside my body, outside my mind."

This LSD-fueled vision of utopia was put into practice at the highest levels of the US government. In 1963, Cord Meyer's estranged wife, Mary Pinchot Meyers, introduced LSD to President John F. Kennedy. Mary approached Leary for supplies and advice.

In Dec. 1963, Meyer called Leary and said they killed JFK because "they couldn't control him anymore. He was changing too fast. They've covered everything up. I'm afraid. Be careful." In Oct. 1964, she was murdered.

MY WEEKEND WITH TIMOTHY LEARY

I had a serious case of hero worship when I visited Timothy Leary around 1990. I had contacted him through his publisher and he phoned me. I wanted to know if the utopian vision Leary represented was still alive.

I was disillusioned. By this time Leary was fixated on the benefits of the "information superhighway." His pantry table was crammed with alcohol. He told me his "vision of God" was depicted in the last scene in William Gibson's book *"Neuromancer."*

"At the end of the world, all the information stored in all the computers will rise up into Cyberspace and mingle together," he said. "That's God."

Wonderful, I thought. All those airline reservations mingling together.

At lunch, I tried to remind him of his original vision: using drugs to awaken our spiritual potential and become more God-like in behavior.

"What do you think God is?" he scoffed. "An old man with a beard?"

Prophets sometimes lose their vision. I think this is what happened with Leary. But he was very generous with his time and hospitality. He was a genuine idealist.

I ferried him around Los Angeles in my rented car. He was appearing in a music video made by an obscure band. He was to earn $300. He lived in a nice house but was not rich. I took him to see his daughter by his first marriage. She lived in public housing in the valley.

CONCLUSION

Too many have given up on protest and social change. They feel that "fighting the darkness" just "brings me down." For me, detachment from the world was a limbo in which I drifted for years. I now believe in the Path of Service. We were put here to do our Creator's work. We become human beings by becoming God's agent in matters large and small.

They didn't expect many of us to find God. We were their marionettes. Popular culture is mostly propaganda and social engineering. The environment, feminism, diversity, you name it. The bankers are pulling our strings. In the case of the drug culture, my generation became self absorbed and quiescent.

Liberal Jews, Sex and the New Satanic Order

Born in 1949, my life span corresponds to a massive social engineering campaign on the part of satanic elites to destroy the institution of marriage and family.

This has been done by separating sex from both love and marriage ("sexual liberation,") and by teaching young women to seek sex and careers instead of marriage and motherhood ("feminism.") They use the media to make people think self-destructive behavior is advanced and "cool."

Reproduction is a very delicate business. If you want children to be born and raised properly, men and women must learn to consecrate themselves for marriage and family. Young girls having random sex, often with each other, aren't going to be loyal wives or good mothers.

LIBERAL JEWS & SEXUAL LIBERATION

New York liberal Jews like Norma Klein probably had no idea she was advancing the satanic Sabbatean agenda in the 1970's and 1980's when she taught teenagers to have sex. The author of 30 books, she thought she was liberating young people from the chains of religious superstition.

I'll bet she didn't know that the Sabbateans are a sex cult, and premarital sex, wife swapping and orgies are part of their dogma. Most liberal Jews are unconscious of the Luciferian role they play by thumbing their nose at what is natural, healthy and decorous.

In a recent article, "Teen Shpilkes," [Yiddish for anxiety] Eryn Loeb revisited this seminal influence on her life and was struck, not by the soft core porn, or the vulgarity, but by the "pervasive Jewishness" of Klein's work. It focuses entirely on "secular Jews... often professors or writers, friendly progressive types who...all own *"The Joy of Sex"* and are happy to discuss its contents with their precocious, introspective offspring... There are affairs, divorces, abortions, ardent feminists, gay characters and lots of sex —all portrayed with Klein's distinctive casualness and honesty at a time when nearly all of these things were destined to stir up controversy."

For example, *"Domestic Arrangements"* (1981) finds 14-year-old Tatiana Engelberg nonchalantly detailing her sexual awakening: "Daddy takes everything very hard which is probably why he got so hysterical when he found Joshua and me having sex in the bathroom at four in the morning."

In *"Beginner's Love"* (1983) 17-year-old Leda Boroff gets pregnant and considers abortion versus adoption. "There aren't very many Jewish babies...I could probably sell it for a year's tuition at Yale."

Norma Klein grew up in New York among "extremely liberal left-wing Jews." Her father was a psychoanalyst and in her home "Freud had replaced God in whom [her] father had decided early on he didn't believe."

There it is in a nutshell. Liberal-Left Jews are going to build a heaven of their own design without God (and without considering anyone else.) God would interfere with their ability to do whatever they like, especially regarding sex.

Liberal Jews are humanists, which means they make men like Freud their Gods and sex their holy grail. They are Luciferians and don't even know it.

CONTRAST

Compare the above "Jewish" or secular position with Vic Biorseth's Catholic point of view.

Biorseth writes:

"In the received wisdom of Western civilization, throughout it's two thousand year history, the primary physical purpose for sex is procreation, and the primary social and spiritual purpose for sex is the foundation of the family. It is therefore reserved for the married state, in which sex has another purpose, that being, bonding of man and wife, the formation of the social "glue" that binds parents more strongly to each other to form the solid foundation of the family unit."

I don't agree with his opposition to contraception. However, it's clear to me that a woman who consecrates herself for husband is more likely to have a successful marriage than one who has had 20 lovers by the time she is 19. Free sex is the ersatz religion of our time, one designed to undermine our social institutions and humanity.

Sex without love is body without soul. It is a rejection of our true identity i.e. soul, which is our connection to God. Physical intimacy without emotional intimacy is self destructive. When there is love, there is commitment.

It's amazing how we are obsessed with healthy food, exercise and air purity but don't care about pervasive pornography, promiscuity, mayhem and Satanism in the mass media. "Man does not live by bread alone."

Sex without love is a denial of God and our humanity. That's why Klein's book is called *"It's OK If You Don't Love Me."* We can still have sex.

Porn — Watching Bruised, Drugged Prostitutes

(Written for HenryMakow.com by David Richards, 22, a UK citizen teaching English in China. See his personal statement at end.)

WARNING!! DISTURBING MATERIAL

Shelley Lubben (right) believed she was ready to shoot her first porn film. She was in for a shock: 'When I walked in, it's like a dark satanic anointing just fell on me. It was creepy, it was dark, it was eerie, and it was nothing like prostitution. I knew I was in the devil's territory; this was the final frontier of Satan.'

During the little satanic ritual that followed, she hit rock bottom: 'I sold what was left of my heart, mind and femininity to the porn industry and the woman and person in me died completely on set.'

Then something remarkable began to happen; Shelley's survival instincts kicked in and she re-connected with the Christian God of her childhood and, after taking a period of rehab to recover from her ordeal, she started on a crusade to expose the reality of porn.

She has marketed herself as a charismatic public figure in the televangelist style, telling her life story in a confessional manner. The hub of her operation is the "Pink Cross," a charity that launches fierce grassroots activism.

There is one overriding truth to Shelley's work; behind whatever thin veil of glamour they masquerade with: porn stars are prostitutes.

MOTIVATION

Porn stars rarely start out from a love of sexual exhibitionism. Along with poverty and broken families, childhood abuse is very common.

Shelley said: 'Many actresses experienced sexual abuse, physical abuse, verbal abuse and neglect by parents. Some were raped by relatives and molested by neighbors. When we were little girls, we wanted to play with dollies and be mummies, not have big scary men get on top of us. So we were taught at a young age that sex made us valuable.'

Often they are teenage runaways picked up by pimps. They only escape one circle of abuse by entering another; they can't run from the pain so they go towards it. Fast forward a few years and they find themselves in a zombified state, drunk and drugged on a porn set as they re-live the same abuse they experienced growing up.

Shelley continues: 'The same horrible violations we experienced then, we relive through as we perform our tricks for you in front of the camera. And we hate every minute of it.'

BRUTALITY

The brutality of most porn videos is obvious to anyone who has seen one. A typical film consists of one or more huge guys on steroids having violent sex with a girl.

Porn users only see a well-edited film. They don't see what happens behind the scenes; the girls that are crying and throwing up because they can't handle the hardcore acts they are being told to do. Jersey Jaxin explains what awaits you on set: 'Guys punching you in the face. You get ripped. Your insides can come out of you. It's never ending.'"

A girl's first time on camera can be horrific. She is disorientated under the bright lights and the sex is shockingly violent. The experience is more akin to an abusive alien abduction than a pleasurable sexual one. This is how Genevieve described her first scene:

'It was one of the worst experiences of my life. It was very scary. It was a very rough scene. My agent didn't let me know ahead of time... I did it and I was crying and they didn't stop. It was really violent. He was hitting me. It hurt. It scared me more than anything. They wouldn't stop. They just kept rolling.'

DRUGS

The sex you see in porn is a lie; sexual enhancement drugs are used on set. 'Drugs are huge. They're using Viagra. It's unnatural. The girls will be on Xanax and Vicodin,' according to Sierra Sinn. No wonder the sex is so vicious.

Perhaps there should be a disclaimer at the bottom of the screen noting what drugs the performers are on: Gary is on Viagra and coke. Candy drank half a bottle of Jack Daniels and then smoked some crack. Enjoy the film.

Most porn stars take drugs, in fact they are often on film to pay for their habit. The girls are traumatized and get high to numb their pain, as Becca Brat will tell you: 'I hung out with a lot of people in the Adult industry, everybody from contract girls to gonzo actresses. Everybody has the same problems. Everybody is on drugs. It's an empty lifestyle trying to fill up a void.'

DISEASE

It should be no surprise that sexual diseases are at pandemic level in the porn industry. With chlamydia, gonorrhea, and herpes being passed from performer to performer, there is a backdrop of sickness to a porn set. In fact, they often act as laboratories for the creation of whole new sexual diseases, such as the novel herpes of the throat.

When disease is added to the already traumatic nature of being a porn actress, it can all get too much, as Tamra Toryn found out: 'I caught a moderate form of dysplasia of the cervix and later that day, I also found out I was pregnant. I had only one choice which was to abort the baby during my first month. It was extremely painful emotionally and physically. When it was all over, I cried my eyes out.'

Most performers develop some form of incurable sexual disease during their career and some are killers; AIDS is still loose in the industry. Every time a performer steps in front of the camera they are playing Russian roulette with their lives.

There is nothing clean about porn; it is diseased prostitutes having sex with other diseased prostitutes.

It is incredible to realize that it has become the norm for young men to grow up watching videos of trafficked women being abused for their amusement. It is legitimized by the silence of the media, education system and religious groups, who rarely denounce it.

A porn habit can terribly pollute a man's image of women and sex. He will become cynical and believe that any nice qualities a girl has mask her true essence; the whore he sees on screen.

Shelley was that girl on screen. It nearly killed her. What saved her was spiritual elevation to a state where she could make judgments on good and evil. When she awoke to see demons running amok in the sex industry, she finally had the strength to leave it.

David's Personal Statement: "My generation have been conditioned to accept porn from a young age…. In primary school I even remember my classmates having soft porn material and phoning sex lines. Then, growing up watching porn online, from 15 onwards, all the way through university, was normal for all the guys my age.

This was all normal to me. What set alarm bells ringing was that I went to a college in university with a diverse range of foreign students and met girls from India, Kenya, China, Japan, Ghana and so on and they were very different. They were warmer, more gentle and caring than English girls and thought English guys acted like sexual animals. So I had to figure out why we were like that and porn is the main reason. I dated a Chinese girl, she was caring and presumed we would always be together, for my English generation that's dinosaur thinking, but when with her I suddenly felt tremendous stability for the first time in my life. She would care and love me no matter what and I felt free to focus on my two main passions, politics and music. I then realized how much pornography and lack of stable relationships were making men too obsessed with sex to focus on anything important. So I came to the conclusion porn was an attack on us."

Rock Music's Satanic Message

Recently *NBC Dateline* had a story about two average American teenagers who murdered and cut up a friend, put the body parts in a garbage bag and hid it in a drain sewer. (Dateline Videos: *It Began as a Teen Drama*)

Church of Satan's Marilyn Manson preaches: "We hate love; we love hate."

The announcer, the parents and the audience shook their heads and asked: "How could they do this?"

I was dumbfounded too. After watching a ten-hour 4-DVD presentation on the satanic agenda infusing much youth music, I have the answer. Incredible and bizarre as it sounds, the younger generation is being inducted into Satanism. It is being taught to murder, rape and hate society in general, and especially Christians and Christianity.

Entitled *They Sold their Soul for Rock and Roll,* the DVD makes a convincing case that espousing Satanism is the price of success in the music industry. Starting with the roots of Rock and Roll, down to Heavy Metal, Goth, Grunge and Rap, this documentary reveals that many famous musicians actually see themselves as evangelists for Satan and say they derive their power from him. They have literally sold their souls to the devil, and their primary goal is to make us do the same. The MTV network is the handmaiden of this agenda.

Produced by "Fight the Good Fight Ministry" the DVD analyses the lyrics, interviews and album art of more than sixty superstars. The consistent espousal of the ideas of Satanists Aleister Crowley, Anton LaVey (Howard Levey) and Madame Blavatsky, and their inclusion in the album art, along with familiar satanic imagery, is part of a deliberate elite agenda. The list of artists exposed includes the Beatles, the Rolling Stones, Michael Jackson, Madonna, Led Zepplin, Kurt Cobain, Marilyn Manson and Eminem. You can see excerpts on line. I recommend you watch Cobain, Manson and Eminem.

This excerpt from "DEMONS" by Rigor Mortis is typical of heavy metal.

"We come bursting through your bodies

Rape your helpless soul

Transform you into a creature

Merciless and cold

We force you to kill your brother

Eat his blood and brain

Shredding flesh and sucking bone

Till everyone's insane

We are pestilent and contaminate

The world Demonic legions prevail"

The DVD explains how music is the most effective means of brainwashing and mind control, especially if the audience thinks it's listening to spontaneous creative expression. The DVD traces the satanic message "Do as thou wilt" (formerly "do your own thing") in many songs advocating free sex, drugs, violence, murder and mayhem. You are God! You can do anything you want! There is no moral order. The rock concert scenes are chillingly reminiscent of the Nazi Nuremberg Rally. Then of course there is the "horned goat" sign fans display, unaware they are pledging allegiance to Satan.

 The unabashed espousal of evil raises the question: why are the world's biggest corporations purveying this poison? Why is tainted spinach intercepted, yet this toxic filth is actually pumped into the minds and souls of millions of unsuspecting youth?

The Illuminati central banking cartel controls these corporations. Its aim is "revolution" i.e. "Communism," banker world dictatorship and the destruction of Western civilization. They need to translate their control of our government's credit (ability to print money) into total control. This is why opposition to socially destructive elements (e.g. promoting homosexuality to straights) is NOT tolerated, but vicious hatred against Christians and society in general is not only acceptable, but actually bankrolled.

"Christianity is our only real enemy since all the political and economic phenomena of the bourgeois states are only its consequences," Christian Rakovsky, a member of the Illuminati explained in the "Red Symphony" document.

The DVD reveals that the Columbine shooters knew the lyrics of satanist bands by heart, and literally were acting out instructions. They deliberately targeted Christian students but the term "hate crime" apparently doesn't apply to Christians.

Student victim Cassie Bernall was asked to reject God to spare her life. She refused. She is a Saint but there is little mention of her in the Illuminati media.

"How could this happen?" Tom Brokaw intoned. With one hand, the mass media pretends to be shocked, and with the other hand it teaches children to kill.

Similarly, media and government pretend to stamp out child predators while at the same time promoting rock groups that encourage children to have sex. The DVD shows a "Spice Girl" serenading a six-year-old with a song advocating self-abandonment. It shows 14-year-old teenage girls who look like hookers admitting that group sex orgies are commonplace.

BRAINWASHING

The Illuminati started off innocently in the fifties and sixties, urging the young to defy authority and indulge their libido. Little did we suspect that "Sergeant Pepper" referred to the Satanist and MI-6 Agent Aleister Crowley and that the Beatles' label EMI stands for "Electrical and Mechanical Instruments," one of Britain's largest war contractors.

Little did we know the music industry is controlled by the mob, and many performers are brainwashed and drugged, and live in fear. Little did we suspect that their rebellious message advanced the Illuminati's "divide and rule" strategy. Or that their prescriptions for living would make us dysfunctional and ruin our lives.

To a large extent, our lives are shaped by popular culture. We are spoon fed our ideas and beliefs instead of learning to apply our common sense to our experience. We are mice in someone else's lab experiment. The "someone else" is Satan's disciple.

Society cannot eschew God and pretend to be neutral and secular. God is synonymous with universal spiritual ideals: truth, love and justice. You cannot turn off the light without being consumed by darkness.

Don't be fooled. People who remove the Ten Commandments from public buildings are making room for golden calves and sacrificial altars.

Mother's Day Perversion— NBC's "Saturday Night Live."

On Mother's Day eve, NBC's flagship satire "Saturday Night Live" did a music video entitled "Mother Love" in which Justin Timberlake and Adam Samberg, rhapsodized about having sex with each others' mother. Veteran actresses Susan Sarandon and Patricia Clarkson played the winsome mothers, indicating how actors now are agents of Illuminati subversion.

The lyrics tell of mom's suffering "since dad passed away" — "We should f--k each others mothers." "I can't wait until I f--k your mother." "It'll be an honor to become your stepfather."

"Hold up/ You thinking what I'm thinking/ I'm thinking I'm thinkin' it too," "Slow up/ What time's it, dog?/ It's time for a switcheroo/ We both love our moms/ Women with grown women needs/ I say we break 'em off, show 'em how much they really mean."

 "I'm a motherlover, you're a motherlover/ We should f--- each other's mothers," the pair sing in perfect harmony, while peering over their designer shades at the camera. " 'Cause every Mother's Day needs a mother's night/ If doin' it is wrong, I don't wanna be right."

This obscenity is an hateful brutal assault on the American psyche. Yet it went largely unnoticed while America debated whether Wanda Sykes was wrong to wish Rush Limbaugh dead. This revolting satire tells viewers that sex is a free-for-all, and human decency, dignity and family can be trampled with impunity. It is all about creating new satanic norms, and illustrates how "liberal" and "progressive" are bound up in Satanism.

SNL has been produced by Lorne Michaels (Lorne David Lipowitz) since 1975. I suppose we should be grateful that the video sidestepped incest but that's coming. The perverts who run the mass media have a thing about sex with mom.

On the other hand, there are rare exceptions. The recent movie "17 Again" upholds family values and illustrates how Hollywood could have had a positive influence.

SEX AS ILLUMINATI WEAPON

Western society has been secretly run by a satanic cult, the Illuminati for hundreds of years. The gradual phasing out of Christianity and the triumph of "secularism" are but stages in the inauguration of Satanism as the new world religion. (Satanism is not really a religion because Satan replaces God. A religion by definition is about obeying God.)

The Illuminati goal is to totally control and dominate every human being. After war and debt, sex is their primary weapon for the degradation and enslavement of mankind. There is a direct line between the "Mother Love" skit on SNL and the US's sexual torture and rape of prisoners in Abu Graib. Both are designed to degrade, dehumanize and enslave.

Sex neutralizes the masses politically. When people are obsessed with their genitals, they are not going to examine who holds power. Leaders can be controlled by their sexual peccadilloes. "As political and economic freedom diminishes, sexual freedom tends to increase," Aldous Huxley wrote.

Western culture is a psy-op, controlled by the Illuminati education and media. The "sexual revolution" has been contrived to destroy the social fabric and enslave us. Human beings tend to experience what they are told to expect. We are brainwashed by countless songs and movies to believe sex (and romantic love) are the Holy Grail. We are pressured to imitate the promiscuous behavior of homosexuals who rarely marry or have children.

In the current issue (May 11, 2009) of *The New Yorker*, there is a review of Helen Gurley Brown who taught young women to have sex outside of marriage. The reviewer writes: "In everything Brown has written or edited, she has promoted the message that sex is great, and that one should get as much of it as possible. (Ditto for money.) Just about everyone knows this and has always known it but in Brown's youth, few women would admit it..." (p.100)

You see how the brainwashing works? Everyone wants to be "hip." Their media tells you "everybody knows" that sex is the best thing.

Social trends are mostly social engineering. Social reality is socially created. Conformity creates norms and the goal posts gradually can be moved.

THE REALITY

Until the "sexual revolution" (1960's) most men and women were quite able to restrict sex to marriage. This ensured that women weren't exploited sexually and children were brought up in an emotionally and financially stable environment. Young children are vulnerable and need the undivided attention of at least one loving parent. Mothers need husbands to support them while raising children. Men and women are less likely to stay together if sex is freely available.

When the institution of marriage is undermined, everyone is sexualized— granny, mom, little sister. Everybody is potentially "do-able."

Modern sex is necrophilia in the sense that the sex partner is just a convenience and not a human being. S/he might as well be a corpse.

In the last 50-200 years, the Illuminati has brainwashed us to see marriage and family in a negative light. It is very hard to find positive images in the mainstream media. This is not an accident.

Sexual desire is largely created by the culture. It is blown out of proportion. Nature made sex appealing so we would propagate, not spend our lives seeking it. — The poet Philip Larkin wrote:

Sexual intercourse began in 1963
(Which was rather late for me)
Between the end of the Chatterley ban
And the Beatles first LP

WEISHAUPT'S WORLD

Remember when the expression "motherhood and apple pie" referred to wholesome, pure and unassailable? We've seen what they've done to motherhood. Apple pie has not been spared either. In the movie "American Pie," the protagonist masturbates into an apple pie. Do you see how no symbol of health and innocence is spared? Do you see how satanic this is? Do you see how they use sex as a weapon to degrade everything?

E. Michael Jones has a 650-page book on the use of sex for political control. It is called *"Libido Dominandi"* which means "the lust to dominate." He writes of the founder of the Illuminati:

"[Adam] Weishaupt wanted to surround "the mighty of this earth" [i.e. the Cabalist bankers] with a legion of men who would run his schools, churches, academies, bookstores and governments, in short a cadre of revolutionaries who would influence every instance of political and social power, and so over the long run educate the society to Enlightenment ideas." (p.17)

This is our world today. The Illuminati is a satanic cult dedicated to supplanting God (i.e. the natural and spiritual order of the universe) with the will of the Cabalist bankers. This bizarre plot is reaching consummation

America's Media-Driven Descent Into Depravity

Many prime time TV programs today would have been considered obscene just 20 years ago. They present outrageous and shocking behavior as if it were normal and this creates cognitive dissonance. Thus, they condition us to accept depravity as the new societal norm.

Thursday at 8 pm, I sat down with my wife to watch one of her favourite shows, NBC's "My Name is Earl" starring Jason Lee.

My wife likes this show because it deals with morality or "karma." The premise is that Earl has a list of people he has wronged and believes he will be rewarded if he makes it right with each one.

Thursday's episode may have been a departure but what a jaw-dropping one! It was a sneak attack in what Senator Jesse Helms called the "systematic psychological warfare" the Rockefellers are waging against the American people.

Wrongdoing: Earl had sexual intercourse with the mother of his good friend Ralph.

Flashback: He and Ralph have a band. One night after a gig, they were partying at Ralph's house with some female groupies. Ralph's mother served rice crispy squares. Everyone else wore nothing but their underwear.

Eventually the group paired off to have sex. (The new party norm?) However Earl's partner had passed out. Not to worry. Ralph's mother, a woman in her fifties, came on to Earl and he was too drunk to resist.

Monkey see; monkey do. Call me old fashioned but this portrayal degrades our image of motherhood and family, something the Illuminati-owned mass media want to do. When motherhood is degraded, we are all degraded.

Readers inform me that often recurring themes on prime time TV are incest, intergenerational and gay-lesbian sex and even bestiality.

Ralph resolves to kill Earl and gives his friend 12 hours to settle his affairs.

Earl appeals to Ralph's mother. Sure, she'll speak to her son; Ralph will do anything for her but, in return, Earl will have to provide regular stud service.

Please do not mistake this for a porn flick. This is prime-time TV watched by children and their parents.

Earl refuses. Resigned to his fate, Earl visits his parents to say good bye. To his surprise, he finds Ralph alone with his own mother. Ralph is wearing nothing but a bathrobe. (He spilled some tomato juice on his pants.) Ralph has determined that he can avoid killing Earl by having sex with Earl's mother. When Earl's mother bends over to get something, Ralph makes suggestive sex doggy-style gestures. Earl apparently is so morally compromised he cannot intervene. (Similarly, I wonder if anyone expressed their disgust to NBC.)

Off camera, Ralph gropes Earl's mother's breasts. Flustered she comes rushing out and leaves the house. Ralph describes how he came up behind her and grabbed them in an "under over" action.

Ralph now determines that Earl can live if he marries his mother. The wedding takes place and Earl is expected to consummate the marriage. Not being drunk,he doesn't want to.

The tables have turned. Now Ralph is threatening to kill Earl if he doesn't have sex with his mother. At this point I switched channels.

An excerpt from this episode was at the show's NBC website. Listen carefully and you'll hear Ralph say to Earl, "Don't touch me with the hand with which you fondled my mother."

When a man wants to really offend and insult another, this is what he says he'll do. Earl has broken a visceral human taboo yet the show treats it as if Earl had broken a favorite fishing rod.

Now you know why Americans are paralysed to act. Like Earl, we are so morally compromised we cannot defend Mother Liberty.

READER'S COMMENTS:

MICHAEL: The following quote comes from none other than "insider" Zbigniew Brzezinski's book "Out Of Control - Global Turmoil On The Eve Of The 21st Century." (1993)

"Television gives the young viewer a first glimpse of the outside world. It first defines - and does so compellingly by combining the visual and audio impact - the meaning of the good life. It sets the standard of what is to be considered achievement, fulfillment, good taste, and proper conduct. It conditions desires, defines aspirations and expectations, and draws the line between acceptable and unacceptable behavior. With audiences around the world increasingly glued to television sets, there is nothing comparable, either in the era of enforced religious orthodoxy or even at the high point of totalitarian indoctrination, to the cultural and philosophical conditioning that television exercises on its viewers...."

Our Leaders Are Sex Addicts

"For a time until there will no longer be a risk of entrusting responsible posts in our States to our brother-Jews, we shall put them in the hands of persons whose past and reputation are such that...if they disobey our instructions, must face criminal charges or disappear — this in order to make them defend our interests to their last gasp."

—Protocols of the Elders of Zion 8

"We replaced the ruler by a caricature of a government -by a president, taken from the mob, from the midst of our puppet creatures, our slaves. This is the foundation of the mine we have laid under the goy peoples."

—Protocols of the Elders of Zion 10

The world is set to drop into the central bankers' outstretched hand like a ripe peach from a tree. Illuminati bankers are harvesting the fruit of their centuries-old plot to destroy Christian Civilization and trap humanity on an eternal treadmill of greed, sex, violence, trivia and political correctness.

They have succeeded because we have no leaders. They select obedient blackmailed perverts to execute their design. I always marvelled that Bill Clinton betrayed the dignity of his office and the trust of 300 million people for a blow job. But, in retrospect, a sex addict is the rule rather than the exception when it comes to our "leaders" (i.e. managers.)

"President Clinton has been very helpful to us," a banker confided in 1998. "We knew of what character he was before we placed him as president. Exposing him was very helpful in adjusting the moral habits of the youth downward. This is to our advantage. Even more agreeable to us were the vain efforts of those who thought they could remove him against our will. He is useful to us and he will not be removed by anyone until we are ready to have him removed." (See my, "Bankers Demand We Obey Them" online or in *"Illuminati"*)

RABBI STEPHEN WISE

Rabbi Stephen Wise was the most prominent American Zionist and Jewish leader from the 1920's until his death in 1949. On the Rockefeller- PBS website he is commemorated as "one of the greatest fighters for democracy and human rights of our generation."

In her book, *"Stranger at the Party,"* (1975), Helen Lawrenson describes how, as a 23-year-old reporter for the *Syracuse Journal* in 1930, she was sent to interview "the most famous rabbi in America."

She made the mistake of saying she admired him: "The next thing I knew he had toppled me backward on the sofa and was making love to me...Before I knew what had hit me, it was over and not a split second too soon either, as someone was knocking at the door and calling his name. "My God!" cried Rabbi Wise, "it's Rabbi Bienenfeld," leaping up and buttoning his fly. And so it was, not only the leading Syracuse rabbi, but with him was Mrs. Wise who fortunately didn't have her hotel key." (p.44)

Later, Wise lured her back to his room and forced her to her knees before him saying, "Kneel before me in prayerful attitude, my darling."

Her worship did not include servicing him "at that time" but she assumed "he acted in the same way in every city he visited" and she wondered if he wasn't afraid of scandal. He replied that, "every dynamic man had a powerful sex drive and should make the most of it."

Three years later, they crossed paths in the course of her work for *Vanity Fair* and she found herself "on [her] back again, this time on the long table in his office, with Wise reciting in Hebrew,"Lift up your heads oh ye gates; and be ye lifted up, ye everlasting doors; and the King of Glory shall come in." Psalm 24:7-10 (45)

Apparently this is a Sabbatean (Illuminati) prayer after sex. The "King of Glory" is obviously the penis. The Sabbateans were a heretical Jewish satanic cult that morphed into Illuminism, Communism, Freemasonry, Feminism, Zionism and "sexual liberation." They were ostracized by Torah Jews for sex orgies and other forms of adultery in the 17th and 18th Century.

The rulers of the world—Jewish and non-Jewish—belong to this satanic sex cult, and in the name of "progress," inducted society into it. They were responsible for WWII and for the Jewish holocaust. Rabbi Wise was feckless when it came to rescuing his fellow Jews from this calamity but better when thwarting the efforts of others.

Helen Lawrenson (1907-1982) was a good-hearted, literate, leftist dupe of the kind the Illuminati liked to have around (for obvious reasons.) The point is she is completely credible. She became the Managing Editor of *Vanity Fair*, and the lover and lifelong friend of both Conde Naste and Bernard Baruch. She and her husband, labor organizer Jack Lawrenson, were regular house guests of Clare and Henry Luce. Her book was published by Random House in 1975.

JORGE W. BOOSHE

According to the late Alan Stang's courageous groundbreaking book, "*Not Holier Than Thou: How Queer is Bush?*" (2007) organized homosexuality, with its belief in sex-for-its-own-sake, is an important Illuminati control mechanism.

Stang speculates that Bush is a homosexual and demonstrates that, despite his Christian family pretensions, he has advanced the homo-sexualization of society and "given organized sodomy considerable control over the federal government." (66)

Stang documents that a well-known male pros-
titute, Jeff Gannon, made dozens of visits to the
Bush White House in 2003 and 2004 often staying
overnight. Apparently the President could be easily
blackmailed. And this doesn't even include Mar-
gie Schrodinger, the Black Texan housewife whose
name has disappeared down the memory hole. She
formally charged the President with rape in 2002
and then conveniently "committed suicide."

Stang's book is a thorough laundry list of homosexual activism within the Republican Party. It came
out before Mark Foley and the Congressional Pages,
Larry Craig and the toilet stall 'wide stance." It tears
the veil off the media's feel-good, sugar-coated image of homosexuality. It is hard to stomach but must
be read. Why? Because some homosexuals by their
own admission hate society and have no morality. Thus these particular homosexuals are perfect
agents of Illuminati subversion.

Alan Stang, who died in 2009, was one of the most
important journalists in America. I highly recommend his book. By now, you should know that
Barack Obama has a homosexual past. Listen to the
interviews with Larry Sinclair by Jeff Rense. Sinclair,
who claims he had sex with Obama, is being ignored
by the mass media, but you can bet his number is
on the Illuminati's speed dial if BO starts to steer
an independent course. (I mean the President, not
his dog.)

CONCLUSION

Every four years, the masses choose which Illuminati sex addict or stooge they want.
The Illuminati banker just smiles:

"We place our proposed leader before you and you vote for what we want. In that way
we give you the vain voting exercise in the belief you had something to do with placing
your president in office."

Is Pedophilia the Next Frontier?

Tween idol Miley Cyrus, 15, has apologized for provocative pictures that appeared in *Vanity Fair* calling them a "mistake," but they are yet another calculated attack on the American psyche, which is being prepared to accept pedophilia.

A society always takes the values of its ruling class, and America (indeed the world) is run by a satanic cult of pedophiles, occultists and criminals known as the Illuminati. They represent the top rung of Freemasonry which is now putting the capstone on their satanic New World Order, which turns Christian civilization on its head.

Cyrus and her father, country singer Billy Ray Cyrus, do not become mega-stars without becoming pawns of the Illuminati. That's Miley flashing the sign of Baphomet. (Of course she has some alibi to gull the wilfully ignorant. They aren't going to tell you they are flashing the sign of the devil. The point is to get you to do it!)

Society will continue to condemn and punish some pedophilia and child porn, while at the same time conditioning the public to its eventual acceptance. Pedophilia is the logical outcome of the values promoted by the New World Order: Sex for its own sake without reference to love, marriage and procreation.

Schools are teaching children to have sex as young as age 13 and to experiment with homosexuality. MTV has taught a generation of young girls to believe their whole value derives from how "hot" they are. Having an adult lover would be a great status symbol.

"Wholesome" 'tween role models like Miley Cyrus (whose favorite TV show is "Sex and the City") "accidentally" pose in sexually provocative ways.

Gay organizations push to lower the age of consent, and you know how important "gay rights" are. Heterosexuals have been conditioned to imitate gay sexual behavior. For example, courtship has been replaced by "hooking up" which in gay terms is "cruisin." Pedophilia is the last gay behavior pattern we must learn.

Photographer Annie Leibovitz says she's sorry her photos have been 'misinterpreted.' Geez, how could a picture of a half-naked 15-year-old on the cover of a national magazine be misinterpreted? And lying in father's lap with her pelvis thrust forward; how could that be misinterpreted? Is this the way fathers and daughters should relate? Are incest and paedophilia the next "next frontier?"

A reader, Rob, writes: The photo has the "devil's salute" with the right hand. The left hand is pointing down, therefore, one hand is pointing up, whilst the other hand is pointing down—indicates the dualistic (marriage of opposites, or reconciliation), cabalistic magical philosophy "As Above, So Below" (The devil goat Baphomet performs the same sign.) What is being said is that, "White magic is the same as black magic." Furthermore, the tongue is out, this is a well known satanic sign."

Sounds to me these pictures are being interpreted correctly.

Oh they'll pooh-pooh and wax indignant, and everyone will rush to see the pictures. This is where it's been going for some time. Sex is the lowest common denominator and the best way to control and degrade humanity and destroy moral values and family.

The satanist Sabbateans who organized the Illuminati in the 18th century are a pagan sex cult. The world is in their grip. They are determined that their values will be ours.

"Times of London" Touts Sibling Incest

From July 2008 until December, *The Times of London* had a permanent feature entitled, "I Had Sex With My Brother and I Don't Feel Guilty" on its "Relationships" web page.

A woman described how from age 14, her brother,15, fondled her and at her age 17, began regular intercourse over a dozen years. Shockingly, the majority of the 600 plus comment writers said that since the sex was consensual, "felt right" and "no harm was done," it was OK.

The article is an example of how the Illuminati changes societal norms. It also illustrates that the "Establishment," which this newspaper has represented for over a hundred years, is not Conservative as commonly thought but Luciferian, i.e. Satanic.

From the Marquis de Sade to Aleister Crowley, the Illuminati goal has been to deny the natural and moral order. "Do as thou wilt shall be the whole of the law" was their motto. Their goal is to re-engineer humanity to serve them by destroying the traditional family as a social institution.

"Do what you will and harm none! " Bill in Truro, Canada unconsciously echoed. "Not my place to judge you." Jana in Somerset: "I think as long as both siblings are willing and aware of what they are doing, it should be 'okay'."

NO HARM?

Few readers recognized that this woman has been harmed. From an innocent age, her sexual feelings had been twisted to focus on her brother and not on her future husband and father of her children.

This article could be a Tavistock Psy-op. It is "told to Joan McFadden" and reads like a Harlequin Romance: "I wasn't scared but I was surprised as [Daniel] started stroking me, though my overriding sensation was one of sheer pleasure...But it hadn't felt wrong and I certainly hadn't felt forced. Rather I felt Daniel had stopped long before I'd wanted him to."

Remember this is a girl of 14. After they began having intercourse, she admits she "had difficulty [being] physically intimate with anyone else" because "sex with Daniel was so amazing."

"So amazing"?

Her claim that this did not affect their sibling relationship does not sound credible: "Sometimes he initiated sex and sometimes I did, but in between times our relationship was as easy, relaxed and affectionate as ever." This reminds me of the way they idealize/sanitize/peddle homosexuality.

Indeed many readers compared incest to homosexuality before it became acceptable.

Eventually Daniel met his future wife "Alison" but he made a strange proposal to his sister. If she agreed, he would live with her instead and continue their sexual relationship. "I know this is meant to be wrong but I've never felt anything so right," he said. Nevertheless, after hours of discussion they decided against it, "parting in tears afterward."

She has become an "academic" and is unmarried although she has met "Derek" and thinks he will be "a lasting relationship." She confides that it is "hard knowing that the one person you love above everything [Daniel] is out of bounds."

Do you think Derek (or any real man) would marry her if he knew she had sex for years with her brother and still carried a torch for him? Any marriage will be based on a major deception. What if Derek finds out after they have children? Another broken marriage?

The reader response shows that many people see sex purely as pleasure rather than part of marriage and procreation. As a result, they can't see that, both in social and personal terms, sibling incest is very damaging.

CONCLUSION

Along with homosexuality, the Illuminati will promote incest as another way to destroy the traditional family. Break down the barrier to sibling incest and they will promote the parental variety, which they practice. The message is: have sex often with anyone but your future husband and father of your children.

The Times of London is owned by Rupert Murdoch, a Rothschild cut-out. Leon Blum, another Illuminati cut-out who became French Prime Minister three times famously wrote: "I have never discerned what there is about incest which is really repulsive. I merely note that it is natural and frequent for sister and brother to be lovers." (*"Du Marriage,"* 1907)

An elite that had the national interest at heart would promote traditional family as the most natural, healthy and personally fulfilling way of perpetuating society. On the other hand, an elite secretly at war with society will do everything to destroy it. A young woman will not dedicate herself to her future family if society (i.e. *The Times of London*) tells her it's ok to have sex with all and sundry, including her brother.

As this story shows, sex is a powerful bond, especially for a woman. Promiscuity of any kind decreases the chance of a successful marriage.

Today in the United States, 40% of all births are out of wedlock. That means close to half of the population will not have a stable, secure upbringing and the love and guidance of a father. The Illuminati is advancing its goal of replacing the nuclear family with the State, which will train people to serve it.

READER'S COMMENTS:

ANONYMOUS: As an incest survivor I am sensitive and observant to the satanic cult (I will not call them "Illuminati" because that means "the enlightened ones." They come from darkness) in power trying to desensitize society to the normalization of incest, child sexual abuse, and pedophilia.

Your article did not mention that nature has a way of telling human beings that degeneracy cannot be accepted. Subsequently, children of incest are often born with defects. Those who feel that incest between brother and sister (or brother/brother, sister/sister) is harmless, have no idea what kind of emotional pain and psychological malignancies can develop in the sibling who is the victim. After four decades, I am still healing from the effects of sibling incest in childhood. The human race can be so ignorant.

Charlotte Roche's Mental Breakdown (and Ours)

Charlotte Roche's repugnant *"Wetlands,"* the best selling novel in the world in 2008, begins with the sentence, "As far back as I can remember, I have had hemorrhoids" and it doesn't improve. It is a disgusting, brutal assault on woman and girls, and on our sensibilities in general.

Disguised as "women's rights," it is the real hate literature, the real face of the NWO Communism and globalism. It is the true Luciferian meaning of "revolutionary" and "progressive," i.e. the destruction of all that is natural, healthy and wholesome.

If a man had written about a degenerate woman who consumes her genital (and other) secretions, and neglects all feminine hygiene, he would be classified as a despicable misogynist. But if a feminist does it, she is celebrated for hammering the last nail into the coffin of femininity.

A reader on Amazon.com commented: "The first chapter was so intensely graphic (describing the protagonist's anal lesion surgery) that I literally had to take breaks between pages, fearing I might pass out."

Roche, 31, is credited with breaking taboos and giving modern women "a new vocabulary" (i.e. to describe their depravity in "positive" terms.) She doesn't know she's actually expressing the self-loathing and desperation of women who have lost their female identity.

EMBARRASSMENT

In a civilized society, Roche would be considered an embarrassing idiot and given counselling. Her manuscript would be returned. But because the global media is owned by an occult sect called the Illuminati, she is turned into a role model and her book become a best seller.

English by birth, Roche was brought up in Germany. She is a garage musician and TV dj with a long history of doing disgusting things for attention. According to a fan site, she "would do virtually anything to scandalize herself and others, including cut herself and use the blood to paint pictures, shaving her head and experimenting with a variety of drugs."

"Wetlands," the story of Helen Memel, a patient in a hospital proctology unit , is a squalid meditation on her genitals, bodily functions and "sexuality." In a recent

interview with *Salon*, Roche reveals the book's flavor, her background and the quality of her self-hate and psychosis.

"You can clean and clean, and you won't ever stop being dirty. My mother tried to raise me in a very liberated way. I was allowed to have sex at a very early age. I was allowed to bring boys over to the house because she didn't want me having sex in the woods. She's a very strong, political feminist, and she raised me in a very feminist way, teaching me that as a girl, I can do everything a boy can do, there's no problem. But still, the sexual stuff ... she never managed to teach me that [onanism] is a good thing. Although my mother was liberated, I still feel that if I have dirty knickers [underpants], I have to hide them from my husband."

"If I'm being really honest, on the one hand I want women to be liberated, but on the other, I have terrible problems. I think I'm too fat, although I'm probably too thin. It's really difficult, for example, to live in a society like this with small tits. I don't even believe my husband when he says he likes the way I look. He has to tell me 10 times a day and I still don't believe him. I think he wants to have sex with a blond, large-breasted lady. You run around and you have complexes about everything. It's so difficult to keep it out of your head.

"And it is not allowed for me as a young feminist to say that women are masochistic. I am and all my female friends are. We stand in front of the mirror, we are naked, and we feel ugly as hell. We see everything as wrong. We try and fight our body to become prettier and work on it. It's not at all free and self-confident. I don't want it to be like that, but I see that it is."

Her special brand of insanity seems inspired by *"The Vagina Monologues."*

"The problem with taboos is that you think you're the only one. And Helen always wants to know: How do other women's vaginas look? We're all completely isolated. It's not a group of women that menstruate; we're on our own. But where does that come from? Mothers still don't think it's a good thing to be a woman."

The interviewer's assumptions are almost as sickening as Roche's answers: "Contemporary women are supposed to be liberated, hedonistic, you can go out and get drunk, sleep around. But if we don't have the words to describe the range of experiences other than the old negative ones, then nothing has really changed....The contemporary woman is supposed to be sexually available, as you say, but when a women is sick, she ceases to exist as a sexual being."

SELF LOATHING

Feminism has made women redundant by depriving them of their natural identity as wives and mothers. Women like Roche are reacting with self-loathing. They are describing their bodily functions in the most disgusting terms. Apparently, this is a widespread phenomenon as documented in a *Salon* article, "The Great Girl Gross-Out."

Femininity is based on being pleasing to a man. Feminine modesty is attractive to men as well. As shown above, Roche's mental breakdown is based on her rebellion against men.

"Very often, lately, people have come up to me and say "You look tired," and I hate it." she says. "Women are supposed to always look fit and healthy and pretty. But everything that is sick and tired is all very human — and I think that being human is a big taboo. When people say that the book is about taboos, I ask them, what do you mean? [Defecation]? [Urination]? [Onanism]?"

Yes, we are animals. But Christian civilization taught that our bodies are the temple of the soul, and the soul aspires to God, i.e. spiritual ideals. We are supposed to mend our behavior according to our spiritual aspirations, to refine ourselves and be beautiful in the sight of God. These ideals are what makes us human, not our animal condition.

A culture looks to women to embody its spiritual ideals and transfer them to the new generation. The attack on women is an attack on civilization. They want to define human beings in purely naturalistic and materialistic terms. They want to mire us in our excrement and become immune to it.

Roche: "I would look at the disgusting thing and describe it in a very detailed way. Maybe even to overcome the disgusting. You look at it as long as you can and then it's not disgusting anymore."

Doing her satanic duty, she is inuring us to the ugly, disgusting and obscene.

Human Rights-
A Higher Form of Discrimination

"Human rights" laws are Orwellian doublespeak for giving "rights" to some people and taking them away from others.

Essentially, homosexuals, atheists and Jews have "human rights" while Christians, Muslims and heterosexuals don't. The laws empower minorities in order to disarm and disinherit the majority. They have nothing to do with justice; they are a tool of state coercion.

This is not hyperbole. In countries where these Masonic concepts of "human rights" and "tolerance" were dominant (i.e. Mexico, the USSR,) Christian schools were closed, churches burned and priests murdered.

This subtle coercion was underlined recently here in Winnipeg when two married lesbians filed a human rights complaint against a Muslim MD. The female MD, from Egypt, suggested the lesbians find another doctor. She didn't refuse to treat them. She just said that in future find someone else because her religion proscribed homosexuality and she had no experience treating homosexuals. (The clinic offered the women another doctor but they declined.)

The local medical association said the MD will have to take more "orientation" courses. Why do the lesbians' genderless rights trump the doctor's religious rights? Because the laws are drafted by Rockefeller-based elitists to undermine heterosexuality and break up the nuclear family. These elitists don't give a fig about homosexuals.

They want to subvert society by pushing homosexual dysfunction on heterosexuals. (They are mainstreaming homosexuality while making heterosexuality seem like a pathology i.e. domestic abuse etc.) Human Rights Commissions are staffed by feminists indoctrinated to uphold homosexual rights over religious rights.

Another example: A few months ago, the Canadian Muslim Congress filed a complaint over a story by Jewish journalist Mark Steyn on the threat of Muslim world domination. The media blitzed the Canadian Human Rights Commission with indignant complaints about violations of free speech. The CHRC dutifully refused to hear the Muslim complaint. Can you imagine this happening if the article were on *Jewish* world domination?

In the UK , a nurse was suspended for offering to pray for an elderly patient's recovery (*The Telegraph*, January 31, 2009) while the Home Office has recognized a "Pagan Police Association" and permitted leave on satanic holidays eight times a year, including summer solstice and Halloween. ("Pagan Police Get Solstice Leave" BBC July 16, 2009)

Have you noticed that, despite the recession, atheists have money to burn? They can afford to take ads on buses questioning the existence of God. This campaign which began in the UK has come to Canada.

"There's probably no God" the ads say. That's "hate" in my book. Believe what you want but don't plaster it over buses. Everyone has their own conception of God. For me, God is synonymous with spiritual ideals like truth, beauty, harmony and love. So don't tell me there is no God. We are all in touch with God whether or not we believe in Him.

Again, this atheist campaign is just a front for the Illuminati cult that funds all "popular" movements (like feminism.) Getting people to be agnostics or atheists is a step toward eventually enthroning the Anti Christ or Lucifer.

This campaign is an affront to the 72% of Canadians who, according to polls, believe in God. How do they get away with it? The Canadian Jewish Congress hauled me up in front of the human rights commission for writing Pharisaic Judaism made its followers into "metaphysical outcasts." I didn't advertise on buses!

It's time we started taking this Luciferian hatred against God and His natural and spiritual (moral) order to "Human Rights" Commissions. Let's expose them for what they really are: instruments of globalist social engineering and discrimination.

The Truth About "Diversity"

We are all affected by "Diversity" but few understand its true nature.

Warning: It isn't pretty.

"Diversity" is a massive long-term behavior modification program that uses minorities to disinherit the majority.

In English, "Diversity" means acknowledging different races, religions and "sexual orientations."

In New World Order Doublespeak, "Diversity" is a devious way to dilute and discriminate against the white, heterosexual Christian majority in Europe, Canada, Australia and the US.

While it pretends to advocate equality, its real goal is to guilt mainly heterosexual White males into yielding position and power. The object is to prepare North America and Europe for inclusion in a "world government" run by the central banking cartel based in London.

This private cartel's power is measured by the fact that virtually every major corporation, educational institution and government agency provides "diversity training" (i.e. political indoctrination) to its employees. Even though studies show it has zero economic benefit, they spend eight billion dollars a year on it. Toyota alone plans to spend that much in the next ten years.

Here is an example of the shaming of Whites that takes place in these sessions. It is from the text, *"Seeing Ourselves: Exploring Race Ethnicity and Culture"* (1999) by Carl James.

A participant, Greg tells the group:

"As for my race, I am white but I never really had to think about it before. I don't feel that it ever affected the people with whom I associated or talked to. My two best friends are Black and (Canadian) Indian. I was brought up in a family that didn't believe in prejudice and I'm proud of that. If I don't like a person, it is because of their personality, not their race or heritage."

Now you'd think that Greg would pass with flying colors.

You didn't consider the hidden agenda. The author, a Diversity trainer, chastises Greg for assuming he is "the norm." Greg fails to acknowledge his "race privilege," that "invisible package of unearned assets" that is the "white colonial legacy." Whites like

Greg deny "the ways in which they socially, culturally and politically produce relations of domination." (p.44)

In other words, Whites naturally oppress other people. That sounds like vicious racism to me.

Can you see what's happening? These Diversity sessions lay guilt trips on Whites, especially males, so they will yield power to compliant & grateful minorities who have not earned it. This is a scam. Anyone who objects to this political agenda commits career suicide. That's political persecution.

I want to be clear that I think the human race is one family and God loves all people equally. Like Greg, I believe people should be judged on their merit alone, regardless of race, gender or sexual orientation.

I have no problem with "minorities" winning positions of power so long as they do it fairly. I welcome the rich contribution immigrants make. I came to Canada when I was a baby in 1951.

But "Diversity" is not about fairness or enriching society. It promotes minorities not for their merits, but as a way to undermine and control the majority.

IRONY

It's ironic that the central banking clique should lay this guilt trip on Whites when they are responsible for imperialism and wars past and present. They grew even richer through the slave and opium trades, and they control organized crime today through their agents.

The US population is more than 75% White and Christian. The plan is for Whites to become a minority by 2050 or sooner. Whites are expected to stand by and become guests in their own house.

When Whites are a minority, no one will champion their rights. There are two million more females than males at US universities. Have you heard of any affirmative action programs for males?

"Diversity" is practically unheard of in China, Japan, Israel, India and Latin America. These countries are allowed to keep their racial character. But because people of European origin have a sense of material, spiritual and political entitlement, they are the hardest to absorb in the New World Order. They are the targets of the "Diversity" program.

The central bankers use the tactic of "divide and conquer" to undermine the four pillars of our identity: race, religion, nation and family.

First, they pretended to champion the workers to get rid of the Tsarist regime in Russia. Then they pretended to champion women and homosexuals to undermine heterosexual values and the family. Finally they are duping Whites to passively accept discrimination and diminished status.

They use the same dog-eared playbook. (Select one) Workers, Jews, Blacks, homosexuals, women have been oppressed for centuries. Let the bankers put their (select one) front men (or womyn) in power.

CONCLUSION

Malleable and conformist, the masses will usually adopt the norm. When evil people set the norm, the masses will succumb to distorted and self-destructive behavior.

The banking cartel creates money using our national credit. As a result, society has been subverted by an alien power with a satanic agenda. Our political and kultural elites consist of traitors who, for example, allowed 9-11 to take place and covered it up. We are subjected to a constant stream of lies from these sanctimonious self-serving pawns.

In a poll taken Oct. 18, 2007, by the Toronto *Globe and Mail*, 63% answered "No" to the question: "Do you think Canada's multiculturalism policies have been a success?" The sample was roughly 11,000 and *Globe* readers tend to be liberals.

The founding peoples of the West have a right to maintain their national character and see it flourish. Immigrants expect to integrate, while retaining their heritage. They don't expect to be used to undermine the majority.

So, let's not fall into their "divide and conquer" trap by focusing our indignation on minorities. They are manipulated as much as we. Let's focus on the central bankers and their lackeys, in politics, education, business and the media.

I know this goes against the grain for some. Ask yourself where did you get your attitudes. They were dinned into you by the media and education. We are being manipulated and duped and it's time we awoke.

May I remind you: the term "politically correct" originated in the Communist Party of the USSR in the 1920's. It is not a coincidence that the term is part of our lexicon today. The same bankers who controlled the USSR then, secretly control the USA, Canada and Europe today.

READER'S COMMENTS:

GARY: Thanks for your recent article on Diversity. I was just fired from a government contract job for refusing to participate in the company's diversity training program. I spent 12+ years in the same facility, received excellent annual reviews every year and gaining the respect of my fellow employees. My immediate manager, site manager and program manager all tried to convince the company not to fire me, but to no avail.

Anyone who stands against the diversity indoctrination while employed by a major defence contractor is, as you said, committing career suicide. When the corporate leaders don't care what their managers say about keeping a good employee, it becomes obvious that they serve the purpose of the central bankers.

Do you know what was interesting about the diversity training in my former company? When the requirement to complete the training was received in our email box, every male in my group griped and complained about it. They all hated it! There is something inside of a man, deep in the gut, that is repulsed by all this diversity training garbage. It is offensive and insulting to a man's intelligence and honor to have to sit through some stupid training video that acts like it is speaking to first graders.

I am a white, married male with strong Christian principles. I am also fortunate to have a wife who supported my decision. She has told me many times how proud she is that I was willing to lose my job with all the benefits for my principles.

ANTHONY: Another insightful article Henry that really hit home for me.

I am a student in Australia who has had the misfortune of studying the social sciences at a so called 'Catholic' university here in Melbourne. My misfortune is even greater as I am often one of only two males in my classes. From day one I have had to listen to lecture after lecture slamming anything good and decent and praising all things feminist, anti-family and anti-Christian (that's right, in a Catholic university!.) I watch as the other students lap this poison up and take every word of it on board as if it was gospel.

Everyone of my lecturers are women and all are militant feminists. I have kept my thoughts pretty much to myself for the first two years (as hard as that's been) but have had to draw the line at a reading that we were presented with written by a homosexual activist who questioned the innocence of children. I wrote, in a journal that was to be assessed, that this sort of writing did nothing to dispel the fears of the pederast nature of SOME homosexuals.

The response (from the head of the sociology department no less) was a 200 word rant (the rest of my work hardly got a mention) branding me as homophobic and warning me in no uncertain terms that this type of writing was unacceptable. All this in a journal that was structured to be a 'critical response' to the readings provided! Thank God for 'diversity' and 'freedom of thought'...oh, as long as you think their way that is.

Canada Pimps Its Girls to Big Pharma

About a month after being vaccinated against the cervical cancer-causing HPV virus, 13-year-old Jenny Tetlock missed the lowest hurdle in gym class, the first hint of the degenerative muscle disease that, 15 months later, has left the previously healthy teenager nearly completely paralyzed. - US News & World Report July 2, 2008

In 2007, the Harper government allocated $300 million to vaccinate thousands of girls as young as age nine against a sexually transmitted disease, human papillomavirus (HPV), which occasionally causes cervical cancer.

The vaccine (Gardasil) only works on girls with no sexual experience. So instead of teaching these children that it is self-destructive and degrading to be promiscuous, the government is inoculating them as if they were going to walk the streets.

Instead of pimping these girls, the politicians are taking their cut up front, from big pharma, profiting from promiscuity in the name of protecting "public health."

In an interview with CBC-TV, a representative of Merck-Frosst, the maker of the vaccine, admitted that lobbying is how pharma business is done in Canada. [Apparently a former adviser to Harper became a lobbyist for Merck.]

The last time the Canadian government took such drastic action was during a polio outbreak in the 1950's. But there is no epidemic of cervical cancer now. In fact, it doesn't even rank in the top 10 cancers affecting Canadian women. Whereas 400 women die of cervical cancer each year, over 5000 die of breast cancer.

BOONDOGGLE WITH CONSEQUENCES

At best, this vaccination campaign is a boondoggle for Merck. At worst it could have many negative effects. A reader from Argentina wrote that last Oct. the government tried to vaccinate girls for Rubeola but was stopped when some doctors revealed the vaccine contained a sterilization agent called prostaglandin.

A report by a McGill University epidemiologist calls the Canadian program "premature and could possibly have unintended negative consequences for individuals and for society as a whole."

While as many as 50% of women get some form of HPV over their lifetime, the report says most of these do not result in cervical cancer and can be cured.

"Most HPV infections are cleared spontaneously. Recent research using available molecular detection technologies suggests that clearance occurs within one year for about 70 per cent of those infected, and within two years for 90 per cent. Thus, HPV infection and cervical cancer must not be conflated: most women who are infected with even a 'high-risk' strain of HPV will not develop cervical cancer."

The report also states that clinical trials were insufficient to test the efficacy of the vaccine since the subjects were too young to be exposed to HPV. The average cervical cancer patient is 47 years old so it isn't clear how long the vaccine will remain effective.

During the last six months of 2006, the (US) National Vaccine Information Center (NVIC) got 385 reports of adverse reactions to Gardasil.

"There are twice as many children collapsing and four times as many children experiencing tingling, numbness and loss of sensation after getting Gardasil vaccination compared to those getting a Tdap (tetanus-diphtheria-acellular pertussis) vaccination."

"There have been reports of facial paralysis and Guillain-Barre Syndrome. And doctors who give Gardasil in combination with other vaccines are basically conducting an experiment on their young patients because Merck has not published any safety data for simultaneous vaccination with any vaccine except hepatitis B vaccine."

In May 2007, Judicial Watch reported 1600 adverse reactions to Gardasil including two deaths.

INSANITY

Next week in Toronto alone, 40,000 young girls and their parents will be pressured to allow an inoculation for a sexually transmitted disease. The reason for the pressure is that three injections are required over a six-months period i.e. the school year.

"My 12 year old daughter is facing this decision — her MD. has suggested we vaccinate her right away," a mother posted on the CBC-TV web site. "I am NOT a skeptical person by any means but something about this whole campaign makes me very nervous. "

At over $400 for the three-doses, this is the most exorbitantly overpriced child vaccine in existence. Apparently Merck will be paying those Vioxx settlements at the expense of Canadian taxpayers and adolescent girls.

The unstated and outrageous assumption behind this vaccination campaign is that promiscuity is the norm. Human papilloma virus will not be transferred if people are selective and monogamous (and use condoms.) These girls have never had sex. Most will not have sex for years. Many will not be promiscuous and will not need this vaccine.

The current Canadian government pretends to be socially conservative and espouse "family values." This is a funny way to do it.

This gratuitous mass inoculation sets a bad precedent. I don't want to speculate what excuse they will find for the next one. This is the shape of socialism in the New World Order: enriching corporations by degrading, endangering and drugging the population.

Movie "Avatar," the Illuminati and The Raelian Connection

(This article was written for henrymakow.com by Steve Thomas)

Is there a connection between the Raelian Cult's belief that we need alien intervention to govern Planet Earth and James Cameron's AVATAR? Is it possible that this screwball cult is manifesting the Illuminati agenda, and that the highest grossing movie of all time is a form of predictive programming?

My research *http://www.henrymakow.com/steve_thomas.html* has uncovered a network of several thousand Illuminati-connected celebrities and politicians, who are also linked to the enigmatic Rael Maitreya *http://www.facebook.com/profile.php?id=694189344,* leader of Raelism (the atheist-alien "religion to encompass all religions") via the Facebook page of his alter ego, "Igor N. Grata." *http://www.facebook.com/grata?v=wall*

Rael has responded to my articles via Igor N. Grata's Facebook Wall (Public Forum diary), confirming the connect between Rael Maitreya and Igor N.Grata.

Names range from Rothschild to Rockefeller, Madonna to McCartney, Olmert to Onassis,Guilderberg-connected Madames *http://www.facebook.com/profile.php?id= 1248453480* to Cardinals and Monarchs. To discover how this world is wired, follow the embedded links. (This verifiable information is accessed via a Facebook account – log in, click name/friends/search.)

On Igor N. Grata's personal friends list, we find 57 Rothschilds & 14 Rockefellers !!!!!

On "Avatar" Director 'James Cameron's' Facebook page, registered friends number approximately 50 world-famous film stars, (Hopkins, Aniston, Collins, Depp…) musicians (Dylan, Joel, Twain…), politicians (Schwarzenneger, Netanyahu), and 'Queen of England Elizabeth.' *http://www.facebook.com/queenofengland.elizabeth?ref=sgm*

Thirty four of these 50 known links each have a direct connect to the Raelian leader Rael Maitreya —via his alter ego IGOR N. GRATA.

AVATAR – THE RAELIAN CONNECTION

To begin, Igor N. Grata's FB page publicizes the film. Raelism promotes the dogma that humans on earth were originally genetically engineered by aliens. Similarly, the avatar creations in the film were 'scientific alien lab constructs' placed on the planet Pandora.

Alien intervention from the skies is the fundamental redemptive expectation of Raelism. Similarly, "Avatar's" Jake Sully came from the skies, a hybrid human-alien saviour-avatar to rescue the Pandoran people from the woes of ignorance and warfare. Thus, Raelism would have us look to the skies for 'alien redemption.'

The spell-binding world of Pandora features: pantheism; planetary energy flows; animism; a mother goddess; sacred trees; telepathic 'sight'; shamanic healing etc. — all features of occult witchcraft and spirit channelling.

Ultimate victory in Pandora is achieved by the intervention of a powerful red dragon with his winged reptilian hordes and red-eyed black beasts. This is a reference to *Revelations*. *http://www.biblegateway.com/passage/?search=revelation%2012:3-12&version=NIV*

The Raelians condemn marriage and family as repressive and promote promiscuous sex as liberating. In the movie, the only 'sex' we see is between alien and avatar. The film induces a preparatory mindset that it is OK to have 'mind sex' / intimate union with aliens. This links into Gaia energy all being one in animal, human, alien etc. The simple message of the film is to be open to intimate connection with aliens.

EX-RAELIAN REVEALS LUCIFERIAN GLOBAL PLANS

Daniel Vandinja, a former high level Raelian, describes the Raelian belief system, where: "God is a fantasy and the human soul is a joke. Eternal life is to be reached through CLONING and the true Gods are E.T.s, who will come to earth to save us from destruction."

In his book, *"RAEL, The Masonic Messiah,"* Vandinja reveals how Raelism reverses truth - God is replaced by aliens - Satan and God are reversed. Rael stated, "All people, made passionate by love... should worship Satan rather than their blood-thirsty God." People are encouraged to welcome aliens who require subservience from humankind. This is reminiscent of the Biblical description of Lucifer seeking to be as God, elevating himself in misplaced pride, resulting in his fall from heaven as he seeks to corrupt and demonize God's creation.

In keeping with the satanic lie, Jesus is blasphemously defined as a "half-breed alien." Vandinja describes the close similarities between misplaced Masonic and Raelian respect for Lucifer, who, as the 'bearer of light and reason' (both groups, he says claim) will "dethrone God" - resulting ultimately in ALIEN-HUMAN HYBRIDS. Is this a last ditch attempt by Satan to avoid his terminal fate in rebellion against God? Ominously, Vandinja quotes Rael: "those who act against the Guide of Guides, and try to prevent him carrying out his mission... will see their life become hell." We discover Raelian contributions to wider plans for: human cloning; *http://www. clonaid.com/page.php?7 depopulation and reforestation; weather control;* Tesla HAARP technology (engineered earthquakes); global cashless currency with personal id chips; 24/7 remote satellite surveillance; world federation government; global universal education; discrediting Christianity and Islam; *http://apostasie.org/english/acte.php* and as world citizen soldier 'peace-keepers.'

Vandinja describes Rael's vision of a 'geniocracy' (*http://raelianews.org/news. php?default.0.84*) where a small number of 'illuminated geniuses' rule the World, described he says, by Thomas Jefferson, as: "the ILLUMINATI, the natural aristocracy, the Intelligencia."

Vandinja suggests Rael's aliens plan to use global surveillance technology to monitor the human population. He describes an intended Raelian-Masonic-Illuminati paradigm shift: "the NEW AGE RELIGION, with the MASONIC MESSIAH (who he defines as ANTICHRIST) at its head, is the very foundation of the new World Government, without which religion, the dictatorship of the NEW WORLD ORDER is completely impossible."

In 1994, Serge Monast, a Canadian journalist revealed the existence of a NASA "Project Blue Beam," a global light show that will pretend to manifest the return of the Messiah from outer space. In fact, he will be the anti-Christ. Is the Illuminati building up to yet another monstrous hoax with the support of the Raelians and the movie "Avatar?"

BOOK THREE

Judaism, Zionism and Communism

Is Lucifer the God of Judaism?

(This was written for Henrymakow.com by Will Newman who attended Jewish synagogue, and has relatives involved in Talmudism, Cabala, B'nai Brith and Masonry.)

In 1976, Walter White, Jr., "a concerned patriot," conducted an interview with a young Jew named Harold Rosenthal who was the assistant to Sen. Javits of New York.

In the interview, later published as "The Hidden Tyranny," the arrogant Rosenthal belligerently boasts (on tape) that the Jewish people have fabricated certain "falsehoods which work to conceal their nature and protect their status and power."

Rosenthal debunks the commonly accepted lie that, "the Jews are Israelites, and thus God's chosen people."

Rosenthal said in part: 'Most Jews do not like to admit it, but our god is Lucifer — so I wasn't lying — and we are his chosen people. Lucifer is very much alive.'" (www.macquirelatory.com/Wallace Interview 1967.htm)

Lucifer's goal is to "be like the most High" (Isa 14:14) and to usurp the worship of God (Mat 4:9).

Lucifer's purpose is to deceive the whole world (Rev 12:9) by transforming himself into an angel of light (2Co 11:4). This is best exemplified by the Freemasons. Their motto of "making good men better" produces a far more favorable public image than the more accurate alternative: "how to become demon-possessed in 33-easy-steps." The Jewish and Masonic religions both worship the same god.

BRIGHT LIGHT

In most Jewish synagogues, a bright burning flame represents their god. The Hebrew word for Lucifer is "Hillel" (Strong's Concordance #H1966) meaning "bright light." Curiously, this is the name chosen for the Jewish student organization. A central text in Cabalism is entitled "the Zohar," which translates to the book of brightness or splendor.

The Jewish six-pointed star is the highest symbol in the occult and goes by various names--the Star of Moloch/Saturn/Chiun/Remphan. It is a symbol of the union of male and female and is identical in meaning to the Masonic square and compass, which is also a six-pointed symbol around the letter "G" representing the generative sexual act. In place of the "G" we find הוהי amidst many Jewish stars.

The Hebrew symbol יח worn around the necks of many Jews ostensibly symbolizes "life" (lachaim). The word literally translates to a "living thing" or "beast" (H2416); this symbol is an idol for The Beast.

The Jewish name for god is represented by the tetragrammaton הוהי (YHVH) can be pronounced Yahweh or Jehovah. The significance of God's name is repeatedly emphasized throughout the scriptures.

When dissected in the Hebrew, the true definition of Jehovah (Yah-Hovah) is revealed. "Yah" (#H3050) means "god." "Hovah" (#H1942) translates to "eagerly coveting, falling, desire, ruin, calamity, iniquity, mischief, naughtiness, noisome, perverse, very wickedness."

Jehovah is synonymous with Baal:

"Baali (#H1180) From ba'al with pron. Suff.; my master; Baali, a symbolical name for Jehovah -- Baali."

The Jewish Encyclopedia ("Adonai and Ba'al") reveals: "The name Ba'al, apparently as an equivalent for Yhwh."

Since the days of Jeremiah, the Jews have forgotten their god's name and replaced it with the title "Baal" or "YHVH": The lying prophets "Which think to cause my people to forget my [God's]name...as their fathers have forgotten my name for Baal." (Jer 23:27).

YHVH and Ba'al both represent the god of sexual perversion and wickedness, Satan.

However, Jews claim that this name (YHVH) is not to be spoken aloud, despite God's command to declare His name throughout the earth (Exo 9:16). Why ignore this commandment?

UTTERING GOD'S NAME

Judaism claims to be the authority on the Old Testament; however they do not practice what they preach. They dress in black, the color of death, in spite of the scriptural precept to wear white (Ecc 9:8), reject Christ as Messiah (who is prophesied throughout the Old Testament) and refuse to speak "God's name" in violation of the scriptures.

By reverencing their name of God (YHVH) by not speaking it, Jews create an air of mystery and holiness around the name while enhancing the curiosity surrounding its pronunciation and power. When curious Jews and non-Jews alike see the "sacred" tetragrammaton being used in occult practice, they are intrigued by the prospective that these sorcerers have harnessed the mystical powers of the name.

Wicca, Satanism, Tarot, occult Catholicism, Masonry and Cabalism use their knowledge of the "sacred name of god" as bait to recruit cult members. If the name were not hidden, these cults would lack a critical tool in their recruitment processes. They could not offer this forbidden knowledge if the Jews, the self-proclaimed authority on God, spoke this name openly.

The mystery religions and witchcraft covens owe a great debt to Judaism for conditioning the mainstream to accept the importance and secrecy of this name. The vocal praise of the name YHVH is reserved for the "elect" who learn the Cabala (and pay money to do so) and is forbidden by the "profane." Judaic doctrine is fundamental to selling the occult as a righteous practice.

Satan is the author of confusion and goes by many names. Many of the ancient pagan deities were Satan and his angels in other forms ("The Two Babylons," by A. Hislop). The Jews employ a number of false names for god in their rituals, which are also alternate titles for Satan and other powerful demons.

In the same manner, the Black Magician and Satanist invokes demons by name. In the Satanic Bible, Anton LaVey (Jewish) provides an extensive list of "infernal names" that, when summoned, provide the practitioner with super human abilities namely intelligence, power, skills in manipulation, enhanced creativity, material wealth, and the satisfaction of diverse lusts.

PRAYER

In Hasidic synagogues, many Jewish prayers are conducted in Yiddish, a composite language far from the intended pronunciation of the original Hebrew. These prayers are nothing more than disguised demonic invocations. They are hypnotic spells, similar to the Enochian language of the Church of Satan.

Young Jews spend countless hours preparing for their Bar Mitzvah, which consists of memorizing long chants and proper cadence and tone. Most who complete the Bar Mitzvah will not be able to translate more than a handful of words. These young men and women have no idea what they are saying or to whom they are praying. Jews are invoking demons named adonai, elohim, el shaddai, zeba'ot, diyenu (Diana) et al in their rituals.

Vain repetitions and head-bobbing during Jewish prayers aid the entrance into a trance state. Large numbers of atheistic Jews engage in the pseudo-religious worship of status and knowledge. As Bill Cooper writes, "The WORSHIP (a lot different from STUDY) of knowledge, science, or technology is Satanism in its purest form, and its god is Lucifer" ("Behold A Pale Horse," 70). Judaism fills its members with the same Satanic powers as the Church of Satan and Freemasonry.

CABALISM

The foundation of Cabalism is identical to Satanism: the reversal of the roles of God and Satan. It is the pursuit of hidden (occult) knowledge which allows one to achieve god-like abilities by calling on the so-called names of god. These are the names of fallen angels/demons/spirit guides who are the gatekeepers to occult knowledge (Gen 6:4, Jubilees, Enoch). While not all Jews actively practice Cabala, they all accept the highest Cabalistic name as their god—YHVH.

The infamous Cabalist and Satanist Aleister Crowley writes, "There are thus 72 'Angels'...these [names] are derived from the "Great Name of God"...The "Name" is Tetragrammaton: I.H.V.H., commonly called Jehovah. He is the Supreme Lord of...the whole Universe ("The Book of Thoth," 43). A number of other secret pronunciations of YHVH are used in the occult in addition to Yahweh and Jehovah.

"Of the 54 sacred names in the Jewish cabala, the primary one is YHWH" (R. Hathaway "Sacred Name of God? Or Blasphemy," remnantradio.org/Archives/articles/sacred_name.htm).

The Jewish creed, the Shema, states: "our Lord is One," so why invoke these other names?

DEMONOLOGY

The secret of the ancient Egyptians, and their modern disciples, the Freemasons, is the art of demonology for gaining power--mainly through the devil, Jehovah. In the Royal Arch degree, the Freemason " acknowledge[s] that the devil, in the guise of Jahbuhlun, is his sacred Lord"—the name Jahbulun being a "composite of Jahweh, Baal, and Osiris." He chants "Jah-buh-lun, Jah-buh-lun, Jah-buh-lun, Je-hov-ah" (Texe Marrs, *"Codex Magica,"* Ch. 4). Albert Pike discusses the Cabalistic/Masonic significance of IAHOVAH in great length in *"Morals & Dogma"* (66, 213, 401, 467, 519).

The name YHVH was injected into the text of the Old Testament by the Pharisees and others who practiced Babylonian Satanism (the precursor to Cabalism and Talmudism). For those who don't believe the Talmud is Satanic it proclaims that Christ is in Hell boiling in excrement and semen (Gittin, 56b,57a).

An agreement was forged between the Jewish Masoretes and the Catholic Church c. 1000 A.D. to change the name of God in the Hebrew Old Testament to the pagan name Yahweh/ Jehovah via the tetragrammaton (remnantradio.org/Archives/articles/sacred_name.htm).

This explains Rosenthal's saying, "We are amazed by the Christians' stupidity in receiving our teachings and propagating them as their own."

In Henry Ford's words, "The Christian cannot read his Bible except through Jewish spectacles, and, therefore, reads it wrong." (*"The International Jew,"* Vol. IV, 238).

GOD'S REAL NAME

The demonic disdain for humanity exhibited by the Luciferian Jew, Harold Rosenthal, typifies the end result of a lethal amalgamation: Jewish religious ritual combined with the worship of knowledge and self. The Jews as a people, by rejecting God and/or accepting Jehovah, have been given over "to a reprobate mind...Being filled with all unrighteousness..." (Rom 1:28-31).

Of course, Mr. Rosenthal was a member of an elite, openly Satanic minority among the Jewish people. Everyday Jews do not know that the god of their faith is in fact Satan hiding behind a mystical name. It is of no consequence to Satan whether he is worshipped deliberately or through subtle lies and deceptions (Gen 3).

The wise Solomon asks, "what is [God's] name, and what is his son's name, if thou canst tell?" (Pro 30:4). God's name is אהיה AHAYAH (sometimes transliterated Ehyeh) meaning I AM. This is the name given to Moses along with the Law. "And God said unto Moses, I AM THAT I AM: and he said, Thus shalt thou say unto the children of Israel, I AM hath sent me unto you...this is my memorial unto all generations."(Ex 3:14-15). "I AM the Lord thy God...thou shalt have no other gods before me" (Exo 32:4-5).

Jews Defined by Occult Ideology, Not Nation/Race

Are the Jews a nation, a religion or a race? None of these apparently.

Shlomo Sand, the author of *"The Invention of the Jewish People,"* shows that the Jews today are not the descendants of Biblical Hebrews but are people of different races who converted to "Judaism" down through the centuries. Unknown to most Jews, Talmudic Judaism is a satanic secret society like Freemasonry, not a religion. This is why you don't have to believe in God to be Jewish. (I expand on this in my Introduction to "Illuminati.")

According to Sand, the description of Jews as a wandering and self-isolating nation of exiles, "who wandered across seas and continents, reached the ends of the earth and finally, with the advent of Zionism, made a U-turn and returned en masse to their orphaned homeland," is nothing but "national mythology."

"I asked myself how such large Jewish communities appeared in Spain. And then I saw that Tariq ibn Ziyad, the supreme commander of the Muslims who conquered Spain, was a Berber, and most of his soldiers were Berbers...who converted to Judaism." (In other words, they converted to an occult secret society, which masqueraded as a religion.)

Elizabeth Dilling said the same thing about race in *"The Jewish Religion: It's Influence Today,"* (1964, Chapter IX) The book is available online.

"Present day Jews are a potpourri of every race of man," she writes, "and they do not have any genealogical or racial derivation from the ancient peoples of the Holy Land."

MY NEW PARADIGM

I had the misconception that Jews were a race because of their antipathy to intermarriage. This was enforced by Hitler's racially-based treatment of Jews. But I couldn't explain why Jews differed racially and discriminated against each other on this basis.

Moreover, I couldn't reconcile the fact that the Illuminati, the secret inner core of Judaism, actively sought intermarriage with non-Jews and sacrificed other Jews to pogroms and holocaust.

My paradigm has now changed. My latest thinking is that, like its proxy Freemasonry, the defining element in Judaism is an occult ideology. Race doesn't matter. Anybody can join the club: Marilyn Monroe, Sammy Davis, Elizabeth Taylor, Madonna, Britney.

As with American Express, "membership has its rewards."

And like Freemasonry, the membership is ignorant of the true agenda. Only the "Illuminated" are in on the secret. The rest are manipulated and expendable.

As with Freemasonry, the hidden agenda is pagan and satanic. Judaism uses the Old Testament to draw people into the fold. But it is actually defined by the Talmud and Cabala which spurn the Old Testament.

Talmudic Judaism used "the Old Testament to cover its negation of every moral law of the Old Testament as its promotes practice of all the occult demonistic abominations excoriated by the Old Testament," Dilling writes.

Dilling shows how Moses' injunctions against bestiality, sodomy, adultery, incest, necrophilia etc. in the Old Testament are overturned in the Talmud. (Chapter V)

The picture of Jews as a nation-race is another way of controlling and manipulating them. It's essential for Jews (and Freemasons) to understand that the best parts of the ideology are for public consumption and to dupe the innocents. From this pool, only the corruptible are informed of the true agenda and allowed to rise. They become part of the Illuminati.

But if there is trouble, the Illuminati will plant the blame on the innocent Jews and Masons, the outer layer of dupes who serve as their human shield.

SATANIC?

The hidden (Talmudic/Cabalistic) agenda of Judaism and Freemasonry is to supplant the natural and spiritual laws of the universe (God) with the tyranny of the Illuminati bankers. They will define reality.

For example, homosexuality, bestiality, incest etc. are being normalized. What is healthy (i.e. marriage, family) is deemed sick; what is false (i.e. climate change) is deemed true; what is obscene and ugly (modern art, entertainment) is deemed beautiful. This is the New World Order.

The Cabalist bankers have been waging war on humanity for centuries. Ordinary Jews and Masons are in jeopardy by virtue of their association with this scourge.

According to the Old Testament, Jews must wait for the Messiah's return before re-establishing Israel. But the Talmud says the Messiah is already here and it is the "Jewish people" themselves. By "Jewish people" they mean the Illuminati bankers who sponsor and run organized Jewry.

For example, the Talmud *Kethuboth* 111a, states: "The Messiah is without metaphor the Jewish people." (Dilling, Chapter VI)

The Cabala teaches that God ("En Sof") is not moral, and has no characteristics. God is composed of nature. Since the highest expression of nature is man, he is God. And since only Jews are human, and above the level of beast, Jews (i.e. Illuminati bankers) are Divine.

According to the Jewish Encyclopedia, the Cabala teaches that the relation between man and God is erotic, "religion being identical with love, sensual pleasure, and especially intoxication." (Ch VI)

The Passover song "Only the Kid" heralds the day when all the world's great nations destroy each other in war, and only Israel is left. (Chapter XIV)

CONCLUSION

Have no illusion, mankind has been inducted into a satanic cult based on the Talmud and Cabala. Gradually we are being sedated and offered up as a tribute to Lucifer by his disciples. Mankind is doomed to an ersatz life, arrested development, a closed loop of sequels, remakes and reruns.

Anti-Semites are protecting the Illuminati by blaming the "racial" Jew. The true villain is the Illuminati banker and his lackeys of every ethnicity and "religion," who embrace the satanic ideology of the New World Order.

Jews Always Exercised Great Power

Jews have an image of a poor, beleaguered people. Even Jews think this is true. In fact, there has always been an elite caste of powerful Jews who allied with local aristocrats, serving as advisers, bankers, administrators, tax collectors, enforcers, doctors and tutors. They used their positions and worldwide contacts to dominate trade and become extremely rich. They rewarded their protectors handsomely.

Their role in the "Enlightenment" and Western imperialism has been discreetly veiled. The neo-feudal New World Order continues this cozy alliance with the Gentile elite. The concept of a "Chosen People" is ideally suited for a tiny plutocracy dedicated to colonizing the human race.

"APOLOGY FOR THE JEWS'

A famous letter, "Apology for the Jews" (1650) provides an unfiltered picture of Jewish power and influence over 350 years ago. The letter was written by Rabbi "Menasseh Ben Israel" (Manoel Dias Soeiro, 1604-1657) a leader of the Amsterdam Jewish Community to convince Oliver Cromwell, (1599-1658) to allow Jews back into England.

Ben Israel's arguments for Jewish return probably were a formality since Cromwell was financed by the Amsterdam Jewish bankers. Nonetheless, he reveals much about the attitude and "condition" of the Jews at this time.

Jews have always used their "religion" as a method of gaining special privileges, including military exemption and their own judiciary. Ben Israel tells Cromwell that God blesses those who aid the Jews and curses those who don't. The Bible decrees that the Messiah won't return until "the People of God" have been fully dispersed to every corner of the world, England included. Only then Jews can return to Israel and never again soil their hands in trade.

The letter makes clear that elite Jews got world power the old fashioned way- they bought it. He says they are extremely loyal to princes and nobles and reward them generously. He mentions numerous princes that welcomed Jews and says it is easy to judge from the trade they generated, "the profit that Princes and Commonwealths do reap, by giving liberty of religion to the Jews, and gathering them by some special privileges into their countries: as Trees that bring forth such excellent fruits."

The accumulation of wealth indicates "the favor of Providence," the Rebbe says, defining his religion. "Profit is a most powerful motive, and which the world prefers before all other things…" Trade and commerce is the proper profession of the Jews, by virtue of their dispersion, and because God has given them a "natural instinct" that allows them to "thrive in riches and possessions" making them useful to their Princes. There arises "an infallible profit, commodity and gain to all those Princes in whose lands they dwell…."

The Jews have no equal when it comes to "merchandising" and "contriving new inventions." Wherever they go, trade flourishes. For example a Jew invented the "Spalatro Scale" which brought the trade of the Levant to the City of Venice. [According to the Jewish Encyclopedia, the Spalato Jews were highly favored by the Venetian republic, and local trade and finance was almost entirely in their hands. Among the noted Jewish families were those of Pardo and Macchiero.]

THE SEED OF GLOBALISM

After being expelled from Spain in 1492, Ben Israel says Jews dispersed to Holland and Italy. They already lived in such disparate places as Egypt, Turkey, and India. There are three synagogues in Cochin, India where the Jews have tawny colored skin. Jews enjoy freedom and prosperity in Baghdad and Persia. In Constantinople, capital of the Ottoman Empire, "there is no Viceroy, or Governor or Bassa who hath not a Jew to manage his affairs and to take care of his estate." Soon they "grow up to be Lords of great revenues: and "most frequently" influence "weighty affairs in government."

The Bassa of Egypt has taken a Jew to be his Treasurer and by virtue of his influence in dispensing favors, he "grows very rich." Many millions of Jews live in the Ottoman Empire and in many cases "they are preferred before the natural Turks themselves."

In Prague, Vienna and Frankfurt there is a "great multitude of Jews" favored by the Emperors but "despised by the people." A far greater number of Jews are found in Poland, Prussia and Lithuania, Although the Cossacks have lately killed 180,000, there is still an "infinite number." All trade is in the hands of the Jews, "the rest of the Christians are either all Noble-men, or Rustiques and kept as slaves."

He says Jews are protected by all the Princes of Italy. They make their HQ in Venice where they possess "about 1400 Houses" [trading companies.] They are received with "great Charity and benevolence" in Amsterdam where they draw a huge trade. They have "no less than 300 houses of their own, [and] enjoy a good part of the West and East-Indian Companies." In Hamburg, there lives a hundred families, protected by the magistrate though molested by the people." Jews enrich the native populations and there are many Gentiles that build themselves great houses and palaces.

CABALIST POWER

In each generation there was a "Ba'al Shem," a Cabala adept claimed magical powers, bilked the faithful and lived in luxury. He was known as "Chief of all the Jews." Did he advise the financiers?

In the 18th Century, the Ba'al Shem of England was Samuel Jacob Falk (1710-1782.) In Sept. 1762 a Dr. Adler published an account of Falk's activities in *"The Gentleman's Magazine."* He described the Cabalist as "a Christened Jew and the biggest rogue and villain in all the world." The Cabalist offered to teach Adler certain mysteries if he could procure "one pound of blood out of the veins of an honest Protestant."

Adler took his own blood to Falk who used it to paint occult symbols and the name of God and the angels around his garden. He then performed "cruelties on a he-goat too loathsome to describe." (This account is from *"Secret Societies and Subversive Movements"* 1924, by Nesta Wester pp. 184-188.)

Cabalism is the basis of a satanic cult, the Illuminati, and the central bankers belong to it. Our leading politicians, including George Bush and Barack Obama, also belong.

In Nesta Webster's words, "it is in the Cabala, still more than in the Talmud, that the Judaic dream of world domination occurs with the greatest persistence." (371) The Zohar relates that the Messiah will declare war on the whole world: "They will all perish when God visits them in His wrath. ...the Holy One, blessed be He, will exterminate all the goyim of the world. Israel alone will subsist..." (374)

CONCLUSION

Menasseh Ben Israel's request was granted. Although there was no official proclamation, Jews were tacitly allowed to return to England. The "British" Empire became a vehicle for the longstanding alliance of Cabalist Jew and Gentile aristocrat to achieve world domination. Now, American imperialism carries the baton, to be replaced eventually by a world government mechanism.

History needs to be rewritten in terms of the actual conflict that took place between the secret hand of the Judeo Masonic alliance against indigenous forces of Christianity, nationalism, race and family. Culture today is Cabalist in character: pseudo mystical, wholly subjective, and amoral. It rejects God, and deifies man and sex instead.

A distinction must be made between the rich Masonic Jews and Gentiles and the ordinary Jews and Gentiles who are their dupes and go'fers. Ordinary Jews have suffered as much as ordinary Gentiles from the megalomaniac vision of the Masonic elite. Masonic Jews guaranteed Jewish solidarity by ensuring that all Jews were blamed for their sins. They funded "anti-Semites" who happily obliged.

This is really about the concentration of wealth and power in the hands of a tiny Lucifer-loving cult, and the serfdom of mankind.

Marranos – The Original Crypto Jews

After Christians took back Spain from the Moors in the 14th Century, they wanted "to root out all non-Catholic elements in the country and unite it under Catholic rule." (Prinz, *"The Secret Jews,"* p.25)

Jews had lived in Spain since the 4th Century BC and had prospered under the Moors. The Church demanded that the more than 400,000 Jews convert or leave. Because thousands had been massacred in anti-Jews riots of 1391, more than 250,000 Jews agreed to convert and became known as "conversos."

However, the Church soon realized its fatal blunder. As you would expect, the majority of these converts were not sincere. These were called "Marranos" (pigs.) But now they were exempt from the taxes and restrictions that governed Jews. They were more influential and powerful than ever.

They intermarried with the nobility and rose to the highest ranks in government and the Church. The founder of the Jesuits, Ignatius of Loyola , was a Marrano, and so was his successor Diego Lainex. Most conversos practised Judaism in secret and were considered "Judaizers."

The "Jews had invaded Spain from within," Joachim Prinz writes. Judaism was not only incurable; it seemed to be invincible....rather than solving the "Jewish question" the mass conversions had created a new problem: a powerful middle class made up of secret Jews." (42)

The Marranos are the original model for the Freemasons and Communists. They pretended to belong to the target group. But, like Masons, the Marranos had handshakes to recognize each other and met in secret at night to rehearse their subversive dogmas.

EXCEPTIONS

There were also many exceptions, sincere converts like St. Theresa of Avila, the greatest Catholic woman mystic. Ironically, when Ferdinand and Isabella restored the Inquisition in 1478, sincere converts took the lead. "The most notorious of these is Tomas de Torquemada, who was descended from a Jewish family, as was his equally violent assistant, Diego de Daza." (39)

The Inquisition is considered one of the most traumatic events in Jewish history. But it had no power over Jews. It only targeted Christian converts who were insincere:

"The Marranos ... appeared not as Jews but as allegedly heretical Christians. The number of Marranos who were executed..is estimated at 30,000. The same Inquisition also punished Muslims ("Moriscos"). However, no unconverted Jews were ever called to the tribunals."

Nevertheless, in 1492 Ferdinand and Isabella expelled all Jews from Spain. Joachim Prinz remarks on the "apparent inability of Jews to understand or predict their own catastrophes. The Jews, whose history consists of one tragedy after another, has yet to be prepared for any one of them." (51)

AFTERMATH

The same process was repeated in Portugal. While many Iberian Marranos eventually gave up their religion, many more left and flooded Europe and the New World (America) with Jews who were able to pass as Christians, i.e. "crypto Jews."

According to Prinz, they prospered wherever they went. Their wealth was "staggering... In Bordeaux, Avignon, Nantes and Marseilles, it became a compliment to characterize a Christian businessman as being "riche comme une juif."

In England, there were only 100 Marrano families in the early 17th century but "they were among the most successful merchants in London." In Germany, 40 Marrano families participated in the founding of the Bank of Hamburg in 1619. The fortune of the Marranos of Altona near Hamburg, was estimated at almost six million marks and some of the finest homes in nearby Amsterdam belonged to newly arrived Marranos." (127)

Everyone knew they were Christians of convenience. "The fiction of their Christian allegiance was a business arrangement...[their] banking house..was a Christian institution with which emperors, dukes, bishops, and heads of government could safely do business." (130)

Inevitably, these Marrano bankers and merchants acted in concert. Prinz tells the story of the Marrano banker (House of Mendes) Joseph Nasi (1524-1579) who controlled the Ottoman Empire as Adviser to Sultan Suleiman and later his son Salim. He tried to create a Jewish homeland at Tiberias but no Jews wanted to settle there. Later, he devised the "Marrano Strategy." He would boycott or ruin anyone who persecuted Marranos. (141)

When a fire destroyed the Harbor of Venice in 1571, many suspected the House of Mendes of paying arsonists to set the blaze. "And while much of the city was still in flames, Joseph Nasi counseled the Sultan to occupy the Venetian island of Cyprus, declaring it a Turkish possession." (142)

CONCLUSION

The real history of the world is the story of how certain rich Jewish bankers and their non-Jewish Masonic allies have conspired to establish the world government dictatorship now emerging.

The outline of this history is becoming visible. Jews or Marranos have always dominated commerce. Their natural allies were the local aristocrats, who provided protection. Intermarriages took place. The royal families of Europe are probably part-Jewish.

Now we are seeing a resurgence of the feudal system, where the masses serve this small, inbred, super rich network of perverts and Satanists. Education and media teaches the serfs to embrace the illuminati's agenda. Taser-wielding cops and soldiers will prod the laggards.

Welcome to the New World Order. It entails some risk for Jews who aren't part of this tiny clique. But Jews never were very good at "predicting their own catastrophes."

Old Testament Believer
Was Ostracized by Jews

Most people think Judaism is synonymous with the Old Testament. But Uriel de Costa (1585-1640) became a famous Jewish heretic because he upheld the Law of Moses.

In 14th & 15th century Spain, over 250,000 Jews were forced to become Christians on pain of death or expulsion. The family of Uriel de Costa was among these "Conversos" or "Marranos." A member of the nobility and very wealthy, Uriel studied at a Jesuit University and became a priest. However, he began to question his faith: "Reason whispered in my ear something utterly irreconcilable with faith."

He read the Old Testament and found it offered "fewer difficulties." He believed in Moses and "decided to live according to his law." So he gave up his ecclesiastical office and beautiful home and sailed to Amsterdam, a "place where

[he] felt the Jews could live in freedom and fulfill the commandments." On arrival he and his brothers immediately "submitted to circumcision."

De Costa had a rude awakening. Biblical Judaism no longer existed. "After the first few days, I began to understand that the customs and institutions of the Jews were not at all in accordance with what Moses had written. ..the Jews were wrong to have invented so many things which deviated...The present day sages have maintained both their customs and their evil character. They still fight stubbornly for the sect and the institutions of the evil Pharisees."

He could not find a basis for most Jewish customs in the Bible nor did the Old Testament speak of reincarnation or immortality of the soul.

Ironically for a man who left his home for religious freedom, Amsterdam Jewry would not let him deviate from their opinion "in the slightest." He was threatened with excommunication and exclusion from the community. He insisted on religious freedom and was expelled. "Even my brothers whose teacher I was, passed me by, so afraid were they of the authorities that they did not even greet me in the street."

De Costa "believed in doing something pleasing to God [by] defending freely and openly the law of Moses," he wrote in his autobiography, *"Example of a Human Life."*

But he lived in isolation from the Jewish community and in great loneliness. After seven years, he sought reconciliation. He describes the humiliation he was forced to endure. He was stripped to the waist, tied to a column and made to recite a psalm while being lashed 39 times. Following this, he dressed and lay down over the threshold of the synagogue while the whole congregation —men, women, children and elderly—walked over him into the street.

"No monkey could have invented a more despicable, tasteless and ridiculous action," he wrote.

The sting of this humiliation stayed with De Costa and he could not effect the reconciliation. He saw no way out but to shoot himself. As a suicide, he could not be buried in a marked grave in the Jewish cemetery.

CONCLUSION

Faced with Christian intolerance, De Costa discovered its Jewish counterpart. Like many Marranos, he was stranded between two worlds.

He belonged to the tradition of the Sadducees and later the Karaites who insisted on adherence to the written law. But these groups had been suppressed by the Pharisees who dominated Judaism with the satanic oral tradition (Talmud) and the satanic pseudo mystical Cabala.

The Old Testament strikes me as a mixed bag. You have to scour it for inspiring parts. Certainly it contains the same kind of xenophobia as the Talmud. But the prophets' denunciation of corruption and decadence rings true.

De Costa should probably have melded back into Christian society. Instead, he remained loyal to his God to the end.

Source: *"The Secret Jews"* by Joachim Prinz (1973)

Michael Hoffman's "Judaism Discovered From Its Own Texts"

"Judaism Discovered," Michael Hoffman's monumental new work on Judaism is subtitled, "A Study of the Anti-Biblical Religion of Racism, Self-Worship, Superstition and Deceit."

But what does Michael Hoffman really think of Judaism?

We are in crisis. It's time we listened to plainspoken pariahs like Michael Hoffman. Anti-Semitism is on the rise and Hoffman's book explains why this is not irrational "hate." It's more important for Jews than anyone to learn that they are associated with a satanic secret society masquerading as a "religion."

Two polls, one on August 9, 2007 and one on January 3, 2009, indicated a sharp growth of anti-Semitism in America. The August poll, conducted for the CIA-controlled RAND Corporation of Santa Monica showed 35% of the American public polled displayed moderate to strong anti-Semitic feelings while a similar poll in January of 2009 showed that percentage had jumped to 62%. This corresponds to the progress of the financial crisis. No doubt, Israel's genocidal attack on Gaza also contributed.

Many people serve as witting and unwitting agents of the central bankers' plan for world tyranny (the New World Order.) Collaboration is a criterion for "success" today. Increasingly, the NWO is called the "Jew World Order" because of the out-sized role Jews play. Most Jews are just trying to please their mother ("be successful dear") but they are part of a sinister force, and if they end up being blamed for it, no one will sympathize.

Is the NWO driven primarily by the bankers' megalomania or by their adherence to a Jewish collective agenda? Since many of the bankers are Cabalist Jews, the answer is probably both. The Jewish bankers have expanded their power base by co-opting the decadent Gentile elite through intermarriage and Freemasonry.

Illuminati bankers are behind the recent financial collapse which is designed to facilitate political change. "Economic crises have been produced by us for the goyim by no other means than the withdrawal of money from circulation." — (*Protocols of Zion*, 20) As Pastor Lindsey Williams said recently, long term, "these people are out to own and control everything...they are out to break us."

HOFFMAN BOOK

Hoffman's book is required reading for understanding the satanic mindset driving both the Illuminati and New World Order.

Normally, a 1100-page book would be daunting. But not in this case. *"Judaism Discovered"* is an encyclopedia in one volume consisting of more than 140 readable articles. The 10 x 7 inch format, large type and generous spacing make the book approachable. Consider it an opulent banquet.

Hoffman is a Talmudic adepts' worst nightmare. The goyim aren't supposed to learn this stuff. Ordinary Jews aren't supposed to know either. Hoffman has research assistants, some of whom are Jews, who read Hebrew, Yiddish, Aramaic and German. He is clearly not motivated by "hate" but rather by a desire to disabuse both Jews and non-Jews. He sees them as victims of an ongoing scam.

A sample of article titles suggests the provocative theme and range:

The Superiority of the Jews
The Inferiority of the Gentiles
Sexual Intercourse with Little Girls is Permissible
Immanuel Kant
The X-Rated Talmud
Sex Magic
Ritual Murder
Hasidic Paganism
Modern Protestant View of Judaism
From Cabala to Aggadah: A Sexual Progression
No "Judeo-Christian" Tradition
The Rabbinic World in the Pre-Modern Age
The Talmud in the Toilet
The Attire of the Pharisaic Male
Who are the Jews Today?
Rabbi Judah Loew and Queen Elizabeth's Dr. John Dee
US Gov't. Lays the Groundwork for Talmudic Courts

SAMPLING THE FEAST

Judaism is a secret satanic cult posing as a religion. Hoffman's main point is that Judaism represents the repudiation by the Pharisees of both the Old Testament and the Mosaic Code. Judaism is not Monotheistic but Luciferian. Its goal is the replacement of God with the secret Jewish leadership. Both the Talmud and the Cabala are dedicated to the proposition that only Jews are human. "The raison d'etre of the Talmud and Orthodox Judaism is the essential spiritual and racial superiority of the Judaic over the non-Judaic," Hoffman writes. This template has been transferred to the Illuminati elite.

I don't know why this information would offend Jews, most of whom consider themselves "secular humanists." Their Jewishness is cultural. They have contempt and even hatred for Orthodox Jews who return the compliment. However, a larger question is, to what extent is the materialistic culture dominant today a form of Judaism? Especially, when you consider the widespread acceptance of Cabala-based New Age beliefs (i.e. human divinity, pantheism, goddess & sex worship and many other occult practices.)

An essay on Moses Hess (1812-1875) suggests modern history and culture have been contrived by Cabalists to overthrow Christian civilization and enslave society.

Hoffman shows how Hess' ideology was at the nexus of Communism, Nazism and Zionism and nurtured all three. In other words, Cabalists control mankind by controlling the Hegelian thesis and antithesis. With Communism, the Cabalist bankers attempted to take our country, property, family, race, religion and liberty (still the goals of the NWO.) The reaction to Communism was Nazism, and the reaction to Nazism was Zionism. All three monsters were built in the same occult laboratory using common parts.

Tellingly, the Nazis did the rabbis' work by killing "unauthorized" opponents of Judaism like Edith Stein, Irene Nemirovsky and Maximilian Kolbe. (Hoffman, p. 650)

A true Christian, Hoffman says the way to stop the Hegelian dialectic is to stop fighting. In a timely reference to Zionist colonizers and Palestinian resisters, he writes that both groups of violent combatants "are mutually draining their enemy and themselves of blood, treasure and most damaging of all, their humanity, since this killing entails the dehumanization of the opposing force and the brutalization of one's own...No authentic Christian engages in this pagan, uroboros, victim-into-executioner cycle. (Mathew 26:52.)" (86)

PAYING THE PRICE

Michael Hoffman writes: "The core of Judaism, like the core of Gnosticism and Egyptian Hermeticism, is magic, the manipulation of the universe, contra God's creation; i.e. against nature. Gershom Scholem, Professor of Cabala at Hebrew University wrote that Cabala embraced a great deal of "black magic, ...a wide realm of demonology and various forms of sorcery that were designed to disrupt the natural order of things..." (Hoffman, p.779.)

Babylonian and Egyptian paganism is the progenitor of Judaism, Hoffman writes. "The rabbis hold Egypt in awe as a magical powerhouse. Pharonic Egypt is the model, root and source for Talmudic and Cabalistic priestcraft." (780) This may explain the pyramid on the US dollar and in the logos of so many corporations.

Hoffman seems mindful of the Illuminati when he writes on his website that, "the evil should NOT be assigned to a particular people denominated as "Jewish," but rather to the spirituality and ideology of Pharisaic/rabbinic origin which can, and does, afflict any people who adhere to its tenets, be they Khazars or Sephardim, WASPs such as George W. Bush, or Germans such as the current Pope of Rome."

Modern history and culture reflect a Cabalistic (satanic) spell and curse on the human race. It is dedicated to the enslavement of mankind by the "Jews" who in practice will be the crazed Illuminati Order.

Jews Must Face the "Dark Side" of Judaism

Stephen Bloom has a love of fairness and justice typical of many liberal Jews. A journalism professor, he saw the opening of a Kosher meat packer by Hasidic Jews in Postville Iowa in 1987 as an opportunity to study the Jewish-Gentile dynamic in microcosm. He discovered more about Judaism and the causes of anti-Semitism than perhaps he wanted to know.

His conclusion from *"Postville: A Clash of Cultures in Heartland America"* published in 2000:

"Initially I had gone to Postville to learn from the Hasidim [orthodox Jews], to share with them a sense of identity and belonging. Instead, what the Postville Hasidim ultimately offered me was a glimpse of the dark side of my own faith, a look at Jewish extremists whose behavior not only made the Postville locals wince, but made me wince, too."

"I didn't want to partake in Hasidim's vision that called on Jews to unite against the goyim and assimilation. The world, even in Iowa, was too bountiful to base my likes and dislikes solely on religion. The word Hasid ...literally means 'the pious one,' but the Postville Hasidim..were anything but pious. You couldn't become casual friends with them...They required total submission to their schema of right and wrong, Jew vs. Christian — or you were the enemy." (291)

In other words, if you're a Jew but don't buy their insanity, then you're no better than the goyim.

ROCKY RIDE

The influx of hundreds of Orthodox Jewish families into a tiny (pop. 1465) Christian farming community in Northeast Iowa was rocky from the start. Yes, the Jews had a seemingly wholesome family life and a pretence of piety. But it soon became apparent they wanted nothing to do with their Christian neighbors. They were there to make money and the non-Jews, (goyim) whether Postville merchants or migrant workers, were barely distinct from the cattle on the assembly line.

The meatpacking plant, Agriprocessors, filed for bankruptcy in Oct. 2008 after the owner Sholom Rubashkin was arrested for bank fraud regarding a $35 million loan. This after the State of Iowa levied $10 million in fines for 9000 violations involving illegal wage deductions and child labor. Then, in June, the company was accused of forging documents for illegal aliens. Four hundred hapless laborers from Guatemala to Palau were arrested and jailed.

When the plant closed, hundreds of workers were left destitute while turkeys languished unfed in trailers outside the plant gates. The town struggled to regain its footing, probably relieved to be rid of this mixed blessing.

In August, a delegation of distinguished rabbis and communal functionaries spent three hours touring the plant, met briefly with local Christian clergy and social activists, and gave the operation a clean bill of health. They found no evidence to suggest, as one rabbi put it, that "someone should not buy things from Agriprocessors."

"A three-hour tour could not uncover the extensive, "egregious" child labor violations that the Iowa state labor commissioner reported... just five days after the rabbis left town. The labor commissioner said he had "never seen anything like it" in his 30 years in the field..." the *Jewish Daily Forward* wrote in an Editorial August 7.

"Three hours wouldn't turn up the voluminous evidence of abuse gathered by the *Forward* when we first broke the Agriprocessors story two years ago. We found compelling indications of sexual harassment, shorted wages, favoritism and bribery in work assignments, inadequate safety training and horrific work accidents in the place we called a 'Kosher Jungle.'"

IN DENIAL

The editorial goes on to suggest that the rabbis were ignoring the precepts of the "Babylonian Talmud." This reflects the naivety of assimilated Jews about the true nature of the Talmud, which is the central document of Judaism. The Talmud regards Gentiles as cattle and preaches hatred against Christians.

This is confirmed by the behavior of the Postville Hasidim. Stephen Bloom was put under the tutelage of one "Lazar," a "model Lubavitcher, a mensch as well as a tzaddik" (wise man.)

"I am a racist," Lazar told Bloom right off the bat. The Jews have persisted throughout history because "we are better and smarter." (192)

"Wherever we go, we don't adapt to the place or the people, Lazar preached..."It's always been like that and always will be like that. It's the place and the people who have to adapt to us."

Bloom reflected: "Lazar's comment underscored the Hasidim's contempt for non-Jews, which wasn't limited to Postville Gentiles but to all Christians...Hasidim like Lazar have a total disinterest in anything or anyone who isn't Jewish...The Hasidim were waging a cultural holy war...Their world was Jew vs. non-Jew...If you didn't agree, you were at fault, part of the problem. You were paving the way for the ultimate destruction of the Jews, the world's Chosen People. There was no room for compromise...no room for anything but total and complete submission." (196-198)

This extends to business, which is a form of aggression against Gentiles. "I don't feel like a Jew unless I bargain," Lazar told him. "A Jew has to feel he got something for the absolute lowest price or he feels rotten." After reaching a deal with a Gentile, the Hasid boasted of not keeping the terms or taking his time to pay. Bloom compared it to hunting: "The Hasidim not only [bargained] with alacrity, but enjoyed boasting about the terrain, equipment, first sighting and ultimate kill." (211)

Bloom relates a particularly shameful incident told by a store owner. A Hasid pretended he had paid in advance for some merchandise, grabbed it and ran out of the store.

Despite being shunned by the Rabbis, a Rev. Miller organized an ecumenical service with two other clergymen from Postville's other two churches. No Jews showed up. "Reverend Miller got stiffed," Bloom writes. (146)

Evidently, tolerance, ecumenicalism, anti-racism, diversity etc. are designed for the goyim not the Talmudists.

CONCLUSION

It doesn't take a genius to recognize that Talmudic behavior is the real cause of anti-Semitism.

But the implications are far more serious. Meyer Amschel Rothschild was a Talmudist. This satanic hatred of humanity, and Christianity in particular, is driving the New World Order. There is a direct line between the Crucifixion of Christ, who represented the God of Love, 9-11 and the New World Order in terms of the degradation of humanity through war and depression. If this logic is correct, humanity's fate is to be crucified like Christ or otherwise slaughtered or enslaved.

Like Stephen Bloom and myself, 90% of American Jews are secular and ignorant of the Talmud. We find its views abhorrent. But these attitudes are the hidden agenda of Zionism and organized Jewry. A Gentile elite consisting of Freemasons has been created to advance this agenda. Barack Obama and most Western "leaders" belong to it.

The New World Order imperils humanity and assimilated Jews. As conditions deteriorate, anti-Semitism will become rampant. Jews must recognize that Judaism is not a religion but a conspiracy against humanity. It is also a conspiracy against Jews, whose security is endangered by its secret agenda.

Society has been brainwashed to reject the *Protocols of the Elders of Zion* which explains the methodology in detail. This document is not anti-Semitic; it is satanic. I first recognized it was authentic when the author chortled that a "cold and forlorn" mood had taken hold of Europe's cities. This is something no "forger" would think of.

Assimilated Jews need to disassociate from organized Jewry and re-invent themselves as a people, recognizing how, like other peoples, they have been deceived and exploited by their so-called leaders. Like Stephen Bloom, assimilated Jews have a strong sense of truth, justice and God's bountifulness, and must join their Christian neighbors in putting America back on track.

Incest Survivor Exposed
Illuminati Satanists

On May 1, 1989, a "nice Jewish girl," age 29, appeared on the Oprah Show and said her family was part of a satanic cult that dates back to the 1700's.

Although they appear to be upstanding citizens —lawyers, doctors, police officers etc. — they engage in satanic ritual human sacrifice, incest and cannibalism, often in synagogues. They drink blood and eat babies.

She is describing the Illuminati which originated in the Frankist Movement in the Eighteenth century. Jacob Frank, born Jacob Leibowitz (1726-1791) led a major satanic heresy that shook the Jewish world. They believed that the Messiah would return if the world went over to evil completely, so they encouraged all sexual licence and satanic Evil as the ultimate Good.

Financed by the Frankist Rothschild banking syndicate, they subverted all religions and national elites by assuming every religious and political hue. They took over Freemasonry and are now in the final stage of establishing their world government a.k.a "globalization."

The abuse Polin suffered is a textbook example of how Illuminati families —Jews and non-Jews— treat their children. George W. Bush and Barack Obama may have suffered similar trauma and, (like Polin,) have multiple personality disorder. Vicki is from Chicago and there is no telling how many Chicagoans surrounding Barack Obama are part of this satanic cult.

THE OPRAH INTERVIEW

Polin told Oprah that she witnessed babies sacrificed and consumed for the "power" this gave. These babies are bred within the extended family for this purpose. She said she was raped several times, and elsewhere says she had five abortions due to intercourse with her father.

Polin said her family was "extremely involved" in these practices. Her mother is "on the human relations commission of the town that she lives in, and she's an upstanding citizen. Nobody would suspect her. Nobody would suspect anybody involved in it. There's police officers involved in it. There's, you know, doctors, lawyers…"

"I mean, to the outside world, everything we did was proper and right, and then there were the nights that things changed, that things just got turned around. What was wrong was right, and what was right was wrong. That's what helps some of them to develop MPD."

Polin's therapist, Tina Grossman was on the show but edited out of the YouTube. She told Oprah that she had treated over 40 survivors from many states and Canada. They have never met each other yet say the "identical same things."

Ms. GROSSMAN: "They are describing identical rituals, just the same as, since I'm Jewish, you could go to New York or California and describe a seder in one state or another and, as a Jew, you would recognize it. This is the belief system in evil and the power that evil gives you, and so it has these certain rituals, so they are very similar with all of the survivors."

OPRAH: "See, but I am very surprised because the Jewish faith is the Jewish faith, and worshipping the devil is not a part of the Jewish faith. I mean, Jewish people do not worship the devil."

Ms. GROSSMAN: "But before there was Christ and before there was a system of one God, there was Paganism- and it still exists in the world, and in many cultures, you still find the belief that there is strength and power in the actual consumption of human flesh or animal flesh."

AFTERMATH

In spite of the fact that both Vicki and Oprah said many times this behavior was not typical of most Jews, the B'nai B'rith-ADL attacked the show as "anti-Semitic." Oprah did her penance and obviously has been forgiven. Vicki was stopped on the street and told her testimony would start "another holocaust." Vicki's response was that denying these crimes was akin to holocaust denial. In July of 1989, she penned this statement and sent it to all concerned:

Vicki Polin

"Our society believes the myth that Jews can't be pedophiles, or abuse their own children. This is a "MYTH," they do abuse children. There are even those who practice cannibalism, and perform human sacrifices. Believe me I saw it with my own eyes. I've come to the point in my life where I feel I need to bear witness. I have and will continue to until I'm sure what I had to endure as a child is believed by you and others like you. I will do whatever is possible so what happened to me doesn't happen to anyone else!"

Vicki became a therapist herself, moved to Baltimore and opened a practice. She has articles about the Frankists on her website, www.theawarenesscenter.org. I attempted to contact her without success. But I found an extensive profile with interviews on Luke Ford's website. Included is an Affidavit from a rabbi Vicki contacted in 2004 regarding an exorcism of her cult upbringing. She described their evil intent to him in these terms:

"The essence of her story was that there are currently many rabbis involved in this cult who brought their satanic rituals with them to the USA from Europe. That she was born into one of the Jewish families owing allegiance to the cult. She claimed to have been used as part of an organized child sexual abuse ring organized by the rabbi of her synagogue, and that the sexual abuse took place on Sifrei Torah Scrolls laid out on the floor of the synagogue. That the abuse began in early childhood and continued over a period of many years, through her teen years and into adulthood, and that she was only one of the many young children, boys and girls used in this manner. I did not ask for specifics of the rituals but she mentioned cannibalism, defecation and the sacrilege of sacred objects." [i.e. the Torah Scrolls]

CONCLUSION

We have been conditioned to think of humanity's satanic possession as normal and natural, like a man who has been sick forever, regards sickness as normal.

Do you think over 180 million people could be massacred in the 20th century merely by accident? That Hiroshima, the holodomor, the holocaust and 9-11 were accidents? That the steady decline of popular culture into degeneracy and obscenity is a coincidence? Do you think the gradual mainstreaming of incest, homosexuality, pederasty and the occult is random? That the destruction of higher education (in the humanities) and the family is also a coincidence? Mankind is in the thrall of a powerful satanic cult.

Robert Edmundson
"Testified Against the Jews"

Our Zionist mind controllers have eliminated al-most all record of Robert Edmondson. Until now, there was no reference to him (or photo) on the Internet. Yet he was thrown into jail in 1936 and again in 1942 for producing hundreds of bulletins alerting his fellow Americans to an International conspiracy financed by the central bankers and consisting largely of Communist Jews. This conspiracy was part of the New World Order.

Robert Edmondson, 1872-195?

A measure of Zionist subversion is when a nation's defenders are defamed and forgotten, while its traitors are rewarded and honored. Other 1930's patriots tarred as "anti-Semites" include Charles Lindbergh. Henry Ford, Charles Coughlin, Elizabeth Dillling, William Pelley, Louis McFadden and Huey Long.

Their fate proves that despite what Americans think, the US is a colony of the London-based Masonic Jewish central banking cartel and its leaders are traitors. Americans haven't been "free" for a very long time.

In 1936, Edmondson was charged with "libelling the Jewish people." In his defence, he wrote, "I am not against Jews because of their religion, as a race, a people or as individuals, but because Jewish leadership [i.e. the bankers] is actively anti-American, is attempting to jettison the American political philosophy and take over the Country, and that I would continue to be anti-Jewish until Jewry repudiated such subversion. Were the offender any other than the Jewish minority, my attitude would be precisely the same. This problem is the biggest and most acute thing in the world today....

"Knowing that pitiless publicity is the only cure for public evils, in 1934 I started on a campaign to expose Jewish Anti-Americanism and Talmudic Communism which has been called the "Code of Hell": a "Rabbi Racket" that victimizes its own followers; an international "Satanic System" subverting France, Britain, Germany and Russia, causing the present depression and moving to take over the United States through the Jewish Radical administration [of FDR.] " (p.69)

Faced with exposure, organized Jewry backed down. Edmondson subpoenaed "Princes of Jewry" Bernard Buruch, Henry Morganthau, Rabbi Wise, Samuel Untermeyer, Mayor LaGuardia, James P. Warburg, Walter Lippmann and Justice Samuel Rosenman. Whereupon the American Jewish Committee petitioned the court NOT to hear the case because the indictment violated the free speech guarantee of the Constitution.

"Jews are afraid of the truth," Edmondson wrote. "They know that a few grains of it will blow the lid off when publicized." (137)

Today more than ever, we are victims of a pathetic disingenuous ruse which equates defending our country, freedom, family and religion with "anti-Semitism." We are under merciless hate-filled attack yet we are accused of "hatred" when we identify them. Remember the little boy who said the Emperor has no clothes? The Zionists put him in jail.

JEWISH LEADERSHIP AGGRESSION

The majority of Jews are not aware of the Jewish leadership's secret agenda, which meshes with that of the central banking cartel. Yet the security of ordinary Jews is jeopardized by this centuries-old plan for world government now reaching fruition. Unless they oppose it, they will be blamed for it.

If they defend it, they are part of it. This includes remaining silent. By their silence, Jews condone the anti-Americanism of their leaders, Edmondson said.

In 1954, Edmondson published a collection of his bulletins entitled *"I Testify Against the Jews."* (All page references are from this text.)

He quotes rare documents such as a letter published in 1880 in the *Review of Jewish Studies,* financed by James de Rothschild. The letter, dating from 1489, is from the head of the Grand Sanhedrin in Constantinople. It advises a rabbi in Arles France to infiltrate Gentile society.

The Grand Satraps and Rabbis told the rabbi to convert to Christianity as the French King demands but "keep the Law of Moses in your hearts;" make your sons merchants so "that they may despoil Christians of their [property]; doctors so that "they may take away Christian lives."

"Make your sons canons and clerics that they may destroy the churches.....Arrange that your sons become advocates and lawyers, and see that they always mix themselves up with affairs of state in order that by putting Christians under your yoke, you may dominate the world and be avenged on them." (71)

Edmondson also quotes a May 11 1933 address at the Hebrew University by the famous Jewish poet N.H. Bialik which confirms a Jewish agenda few Jews are aware of. He says Jews have undermined Christianity by "deliberate Jewish conniving...it has been effected in great measure by crypto Jews (secret Jews) who have permeated Christianity and spoken through the mouth of Christianity." (51)

He says these crypto Jews are also the creators of "the Renaissance, of Liberalism, of Democracy, of Socialism, and of Communism." (151)

Remember he was speaking in 1933: "The Gentiles have at last realized this secret—that Judaism has gradually penetrated and permeated them like a drug. The Gentile nature is in revolt, and is trying to organize the final battle...They would 'smoke us out' of all the cracks and crannies where we have hidden. They would exterminate us like bacilli and be rid of us." (152) (*Judaism in History-A Jewish Conception* in "Lines of Communication" July 1933)

This is proof that millions of innocent Jews, including my grandparents, died partly because of the demented megalomania of the Jewish leadership. Ironically, the Nazis were financed by the Masonic Jewish bankers as a way of bringing war upon the Gentiles and forcing Jews to support Zionism.

CONCLUSION

The conspiracy against Christian Western civilization has succeeded so much that it cannot even be mentioned.

We live in a decadent, superficial, hypocritical society where people sell their souls for money and sex, and where mass media and education are devoted to propaganda and indoctrination. Denied the truth, we are kept in a state of arrested development, befitting children or "cattle." The peoples of the world and even their governments are "only children under age." (*Protocols of Zion*, 15)

We can be politically correct or we can admit that mankind is in the thrall of a satanic force bent on enslaving us.

Henry Klein – Anti Zionist Martyr

Shortly before his "suicide" in 1955, Henry H. Klein, a righteous Jew, uttered these prophetic words:

"Zionism is a political program for the conquest of the world…Zionism destroyed Russia by violence as a warning to other nations. It is destroying the United States through bankruptcy, as Lenin advised. Zionism wants another world war if necessary to enslave the people. Our manpower is scattered over the world. Will we be destroyed from within or will we wake up in time to prevent it?" (Pamphlet, *"Zionism Rules the World"*)

Like Robert Edmondson, Klein is another American hero flushed down the memory hole for defying the Rothschild -Rockefeller cartel. There is no Wikipedia entry for this Jew who

Henry Klein (1879-1955)

fought the Masonic bankers all his life as a crusading NYC reporter, editor, author, city official and Mayoral candidate. (He said the Rockefellers and most other tycoons are under Zionist control.) He became a lawyer and defended pro bono Christian patriots in the famous "Sedition" Show Trial of 1942-1944.

Klein represents the true Jewish spirit, not exclusive to Jews, of serving God, the inborn universal principle of absolute truth and justice. Like other groups, Jews have been betrayed by the Luciferian (Illuminati) central bankers using various 'isms including Zionism, Communism, Liberalism, Fascism, Socialism and Feminism.

Klein dedicated his 1935 autobiography *"My Last Fifty Years"* to his mother "whose Instincts and Spirit were transmitted to her son." He can truthfully say, "In a world ruled by Mammon, I have tried to serve my Fellowman…If I have exposed some hypocrites, humbugs and liars, I feel I have only further served God."

ZIONISM AND BARAMA

Klein's criticism of Zionism was confirmed when Barack Obama proved that even a Black man can become President if he is prepared to be a Zionist chore boy. His first act was to appoint Rahm Emanuel, an Israeli dual citizen, as his Chief of Staff. This is fitting since Obama's own citizenship is in doubt. The height-challenged Emanuel is rumored to be Mossad.

Sit back and enjoy Barama's black-faced imitation of JFK while he executes the Illuminati agenda inflicting more war and hardship on the US people.

At least now the Conservatives are outside the tent (instead of being deceived inside) and the Liberals are discovering the real meaning of "Change."

To digress from Klein's story for another moment, there is a revealing item in the *Jerusalem Post* about how Rahm Emanuel called his rabbi on Rosh Hashanah to ask if he could violate the holiday for a conference call about the $700 billion bank bailout.

Rabbi Asher Lopatin gave his permission "as long as the violation was kept to a minimum" since "this was a matter of life and death" and "modern Orthodoxy" is "committed to making it a better world."

Leaving Tap Dancing class

Jewish author Arthur Koestler once quipped that Judaism "teaches Jews how to cheat God." The rabbi justifies violating religious law to bail out bankers and calls it "making it a better world." This self deceit is a reminder that Jewish rabbis are mere "scholars" and not holy men in the sense of renouncing the world.

THE SHOW TRIALS

The election of Barack Obama will polarize Liberal and Conservative. We will see the typical Zionist- Communist practice of curbing free speech and persecuting dissenters in the name of curbing "bigotry" and anti-Semitism.

In 1942-44, FDR ordered a Stalinist Show Trial to punish American patriots and anti-Communists. Since Russia was an ally, he wanted to paint his critics as Nazis and anti-Semites. About 45 disparate activists, including Robert Edmondson, were charged with inciting rebellion among American soldiers and put in jail. The investigation against them was conducted by the B'nai Brith, the FBI and reporters for the (Illuminati Jewish banker owned) *Washington Post*.

Henry Klein represented Elmer J. Garner of Wichita, Kansas, the first cousin of FDR's first Vice President John Nance Garner, a deaf 83-year-old American patriot who died three weeks after the trial began. He had been held in the [Washington, D.C.] jail for several weeks, for lack of bond fees, and died alone in a Washington rooming house with 40 cents in his pocket.

Among the other persecuted patriots were: a sign painter who was 80 percent deaf, a Detroit factory worker, a waiter and a maid. (This account is indebted to *"A Mockery of Justice - The Great Sedition Trial of 1944"* by Michael Collins Piper & Ken Hoop.)

More prominent targets included former American diplomat and economist Lawrence Dennis, who said "Pearl Harbor did not suspend the Bill of Rights"; Mrs. Elizabeth Dilling of Chicago, an outspoken and articulate anti-Communist lecturer; Rev. Gerald Winrod of Kansas who had run for the Senate; and William Griffin, a New York-based publisher with connections in the Roman Catholic Church.

By jailing these people, FDR hoped to intimidate his more serious critics, men like Col. [Charles] Lindbergh or Senators [Burton] Wheeler [D-Mont.], [Robert] Taft [R-Ohio] and Gerald Nye [R-N.D.]

KLEIN'S DEFENCE

After Garner died, Klein represented Col. Eugene N. Sanctuary,73, who ran the Presbyterian foreign mission office in NYC. Sanctuary had written a pamphlet *"Is the New Deal Communist?"* in which he made a 35-point comparison of it to Marx's 1848 program.

He also wrote *"The Talmud Unmasked: The Secret Rabbinical Teachings Concerning Christians"* (New York, 1939 and he authored several hundred sacred and patriotic songs including *Uncle Sam We Are Standing by You*. He was hardly the dangerous seditionist that the prosecution and the sympathetic press painted him to be.

"This alleged indictment," Klein said in his opening address to the jury, "is ... under a Constitution which guarantees free press and free speech at all times, including during wartime...These people believed in the guarantees set forth in the Constitution, and they criticized various acts of the administration."

Klein's defence included the following:

"We will prove that the Communists control not only our government but our politics, our labor organizations, our agriculture, our mines, our industries, our war plants and our armed encampments."

"We will prove that this persecution was instigated by so-called professional Jews who make a business of preying on other Jews by scaring them into the belief that their lives and their property are in danger through threatened pogroms in the United States [and that] anti-Semitism charged in this so-called indictment, is a racket, that is being run by racketeers for graft purposes."

"We will show that the most vicious written attack on Jews and on the Roosevelt administration emanated from the office of the FBI by one of its agents, and that the purpose of this attack was to provoke others to do likewise. We will show that this agent also drilled his underlings in New York with broom sticks preparatory to "killing Jews."

"We will show that large sums of Hitler money helped finance Mr. Roosevelt's campaign for re-election in 1936 and that right at this moment, British, American and German capital and industry are co-operating together in South America and other parts of the world." [This points to the Illuminati as a worldwide elite conspiracy controlling both sides of every conflict.]

Klein's speech was a critical turning point in the defence. Lawrence Reilly wrote that "Klein did much in his brief speech to torpedo [Prosecutor] Rogge's case by bringing to light the hidden agencies responsible for its existence."

As a direct consequence, Klein was targeted, specifically because he was Jewish. Klein wrote that "attempts were made to poison me in Washington DC and to knock me off otherwise in NYC. My telephone has been tapped for more than 10 years and my mail stolen. Clients and friends were warned to keep away from me and word was sent out by the Jewish cabal to starve Klein."

According to Revilo Oliver, Klein committed suicide in 1955 but quite likely he was murdered. Louis McFadden, the chairman of the House Banking Committee was similarly murdered in 1936.

CONCLUSION

Our society is like a snake shedding its skin. The old skin was Western civilization, devotion to God, country, human development and freedom. The new skin is a banker-controlled socially engineered plantation where the slaves watch porn and think of nothing but sex.

Henry Klein fought this takeover but America doesn't even know he existed. This is the fate of patriots in a land subverted by an international satanic cult bent on translating its economic monopoly into a total monopoly over politics, culture and religion. Zionism, including organized Jewry, is an unwitting agent of this demonic drive to own everything and everyone.

But Zionism is just one arrow in the Illuminati quiver, which includes Freemasonry, most religions including fundamentalist Islam (Salafis/Wahabis,) intelligence agencies, corporations, governments, foundations, think tanks, the mass media, education, professional associations, universities, charities NGO's etc. Essentially they have control over money and everyone dances to their tune, while oozing unction. They pit their various agents against each other in order to achieve their goal, the degradation and enslavement of mankind.

It's hard to say whether the Illuminati expresses a Pharisee Jewish need to control the world, or a satanic one, or whether there is any difference between the two. But one thing is clear. Like everyone else, exceptional Jews like Henry Klein have an innate connection to God. Once we realize we are victims of a monstrous hoax, we can follow Klein's example and express His Spirit anew.

Hitler Was a Godsend for Israel

If Hitler didn't exist, Zionists would have had to create him. Maybe they did.

The numbers (from Edwin Black's *"The Transfer Agreement"*) tell the story. In 1927, about 15,000 of Germany's 550,000 Jews considered themselves Zionists. That's less than 2%.

The vast majority of German Jews "vehemently rejected Zionism as an enemy from within." They were Germans. Eighty thousand had fought in the trenches and 12,000 had died. "Nowhere was the opposition of Jews [to Zionism] so widespread, principled, and fierce as in Germany," a Zionist historian wrote. (168)

Thanks to Hitler, 60,000 German Jews emigrated to Israel between 1933 and 1941. Thanks to a "Transfer Agreement" between Nazis and Zionists, Jewish property valued at $100 million was transferred to Israel in the form of German industrial exports used to build Israel's infrastructure. The Transfer Agreement brought in tools, raw materials, heavy machinery, appliances, farm equipment as well as labor, and capital to finance expansion. Many of Israel's major industries, like textiles and the national waterworks, were thus founded. (373,379.)

This at a time when there were only 200,000 Jews in Palestine, mainly anti- Zionist religious Jews. The daily wage of a Jewish worker in Palestine was $1 a day. There were 800,000 Palestinian Arabs.

THANKS TO HITLER

Thanks to Hitler, the kernel of the German Jewish community was lifted up and transferred to Palestine along with their property. "Many of these people were allowed to transfer actual replicas of their homes and factories —indeed rough replicas of their very existences." (379)

In 1937, when the British proposed dividing Palestine into two states, the Nazis wondered if they hadn't made a mistake by creating "a Jewish Vatican" dedicated to Germany's demise. But Hitler overruled all dissenters and insisted the Transfer Agreement be continued and even expanded to other countries. Italy, Rumania, Hungary and several other countries under fascist influence signed similar agreements. (378)

Hitler hated Jews so much he built a country for them. He could have taken all their property and kicked them out but that would have been anti-Semitic.

What did he get out of it? Well the Zionists actually expanded Nazi trade by reselling German goods throughout the Middle East. Yes, they didn't just trade with the Nazis, they acted as their agents. The Nazis got rid of a lot of Jews and got a lot of Jaffa oranges in return.

The World Jewish Congress had to act pretty offended because they sponsored a world boycott of Germany goods. But this only endeared the doughty Zionists to the Nazis. And gave the Nazis an excuse to boycott and persecute German Jews which helped their Zionist pals.

ZIONIST-NAZI COOPERATION

As soon as the Nazis assumed power in 1933, the Zionists gained a visibly protected political status. After the Reichstag fire, the Nazis crushed virtually all political opposition and closed 600 newspapers. But not the Zionists nor their newspaper which was hawked from every street corner, and saw its circulation multiply five times to 38,000.

Zionism was "the only separate political philosophy sanctioned by the Third Reich." (174)

The Zionist uniform was the only non-Nazi uniform allowed in Germany. Same with their flag. Hebrew was mandated in Jewish schools. Still German Jews wanted to stay in Germany "even as second class citizens, even reviled and persecuted." (175) Zionists scorned the German Jews saying they deserved to be persecuted for wanting to assimilate.

Zionists pandered to the Nazis: "a common fate and tribal consciousness must be of decisive importance in developing a lifestyle for Jews too." (175)

This explains how " a fringe minority of German Jews [i.e. Zionists] took emergency custody of 550,000 men, women and children..." Black says. This was confirmation "of what Diaspora Jews had always feared about Zionism—it would be used as the legal and moral pretext for forcing Jews out of European society." (177)

It explains also why Israel behaves like Nazi Germany. They have a common racist pedigree.

At the post war Nuremberg trials, Julius Streicher affirmed that the Nuremberg Laws of 1935 were patterned after racist religious Jewish Law: "I have repeatedly emphasized the fact that the Jews should serve as an example to every race, for they created a racial law for themselves-the law of Moses, which says, 'If you come into a foreign land you shall not take unto yourself foreign women.'

...These laws of the Jews were taken as a model for these laws. ...That was the beginning of Jewry which, because it introduced these racial laws, has survived throughout the centuries, while all other races and civilizations have perished."—Trial of the Major War Criminals Before the International Military Tribunal, Nuremberg, 14 November

1945 - 1 October 1946, Volume 12, Secretariat of the Tribunal, Nuremberg, Germany, p. 315. (Thanks to Chris Jon Bjerknes.)

It's conceivable that Nazism was created in the image of Zionism (and Communism.) Certainly, Nazism and Zionism were complementary Illuminati movements. Not only did the Nazis build Israel, but Israel built Nazi Germany by providing an export market. They worked together. Many Jews didn't get all their money when they arrived in Israel. Thus, the Zionists also participated in the looting of Europe's Jews, which was called "Aryanization."

CONCLUSION

Increasingly Israelis, and Jews in general, realize that Zionism is a ruse and Israel's behavior bears an uncanny resemblance to Nazi Germany's. For example, Israeli academic Yeshayahu Leibowitz said everything Israel has done since 1967 is "either evil stupidity or stupidly evil." He refers to the Israeli army as "Judeo-Nazi."

This is not the place to show how Hitler was put into power by Anglo-American (i.e. Illuminati Jewish) finance. But it is the place for Jews and Americans to consider this lesson: Historical events are created to trick people into advancing the New World Order.

European Jews were uprooted, robbed and massacred in order to build the capital of Rothschild world government in Israel. Americans are dying in Iraq and Afghanistan and possibly Iran to stamp out Islam. Economic turmoil is making desperate people embrace world government "socialism." And so on...

Zionism Means
Never Saying You're Sorry

"The Jewish elite, the academics, politicians and media consider themselves to be great moralists, with very little self-introspection. Their self-righteousness, arrogance, and inherited Jewish prejudices against Christians has led to a huge amount of anti-Christian sentiment."

In Canada, this is called "hate speech" and would draw "human rights" complaints from organized Jewry.

In fact, this statement was made by an Israeli Jew to the *Jerusalem Post,* (March 30, 2009) and referred to anti-Semitism in Norway. I changed "Norwegian" and "Lutheran" to "Jewish," and "Israel" and "Jews" to "Christians."

Manfred Gerstenfeld, Chairman of the Jerusalem Center of Public Affairs was commenting on the "latent anti-Semitic feelings in Norwegian society" released by Operation Cast Lead, the Israeli slaughter of Gaza civilians. This shows that Zionists claim carte blanche when it comes to ethnic generalizations about others but cry "anti-Semitism" to silence criticism of themselves.

Rabbi Yoav Melchior, the leading rabbi of Norway, echoed this parochial view that the Norwegian outrage at the Israeli massacre of Gazans was the result of latent anti-Semitism.

The rabbi said he had been "very scared during the war. Hatred spread in a fast, dangerous way. This was blind emotionalism against Israel and against Jews. It gets deep at the heart of Norway's emotional anti-Semitism. The current wave of anti-Semitism shows what people have been holding inside them," he said.

Gerstenfeld, who authored and recently published *"Behind the Humanitarian Mask: The Nordic Countries, Israel, and the Jews,"* noted that "considering that there are only 700 Jews in a population of 4.6 million, there is a lot of hatred against Israel and the Jews."

Norway's government has been vocal in its criticism of Israel in recent months. At the outbreak of the Gaza hostilities, Foreign Minister Jonas Gahr Støre declared that "Norway strongly condemns any form of warfare that causes severe civilian suffering, and calls on Israel to withdraw its forces immediately."

In addition, "the Norwegians are pioneers in boycotting Israel," Gerstenfeld said, citing many Norwegian trade unions' tendency to support Palestinian interests at Israel's expense.

According to Gerstenfeld, "because Norway is a very tiny country with a language most don't understand, nobody gives them much attention. Their anti-Semitism flew completely under the radar for a long time." Now that the world is becoming aware of the situation in Norway, "the Norwegian elite won't get away with this incredible arrogance any longer," he asserted.

THE ZIONIST MINDSET

This article illustrates two disturbing characteristics found in the Zionist (and perhaps Jewish) psyche.

1) Zionists never say sorry because they are never wrong. They have suspended the law of cause and effect. Criticism is never the result of their own actions or behavior. It is always due to an irrational inbred hatred or prejudice on the part of others. "Anti-Semitism" gives them infallibility and immunity.

But as long as Jews support Israel, they will be held responsible for Israel's actions. Zionism is all about creating anti-Semitism to force Jews to back their aggressive hidden agenda. (See my "The Zionist Protection Racket" online.) Jews are being used to build the Rothschild's Thousand Year Kingdom, and when they are no longer needed by the Illuminati, they will be tossed aside.

Zionists demonize and treat their opponents like subhumans and "haters" because they won't admit wrongdoing. At some level, they think they are God and can do no wrong. Thus while some righteous Israeli soldiers reported numerous war crimes in Gaza, the IDF blithely concluded that these reports were "hearsay." This trimming of the truth to fit the agenda has become commonplace in the world today.

2) Gerstenfeld's threat that "the world is becoming aware of the situation in Norway" and the Norwegian elite "won't get away with it any longer" reveals an authoritarian tendency.

Zionists, like Communists, do not respond to criticism with rebuttals because they can't. After marginalizing critics, they respond with ad hominem attacks, ridicule, smears, threats, legal actions, and attacks on their livelihood. Disingenuously, they cry "hatred" when in fact they are a major source of hatred. They are a big part of the dynamic of the emerging totalitarian world government.

In the West (the US, Canada, Australia, the UK, Germany and France) this totalitarian system is synonymous with support for Zionism. Criticism of Israel is banned. In the UK, a diplomat faces jail for expressing disgust at Israeli atrocities. British MP George Galloway is refused entry to Canada because of his support for Palestinians. Canadians never debated this "security agreement" whereby critics of Israel, a country built by Zionist terrorism, were accused of supporting terrorism.

The way Zionists and Communists work, the way the New World Order works, is to control people by controlling thought and discourse, and ultimately by intimidation.

CONCLUSION

Anti-Semitism has increased due to two factors. 1) Israel's attack on Lebanon in 2006 and Gaza in 2008. This reaction was wildly disproportionate to the provocation, unequal in strength, and targeted civilians. 2) The perception that Jews were behind the credit crisis.

Indeed, the Illuminati Jewish dominated Federal Reserve is responsible, according to G.H.W. Bush Assistant Secretary of Housing, Catherine Austin Fitts.

"Alan Greenspan is a liar. The Federal Reserve and its long standing partner, the US Treasury, engineered the housing bubble, including the fraudulent inducement of America as part of a financial coup d'etat. Our bankruptcy was not an accident. It was engineered at the highest levels."

The cause of anti-Semitism is no mystery. Too many Jews have served as dupes and agents of the world's central banking cartel's (i.e. Rothschild's) plan for world government tyranny. Masons, Mormons, Jehovah Witnesses, Republicrats and practically every other "successful" religion or organization also serve. (Anyone who espouses diversity, "women's & gay rights," climate change etc.)

But if history is an indication, popular indignation will grow, and be funnelled against Jews who play little or no role in this diabolical conspiracy. These Jews must stand up now and, in the words of Sam Goldwyn say, "include me out."

Zionists Endorse Anti-Semitism

Anti-Semitism used to refer to a racial prejudice against Jews. Now "hate" is a code word for something else: Opposition to Zionism, a political program that even many Jews find repugnant.

By equating "hate" with opposition to Zionism, organized Jewry has given everyone permission to be an anti-Semite.

In Soviet Russia, anti-Semitism was considered "counter revolutionary" and severely punished. Similarly, anti-Semitism is now a political crime in the West because it runs counter to the Zionist New World Order.

For example, a Winnipeg journalist, Leslie Hughes, was dropped as a Liberal candidate in the 2008 election for remarking on Israeli foreknowledge of the 9-11 attack in a 2003 article. She was quoting an Israeli newspaper. She taught courses on tolerance and had no feelings of hostility against Jews. Her crime was political. She got the news while she was canvassing in her riding.

She has filed a lawsuit against the Canadian Jewish Congress and the Liberal Party.

My writing warns Jews they are being used to advance the central banker's plan for world government dictatorship. I emphasize that every significant nation, religion and organization also is being used.

Nonetheless, the Canadian Jewish Congress accuses me of "hatred against Jews" and wants to suppress my writing. The absurdity of accusing the son of holocaust survivors of anti-Semitism underlines the true "counter revolutionary" nature of my crime.

YOU ARE AN ANTI SEMITE IF ...

Rev. Ted Pike extrapolates from the 2004 US "Global Anti-Semitism Review Act" to define the kind of political activity that is being criminalized. ("The Real Motive Behind Dept. Of Global Anti-Semitism")

1. Any assertion "that the Jewish community controls government, the media, international business and the financial world" is anti-Semitic.

2. "Strong anti-Israel sentiment" is anti-Semitic.

3. "Virulent criticism" of Israel's leaders, past or present, is anti-Semitic.

4. Criticism of the Jewish religion or its religious leaders or literature (especially the Talmud and Cabala) is anti-Semitic.

Criticism of the U.S. government and Congress for being under undue influence by the Jewish-Zionist community (including AIPAC) is anti-Semitic.

6. Criticism of the Jewish-Zionist community for promoting globalism (the "New World Order") is anti-Semitic.

7. Blaming Jewish leaders and their followers for inciting the Roman crucifixion of Christ is anti-Semitic.

8. Diminishing the "six million" figure of holocaust victims is anti-Semitic.

9. Calling Israel a "racist" state is anti-Semitic.

10. Asserting that a "Zionist Conspiracy" exists is anti-Semitic.

11. Claiming that Jews and their leaders created the Bolshevik Revolution in Russia is anti-Semitic.

12. Making "derogatory statements about Jewish persons" is anti-Semitic.

13. Denying the right of mostly atheist Jews to re-occupy Palestine is anti-Semitic.

14. Alleging that Mossad was behind the 9/11 attack is anti-Semitic.

Essentially if you believe in truth and justice, you're an anti-Semite. If you believe in free speech, free inquiry and the democratic process, you're an anti-Semite. If you oppose tyranny, corruption and murder, you're an anti-Semite.

If you're not an anti-Semite, you're uninformed at best, and a sell-out ("vendu") at worst.

Ultimately, the New World Order will turn 90% of the world's population and at least 50% of Jews into anti-Semites. Is this the real agenda? To divert blame away from the central banksters and their non-Jewish Masonic minions?

THE SYNAGOGUE OF SATAN

Andrew Hitchcock's *"The Synagogue of Satan"* is a compelling chronology of the Jewish role in the central banker's Satanic conspiracy a.k.a The New World Order. Together with my *"Illuminati,"* it provides as an excellent introduction to the subject.

The only knock is that Hitchcock does not provide any references. For example, he lifts the above list from the Internet without giving credit to Rev. Pike. Nevertheless Hitchcock's sources can be verified online.

I was impressed by the amount of new information and insight I found. Hitchcock explains how the "nationalization" of the Bank of England in 1946 was a sleight-of-hand. He provides new information on the art of money creation. He lucidly explains the significance of the Noahide Laws.

You read this book with growing fury at the scale of ruthlessness, criminality and chutzpah of certain Jews. These Jews are not God's Chosen people, but Satan's, a matter that should be of concern to other Jews who are guilty mostly of naivety, complacency, conformity, cowardice, and opportunism. The same can be said of Americans and Canadians who support war crimes in Afghanistan with their taxes.

Hitchcock quotes Werner Sombart who says that from 1820 onward, there was "only one power in Europe, and that is Rothschild." He says modern capitalism and Americanism are nothing but "the Jewish spirit distilled."

CONCLUSION

Zionists will label everyone an anti-Semite because anti-Semitism is their bread and butter.

Jews have the naive misconception that Zionism is there to protect them from anti-Semitism. In fact, Zionism is there to create anti-Semitism in order to force Jews to carry out the Illuminati agenda, i.e. central banker world government. The goal of Zionism is to make Jews a pariah, the better to use them.

Zionism is the primary source of anti-Semitism in the world today jeopardizing all Jews whom they claim to represent. Imagine if the Illuminati decided to make Jews their scapegoat. Imagine if one day they revealed the Mossad role in 9-11. Imagine if the word was spread: "the Jews did 9-11." We could have pogroms in America. Yet many Jews, who had nothing to do with 9-11 and will suffer, stubbornly support Israel.

Israel is the Rothschild's private fiefdom; their private army, secret service and nuclear arsenal. All these are being used to advance the Rothschild world government agenda. In the future, Zionist Jews and their supporters will have alot of 'splaining to do.'

NWO : Front for
Cabalist Jewish Tyranny

In the expanded edition of *"Under the Sign of the Scorpion"* (2002) Estonian writer Jyri Lina unearths Cabalist (Masonic) Jewish authors who take credit for Communism, and by extension World Government. While long suspected, this has rarely been confirmed by Jewish sources.

The Bolshevik Revolution "was brought about through the hands of the Jews," M. Kohan wrote April 12, 1919 in the newspaper *Kommunist* (Kharkov.)

The article is entitled:"The Jews' Service to the Working Class" and continues: "Could the dark and oppressed masses of Russian workers and peasants throw off the yoke of the bourgeoisie themselves? No, it was Jews from beginning to end who showed [them] the way to the rosy dawn of internationalism and who to this day rule the Soviet Russia." (p.161)

Lina cites a Zionist document found on the body of a Jewish Communist Battalion Commander published in an Estonian newspaper on Dec 31, 1919 that suggests Communism in fact was a disguised economic, race and religious war:

"Sons of Israel! The time of our final victory is near. We stand at the beginning of our world dominion and our renown....We have transformed Russia into an economic slave and taken nearly all of its riches...We must eliminate their best and most talented individuals...We must provoke class war and dissension among the blind peasants and workers [and] ...annihilate the cultural values the Christian peoples have acquired... faithful sons of Israel hold the highest posts in the nation and rule over the enslaved Slavs." (p.162)

Lina's book provides substantial support for the view that mankind is the victim of a long-term satanic (Cabalist Jewish, and Masonic) conspiracy to enslave and despoil it. The Masonic & Jewish central banking cartel used the rhetoric of Communism (class warfare & public ownership) to conquer Russia and China. These were basically foreign (Jewish, Masonic, British) invasions disguised as "revolutions." The New World Order is an extension of Masonic Jewish ("British") imperialism.

Naturally, the Communists didn't want this connection made. They outlawed "anti-Semitism" on pain of death. Russian patriots were regarded as "anti-Semitic" and exterminated. People in possession of the *Protocols of Zion* were executed.

TERROR

The fact that Communist atrocities are soft pedalled here in the West and "hate laws" introduced, confirms that the same power is in control. Unless they have changed, we could be in grave danger.

Communist executions were published in the Cheka's weekly newspaper. In 1917-18, 1.7 million people were executed. From Jan 1921 to April 1922, 700,000 were executed. Among the victims was the cream of Russian society: Bishops, professors, writers, doctors— all accused of "anti-social thinking." Lina writes that "the eyes of church dignitaries were poked out, their tongues were cut off and they were burned alive...The Bishop of Voronezh was boiled alive in a big pot and monks forced to drink this soup." (pp. 110-112)

Lina cites the Old Testament (*Isaiah, Deuteronomy*) as the ideological source of this barbarism. Their God commanded the Jews to slaughter and enslave the goyim and take their property. (p.113) (Lina, however, is no Christian—calling Christianity the "religion of slaves.") He names 60 top members of the murderous CHEKA in the 1930's. All but two were Jewish. (290)

Most Jews today were not alive in 1918-1922 and are not a conscious part of the Illuminati conspiracy. Most haven't a clue about the Talmud or the Cabala. They do not realize that Zionism and organized Jewry are run by these fanatical bankers and have a secret agenda.

The constant calls for non-democratic world government by banker- owned politicians are proof that this conspiracy is very real indeed. The devil operates by deceit and seduction. He will make the New World Order look benevolent. By the time the truth is apparent, it will be too late.

REVOLUTION AS GANGSTERISM

Jyri Lina has performed an invaluable service by exposing the Russian Revolution. He puts it in the context of the French Revolution which was instigated by the same forces. In both cases, the "revolutionaries" had no interest in the welfare of the people. Quite the opposite, they dismantled what was good and stole everything of value:

"The Russian workers became slaves to the international extremist Jews..formerly secret Communist Party archives reveal Trotsky had $80 million in US banks and 90 million Swiss Francs in Swiss banks." (157) In Oct. 1918, Jewish bankers in Berlin received 3125 kilos of plundered Russian gold. (278)

Similarly Lina describes how the Masonic Jewish bankers started World War One. He cites an article by a Rabbi Reichorn July 1, 1880: "We shall force the goyim into a war by exploiting their pride, arrogance and stupidity." (182)

The Masonic newspaper *British Israel Truth* wrote in 1906: "We must prepare ourselves for big changes in a great war which faces the peoples of Europe." (181)

In 1919, a Zionist newspaper wrote that International Jewry forced Europe into the war so "a new Jewish era could begin throughout the world." (181)

We are in the grip of a pernicious power. The true meaning of "Enlightenment" and "Revolution" is to overturn the natural and spiritual order of the universe and replace God with Lucifer who represents the pretensions of the Illuminati (Masonic) and Jewish bankers. Our social, political and cultural life is orchestrated by them.

But like cockroaches, they fear exposure. Juri Lina has shone the light. His book can be purchased for $30 by writing to him directly. jyrilina@yahoo.com

USSR - Illuminati Experiment Was A "Social Catastrophe"

As we edge toward world government, it pays to recall the Illuminati's last great social experiment, Soviet Communism, which Jyri Lina describes as a "social catastrophe."

In his book, *"Under the Sign of the Scorpion"* (2002), the Estonian writer says about 150 million people died as a result of the Bolshevik Revolution, subsidized by the Illuminati (Masonic Jewish) banking cartel. The West pretended to oppose the Bolsheviks but in fact defended them and betrayed the White Russians who were our allies in WWI. The Bolsheviks would have lost except for Western intervention. (322)

An additional 60 million people were murdered under Chinese Communism. These satanic regimes "gripped the... people by the hair of their heads" (Winston Churchill) and brutally destroyed two advanced civilizations. The Illuminati central bankers still run the world. If "Past is Preface," are we being set up for similar brutal treatment? Is this the reason why the truth about these "revolutions" is suppressed?

INSIDE STORY

Juri Lina claims that the USSR was ruled by Jewish gangsters. Soviet "anti-Semitism" was the spin they put on their gang wars. Marxist ideology was a smokescreen. Josef Stalin was a Jew who spoke Yiddish and married Jewish women. He was diagnosed as a "paranoid hysteric" by a doctor who he was murdered for revealing this.

He had an inferiority complex due to being only five foot one inch tall and employed a stand-in for public appearances. He murdered his second wife in 1932 when she accused him of genocide. Like Lenin, another Jew (who died of syphilis) Stalin was also bisexual. (pp. 284-286.) These are the freaks the Illuminati bankers put in power.

Stalin was under the influence of another Jew, Lazar Kaganovich (and married his sister.) Kaganovich played on Stalin's paranoia to murder over 20 million Communist party leaders, functionaries, and army officers, especially those aware of his nefarious deeds. Stalin and Kaganovich were after their rivals' gold. During the Great Terror of 1934-38, NKVD Officers began wearing a new symbol on their sleeves, a sword and serpent. "This symbolized the struggle of the cabalistic Jews against their enemies," Lina writes. "There is no devil according to the Talmud. Satan and God are united in Yahweh." (301)

At the peak of Stalin and Kaganovich's terror in 1937-38, executions reached 40,000 a month. Alexander Solzhenitsyn estimated a million were executed and another two million died in death camps. *Literaturnaya Rossiya* estimated total deaths due to murder, induced starvation and maltreatment at 147 million, five million a year for the period 1918-1938. Lina points out that many killed were women and children who were classed as "enemies of the people." After all "they cost money" i.e. were "useless eaters" in Communist eyes.

Huge mass graves surround the major cities of the USSR. One containing 100,000 bodies was found in Kuropaty, six miles from Minsk. Every night from 1937 to June 1941, the NKVD lined people up at the grave side, gagged and blind-folded. To save bullets, the executioners tried to kill two people with one shot. (303)

At the peak of the terror, the NKVD began gassing people in lorries. The West considered all this to be normal. Bernard Shaw said nations had the right to eliminate undesirables. The US ambassador to Moscow, Joseph Davies, a Freemason, was especially enthusiastic about the show trials. (304)

The USSR lost an additional 35-45 million people during the Second World War. The historian Nikolai Tolstoi claims that half of these were actually killed by the Bolsheviks and blamed on the Nazis. During campaigns against counter revolutionaries in 1949-1952, another five million people were murdered. (307)

In addition to the holomodor (1932-32) which killed 15 million Ukrainians, there was another (lesser known) organized famine in the Ukraine in 1946-1947 to put down political resistance. This killed two million. Another million Russians were killed or irradiated in 1954 when the Communists tested an atomic weapon on Russians. (318)

SATANIC GENOCIDE SPONSORED BY THE WEST

The Bolshevik Revolution was totally organized and financed by Illuminati bankers (Schiff, Rockefeller, Warburg etc.) and the German government, which they controlled. (206)

Anthony Sutton found that 95% per cent of Soviet technology came from the US or their allies. He said the Communists couldn't have lasted "one day" without Western aid. While pretending to be engaged in a "Cold War," the West actually provided billions in direct military and economic subsidies to the Soviets. How else can you have a war? (322)

A quarter million tractors were needed for the "collectivization" of the Kulak farmers land. With financing from Kuhn Loeb, 80 US companies participated in building three huge tractor factories. These were also used for building tanks.

Under the Rapallo Treaty signed in April 1922, German consortiums built numerous airplane, locomotive and munitions factories throughout the USSR. Krupp built tanks and submarines in Leningrad and Rostov. German troops rehearsed Blitzkreig tactics on Russian soil. Clearly the Illuminati sponsors both sides of every conflict. Without this industrial activity and economic aid, the USSR would have failed.

The West's Illuminati politicians and financiers didn't lose any sleep over the executions or the 15 million sent to the Gulag. (343) Their newspapers suppressed this information. They are as guilty as the NKVD executioners, and it was all done on our dime.

"The Western financial elite wanted to use market economy capitalism as an anvil and Communism as a hammer to rule the world and entirely subdue it," Lina writes.

Eventually the cost of maintaining the USSR became prohibitive, and the new Russia was born, under the Freemasons Yeltzin and Putin.

The same gang of Satanists and mass murderers continue to rule our planet. Our politicians are their conscious or unconscious agents. This doesn't bode well for the New World Order. A thin patina of law and civilized tradition separate us from the barbarism and chaos experienced in Russia.

We live in a fool's paradise. The price of not bringing these monsters to justice for crimes like 9-11 is that they continue to inflict their madness on the human race.

Will "Lean Years" Lead to Communism?

Right on schedule, the politician-puppets are promising to save us from the crisis caused by the banker-puppets by creating "a new world financial order."

Nicholas Sarkozy and Gordon Brown are calling for a "new international financial architecture for the global age" which will establish Rothschild global governance under the guise of "reforming and regulating" markets.

In an article *"The Joseph Principle and Crisis Economics,"* Carl Teichrib, a young Manitoba researcher-farmer says the manipulation of calamities to re-make society can be traced back to Biblical times. Joseph, one of

Carl Teichrib

the first Court Jews, is best known for predicting seven years of abundance (inflation) followed by seven years of famine (credit-contraction or deflation.)

He is less well known for using this "business cycle" to establish a form of Communism. All the cultivated land in Egypt became the property of the crown, and the people farmed it for the king, giving him one-fifth of the produce.

Teichrib, a devout Christian, writes:

"In *Genesis* 47, Joseph, second in command to Egypt's Pharaoh, warned of a coming famine, and prepared stock-piles of grain to aid the people through the crisis. When the famine hit the land, the people came to Joseph to buy food stock. A simple transaction was made; the citizens used the national currency to purchase grain.

"In verses 14 and 15 we find an unusual development. After the grain was purchased, Joseph intentionally holds the money back, keeping it from being re-circulated into the local economy. The result is predictably catastrophic for the people: Economic crisis.

"According to the King James Version, "the money failed" (vs.15), and in the New International Version it says that the "money is used up." Egypt experienced intentional, government-sponsored deflation in the midst of a natural calamity. The money collapsed.

"Needing to eat, what did the citizens do? They brought Joseph their livestock in exchange for grain (vs.16-17.) As an agrarian society, livestock represented the industrial basis of the people. Hence, placing this power in the hands of the government, the people's commercial activity was effectively abolished.

"In relating this series of events to others, some have asked me; "Why didn't the people just eat the animals instead of trading them for grain?"

"Refrigeration didn't exist. And while the people could have dried some of the meat for long-term use, grain would have been the most valuable and stable food source during a drought. Now the people had neither money nor livestock; and a year later they were out of food.

"Returning to Joseph, who obviously was in charge of the storehouses, the people begged their leader to take their land and themselves in trade for food (vs.18-19.) Property was therefore consolidated under the state, and the citizens literally became slaves in their own country (vs.20-21.) In the King James Version the language goes even further: Joseph depopulates the rural areas and moves the people into the cities.

"This is a masterful population control strategy. Once the wealth of the nation had been consolidated under the Pharaoh's banner via Joseph's actions - monetary wealth, the industrial base, land and productivity, and the people as economic assets - then Joseph instituted a new farming and taxation system (vs.20-24.) How did the people respond? They gladly relinquished control of their wealth, property, and themselves (gave up their freedom) for the promise of state-dictated security.

"Keep in mind; all of this started through a debasing of the currency system. The manipulation of money is, arguably, the most potent method - outside of war - used to rearrange the fabric of society.

"Am I suggesting that our current crisis will be used as leverage to re-structure our Western world? The odds are in favor of it. Consider what the father of modern economics, John Maynard Keynes, had to say in 1919.

"There is no subtler, no surer means of overturning the existing basis of society than to debauch the currency." - John Maynard Keynes, "The Economic Consequences of the Peace," (1919), 236.

"Keynes economic model is what we have been using since the end of World War II. Roughly speaking, it's the idea that governments can stimulate the economy through interest rate management - the heart of credit and debt - taxation programs, and other state-instituted incentive programs. Although the above quote was aimed primarily at inflationary actions, the same conclusion could be made regarding deflationary leveraging."

When alien bankers control the purse strings of the State, inevitably the State becomes synonymous with these bankers. The State is "public" in name only. This is the true face of Communism.

Obama's Jewish Grandfather

If you Google "America's First Jewish President," you'll find links to many Jewish publications "kvelling" (yiddish for boasting) about how Barack Obama was sponsored by Jews and is "one of us." This may be literally true. I suspect his mother's father Stanley "Dunham" was Jewish. Obama's mother "Stanley Anne Dunham" certainly looked and acted like a Communist Jew. (My first mother-in-law was one.)

As we have seen, the modus operandi of the satanic Sabbatean Frankist cult (Illuminati) is to intermarry and impersonate all other religions, ideologies and nationalities. Reinhard Heydrich's grandfather was Jewish. Hitler's grandfather was Jewish. Churchill's mother was half-Jewish. Sonya Sottomayer parades as a "Latina" but her mother was Jewish. It wasn't

26 October 1944   Somewhere in France

To:

Your son, Stanley

just Jewish actors in Hollywood who changed their name and their persona. The object is power. By controlling all sides, they create divisions, chaos and war. Ultimately the aim is to destroy Western civilization and bring about the New (Communist, some say Jewish) World Order.

To call Barack Obama "America's First Jewish President" is disingenuous. Many other presidents are rumored to have had Jewish blood: Theodore Roosevelt, FDR, Truman, Eisenhower, Johnson and the Bushes to name a few. So it's not surprising to read in Wikipedia that, Stanley Dunham, a lowly furniture salesman from Kansas was related to six US Presidents.

"Stanley Armour Dunham's distant cousins include six US presidents: James Madison, Harry Truman, Lyndon Johnson, Jimmy Carter, George H. W. Bush and George W. Bush. [19] Through a common ancestor, Mareen Duvall, ...Stanley Dunham is related to former Vice-President Dick Cheney (an eighth cousin once removed.)[2] Through another common ancestor, Hans Gutknecht, ...Stanley Dunham is President Harry S. Truman's fourth cousin, twice removed."

In contrast to her husband, non-Jew Madelyn Payne Dunham is related to no Presidents. Wikipedia waxes on about Stanley's "Irish" antecedents but my Jew-dar isn't buying it.

Other clues. Stanley's mother Ruth (a common Jewish name) Lucille Armour committed suicide when Stanley was eight-years-old. His father abandoned him and his brother to their grandparents. What would cause a mother of two boys to commit suicide?

As a furniture salesman, Stanley was described as "gregarious, friendly, impetuous, challenging and loud...could charm the legs off a couch."

Stanley Dunham and his wife Madelyn (not Jewish) raised Barack from age 10 in Honolulu in the 1970's. Although Madelyn didn't have a university degree, she became Vice-President of a bank. Madelyn and Stanley are described as "Methodists." But Barack was raised as a "Unitarian" which like Freemasonry and Judaism, doesn't require members to believe in God. It is yet another stalking horse for the NWO.

Obama's mother, "Stanley Anne," became a Communist and fought the "Establishment," not realising the Communists ARE the Establishment. She allowed a Communist degenerate Frank Davis to take pornographic pictures of her, which are on the Internet. (Google Images) Davis boasted of bedding white women and some believe Davis is Obama's real father. Certainly Barack Obama Sr. didn't waste any time abandoning mother and son.

"Stanley Anne" was an "idealistic" part-Jewish woman who got her Ph.D. and worked for Timothy Geitner's father in Indonesia at the elite Ford Foundation. Some suspect she did double time for the CIA.

ROTHSCHILD'S CHOICE

My interest in Obama's antecedents was piqued by Texe Marr's new DVD about Barack Obama called "Rothschild's Choice." Packing the punch of an old fashioned sermon, this DVD demonstrates convincingly that Barack Obama's role is to roll America into a Jew World Order. Anyone wishing to understand "anti-Semitism" need go no further than this video which I recommend to Jews and non-Jews alike. It's a disgrace that America has produced only a handful of courageous and effective defenders like Texe Marrs.

Although Jews make up no more than 2.5 % of the US population, Marrs shows how Jews (and Israel) dominate business and government, not to mention entertainment to the detriment of Americans. The recent credit crisis is portrayed as outright theft from the US taxpayer by Jewish bankers. Although I considered myself well versed on the subject, the video contained a lot of new information. For example I wasn't aware that the whole American Black leadership are Prince Hall Masons like Barack Obama, and therefore instruments of the Illuminati Jewish bankers.

The list includes NY Governor David Paterson, Jesse Jackson, Eldridge Cleaver, Louis Farrakhan, Al Sharpton., Andrew Young, Julian Bond, Kweisi Mfume and entertainers like Count Basie and Nat King Cole.

The Illuminati Jews are Satanists who breed with generational Satanists from other backgrounds and impersonate every race religion or nationality. Obama is a "Christian," a "Muslim" and even a Jew. He is an Indonesian, Kenyan and an American. He is Black and White. He is a perfect leader for a new world bereft of race, nation and religion. In fact, he represents an alien satanic force, the Illuminati, intent on gradually enslaving mankind.

The Illuminati have usurped the leadership of Jews in the same way as they have usurped the leadership of Blacks, Christians, Americans and Europeans in general. We are all equally culpable.

'CHANGING THE WORLD'

It is a tragedy that mankind's collective and idealistic impulses have been co-opted by the Illuminati bankers and used to increase their power and wealth. "Equality" and "social justice" are ruses to cover their real agenda: the reduction of the human race to the status of worker-consumer drones. Now, they are taking our racial, religious, national and gender identity. Eventually they will take our freedom and property. Perhaps then, too late, we'll get the message.

Obama's Slip Showed His Real Colors

During the 2008 election campaign, Barack Obama caused an uproar with a slip of the tongue. Americans want to be deceived but they demand a certain level of competence. They don't want the harsh truth thrown in their face.

Obama's remark was incendiary because he let his mask slip and showed his true feelings. He is a Communist. His father and mother were Communists and he is proud of his heritage.

We're past the idea that Communism is a working class rebellion for public ownership and social justice. That's just window dressing to capture idealistic "useful idiots." Communism is government tyranny designed by the London-based Illuminati bankers to absorb all wealth under the facade of "public ownership." Some form of Communism will be the face of the New World Order.

PARSING OBAMA'S REMARK

The Illuminati is reshaping humanity by destroying the four pillars of human identity: race, religion, nation and family. This is also the Communist platform.

Obama's statement demonizes people who resist this rapacious and evil program. This is what Communists (and Socialists and Liberals) do as a reflex. They need to dehumanize people who cling to their God, country, heritage and family. They need to believe we are prejudiced, hate-filled fanatics, yokels and fascists.

Here is what he said:

"You go into these small towns in Pennsylvania and, like a lot of small towns in the Midwest, the jobs have been gone now for 25 years and nothing's replaced them. And it's not surprising then they get bitter, they cling to guns or religion or antipathy to people who aren't like them or anti-immigrant sentiment or anti-trade sentiment as a way to explain their frustrations."

Obama depicts religion as an irrational prejudice fed by economic frustration. "Antipathy to people who aren't like them" refers to the homosexual and feminist activists who are destroying the institution of the family. "Anti immigrant or anti trade sentiment" refers to policies that protect national or racial character. "Guns" refers to the necessity to render these people powerless.

Obama managed to touch all the bases.

A faux Presidential race makes Americans believe there is a chance for democratic change. There is not. This should be obvious from the Congressional elections when the public gave the Democrats a mandate to end the Iraq war. What happened? The opposite. Bush sent more troops.

Clearly the Iraq war will end not when the Democrats or anyone says, but when the Illuminati bankers decide it will. It was the same with Vietnam.

[Obama campaigned on a mandate for "Change." But we know now, he kept Bush's Defence Secretary Robert Gates and ordered a "Surge" in Afghanistan.]

CLINTON'S LIES

Hillary Clinton's slip about dodging sniper fire in Bosnia caused an uproar for the same reason. It was a reminder that the candidates are telling boldfaced lies and the process is a charade.

When she was asked how she could "oppose" Free Trade when her husband is getting millions of dollars to lobby for it, she just laughed and shrugged. Caught red-handed again.

Look at the choice the Illuminati have given Americans. A Black Communist; a crooked lesbian; and a fossil who represents a continuation of the disastrous policies of the Bush administration. Who represents the majority of good hardworking honest Americans? Who really represents change? No one.

Obama is related to both Bush and Cheney.

When will Americans recognize that the Illuminati is destroying their country and laughing at them? Humiliating and ridiculing and killing them? When will they realize that 9-11 was perpetrated by the Illuminati, that their leaders and mass media are betraying them? When will they realize US democracy has been hijacked?

When they do, Americans will take to the streets with guns. And that is what the "war on terror" is really about: creating a police state to oppress Americans who then will be called "terrorists."

That's when soldiers and policemen will have to ask, where do their loyalties belong? With the foreign-based satanic cult that runs the government or with their fellow citizens.

BOOK FOUR

Hidden History

Catholics Unveiled
Masonic Jewish Plot in 1936

In the London Catholic Gazette of February 1936 a sensational article was published under the heading: "The Jewish Peril and the Catholic Church." The monthly organ of the Catholic Missionary Society of England was quoting speeches delivered in a series of secret Jewish meetings in Paris. A few weeks later, the Parisian weekly "Le Reveil du Peuple" published a similar account, adding that the statements had been made at a recent convention of the B'nai Brith (secret Masonic order in which no Gentile is admitted) held in Paris.

The article of the "Catholic Gazette" read as follows:

"THE JEWISH PERIL AND THE CATHOLIC CHURCH"

That there had been and still is a Jewish problem no one can deny. Since the rejection of Israel, 1,900 years ago, the Jews have scattered in every direction, and in spite of the difficulties and even persecution, they have established themselves as a power in nearly every nation of Europe.

In view of this Jewish problem, which affects the Catholic Church in a special way, we publish the following amazing extracts from a number of speeches recently made under the auspices of a Jewish society in Paris. The name of our informant must remain concealed. He is presently known to us, but by reason of his peculiar relations with the Jews at the present time, we have agreed not to disclose his identity nor to give away any further details of the Paris meeting beyond the following extracts which, though sometimes freely translated, nevertheless substantially convey the meaning of the original statements.—Editorial Note glories in the fact that without detriment to their own racial unity and international character, the Jews have been able to spread their doctrines and increase their political, social and economic influence among the nations..

"As long as there remains among the Gentiles any moral conception of the social order, and until all faith, patriotism and dignity are uprooted, our reign over the world shall not come.

"We have already fulfilled part of our work, but we cannot yet claim that the whole of our work is done. We have still a long way to go before we can overthrow our main opponent: the Catholic Church...

"We must always bear in mind that the Catholic Church is the only institution which has stood, and which will, as long as it remains in existence, stand in our way. The

Catholic Church, with her methodical work and her edifying and moral teachings, will always keep her children in such a state of mind, as to make them too self-respecting to yield to our domination, and to bow before our future King of Israel...

"That is why we have been striving to discover the best way of shaking the Catholic Church to her very foundations. We have spread the spirit of revolt and false liberalism among the nations of the Gentiles so as to persuade them away from their faith and even to make them ashamed of professing the precepts of their Religion and obeying the Commandments of their Church. We have brought many of them to boast of being atheists, and more than that, to glory in being descendants of the ape! We have given them new theories, impossible of realization, such as Communism, Anarchism, and Socialism, which are now serving our purpose...The stupid Gentiles have accepted them with the greatest enthusiasm, without realizing that those theories are ours, and that they constitute our most powerful instrument against themselves...

GENTILES BUILDING THEIR OWN JAILS

"We have blackened the Catholic Church with the most ignominious calumnies, we have stained her history and disgraced even her noblest activities. We have imputed to her the wrongs of her enemies, and thus brought these latter to stand more closely by our side... So much so, that we are now witnessing to our greatest satisfaction, rebellions against the Church in several countries... We have turned her clergy into objects of hatred and ridicule, we have subjected them to the contempt of the crowd... We have caused the practice of the Catholic religion to be considered out of date and a mere waste of time.

"And the Gentiles, in their stupidity, have proved easier dupes than we expected them to be. One would expect more intelligence and more practical common sense, but they are no better than a herd of sheep. Let them graze in our fields till they become fat enough to be worthy of being immolated to our future King of the World...

"We have founded many secret associations, which all work for our purpose, under our orders and our direction. We have made it an honour, a great honour, for the Gentiles to join us in our organizations, which are, thanks to our gold, flourishing now more than ever. Yet it remains our secret that those Gentiles who betray their own and most precious interests, by joining us in our plot should never know that these associations are of our creation and that they serve our purpose...

"One of the many triumphs of our Freemasonry is that those Gentiles who become members of our Lodges, should never suspect that we are using them to build their own jails, upon whose terraces we shall erect the throne of our Universal King of Israel; and should never know that we are commanding them to forge the chains of their own servility to our future King of the world.

INFILTRATION

"So far, we have considered our strategy in our attacks upon the Catholic Church from the outside. But this is not all. Let us now explain how we have gone further in our work, to hasten the ruin of the Catholic Church, and how we have penetrated into her most intimate circles, and brought even some of her Clergy to become pioneers of our cause.

"Apart altogether from the influence of our philosophy, we have taken other steps to secure a breach in the Catholic Church. Let me explain how this has been done.

"We have induced some of our children to join the Catholic body, with the explicit intimation that they should work in a still more efficient way for the disintegration of the Catholic Church, by creating scandals within her. We have thus followed the advice of our Prince of the Jews, who so wisely said: 'Let some of your children become canons, so that they may destroy the Church'. Unfortunately, not all among the 'convert' Jews have proved faithful to their mission. Many of them have even betrayed us! But, on the other hand, others have kept their promise and honored their word. Thus the counsel of our Elders has proved successful.

REVOLUTION

"We are the Fathers of all Revolutions - even of those which sometimes happen to turn against us. We are the supreme Masters of Peace and War. We can boast of being the Creators of the REFORMATION! Calvin was one of our Children; he was of Jewish descent, and was entrusted by Jewish authority and encouraged with Jewish finance to draft his scheme in the Reformation.

"Martin Luther yielded to the influence of his Jewish friends, and again, by Jewish authority and with Jewish finance, his plot against the Catholic Church met with success...

"Thanks to our propaganda, to our theories of Liberalism and to our misrepresentations of Freedom, the minds of many among the Gentiles were ready to welcome the Reformation. They separated from the Church to fall into our snare. And thus the Catholic Church has been very sensibly weakened, and her authority over the Kings of the Gentiles has been reduced almost to naught.

"We are grateful to Protestants for their loyalty to our wishes - although most of them are, in the sincerity of their faith, unaware of their loyalty to us. We are grateful to them for the wonderful help they are giving us in our fight against the stronghold of Christian Civilization, and in our preparations for the advent of our supremacy over the whole world and over the Kingdoms of the Gentiles.

"So far we have succeeded in overthrowing most of the Thrones of Europe. The rest will follow in the near future. Russia has already worshiped our rule, France, with her Masonic Government, is under our thumb. England, in her dependence upon our finance is under our heel; and in her Protestantism is our hope for the destruction of the Catholic Church. Spain and Mexico are but toys in our hands. And many other countries, including the U.S.A., have already fallen before our scheming.

CHURCH WAS LAST BASTION

"But the Catholic Church is still alive.

"We must destroy her without the least delay and without the slightest mercy. Most of the Press in the world is under our Control; let us therefore encourage in a still more violent way the hatred of the world against the Catholic Church. Let us intensify our activities in poisoning the morality of the Gentiles. Let us spread the spirit of revolution in the minds of the people. They must be made to despise Patriotism and the love of their family, to consider their faith as a humbug, their obedience to their Church as a degrading servility, so that they may become deaf to the appeal of the Church and blind to her warnings against us. Let us, above all, make it impossible for Christians outside the Catholic Church to be reunited with that Church, or for non-Christians to join that Church; otherwise the greatest obstruction to our domination will be strengthened and all our work undone. Our plot will be unveiled, the Gentiles will turn against us, in the spirit of revenge, and our domination over them will never be realized.

"Let us remember that as long as there still remain active enemies of the Catholic Church, we may hope to become Masters of the World... And let us remember always that the future Jewish King will never reign in the world before the Pope in Rome is dethroned, as well as all the other reigning monarchs of the Gentiles upon earth."

Why the Bankers Love the Left

Count Cherep-Spiridovitch was a Czarist general who battled the Bolsheviks in the 1917 Russian Revolution.

In 1926, he published a book entitled *"The Secret World Government"* which shows how the Rothschild's plan for world tyranny dominates modern history.

The fact that *"The Secret World Government"* is generally considered "right wing" and "anti-Semitic" is revealing:

1) It shows that society has been brainwashed and subverted by the Rothschild conspiracy.

2) It reveals how the bogus issue of anti-Semitism diverts attention from a genuine mortal threat to humanity.

3) It explains the true meaning of "right wing crackpot" and why the Left is an instrument of the bankers.

EXAMPLE: THE US CIVIL WAR

Compare the treatment of this war in *"The Secret World Government"* with *"A Peoples History of the United States"* by Howard Zinn, a leftist Jew who cannot utter the word "Rothschild."

Cherep-Spiridovitch cites an interview with the German chancellor Otto von Bismarck in 1876. Bismarck explained that the Rothschilds who controlled Europe were afraid the United States would become independent of them if it remained one nation.

"They foresaw tremendous booty if they could substitute two feeble democracies indebted to the Jewish financiers for the vigorous republic confident and self providing. Therefore they [instructed] their emissaries ... to exploit the question of slavery and thus to dig an abyss between the two parts of the republic." (180)

The Illuminati used the Masonic "Knights of the Golden Circle," formed in 1854 by George W. L. Bickley, to spread racial tension by making slavery an issue. Members included Lincoln assassin John Wilkes Booth, Confederate President Jefferson Davis, and his adviser Judah P. Benjamin, the Confederate Secretary of War, a Rothschild agent.

The plan was to divide the United Sates between England controlled by Lionel Rothschild and France, controlled by James Rothschild. France was to take over the whole South while Canada annexed the defeated North. In 1863, France and Spain invaded

Mexico with 30,000 troops. The embattled Confederate States offered Louisiana and Texas to France in exchange for assistance.

Britain and France were ready to snuff out the young republic but were deterred by Russia, the only European power not yet in the Rothschild's thrall. Czar Alexander II sent his fleets to New York and San Francisco and declared that an attack on Lincoln would be an attack on Russia.

Meanwhile Lincoln created "greenback" dollars to finance the war and escape indebtedness to the foreign financiers. "They understood at once that the United States would escape their grip," Bismarck said." The death of Lincoln was resolved upon. Nothing is easier than to find a fanatic to strike." (180)

Compare this with Howard Zinn who although a "socialist," makes no mention of European financiers. His book is a soap opera of the exploitation of the poor. He depicts the Civil War as a clash of different capitalist "elites."

"The Northern elite wanted economic expansion.... The slave interests opposed all that. " (189) Again, "The American government had set out to ... retain the enormous national territory and market and resources. " (198)

In other words, "capitalism" and not the Rothschild Illuminati caused this heinous war that cost 500,000 soldiers' lives and eight billion dollars. Is it any wonder these bankers, who are the real establishment, love the Left? Is it any wonder they populate our universities with pious Marxists (and feminists) who never question why they are pulling down big salaries if they are *really* defying the establishment?

Another Pied Piper is Noam Chomsky who attributes all evil to capitalism and American imperialism. As far as I know, he never mentions the Rothschilds, the Illuminati, the Council on Foreign Relations or the New World Order. He pretends that Oklahoma City and 9-11 were NOT inside jobs.

"We shall erase from the memories of men all facts of previous centuries which are undesirable to us," say the *"Protocols of the Elders of Zion."* "And leave only those which depict all the errors of the government of the goyim." (*Protocol* 16)

The problem is not American capitalism but the control of the nation's credit by a small private international cartel. This international group is behind Western imperialism and every war.

The big government vs. big business paradigm diverts attention from the Illuminati bankers who run both. This paradigm places the blame on capitalism and the US, which has been under Illuminati control for at least a century.

It teaches each new generation to be alienated from their country and to rail against free enterprise, thus helping the bankers advance their communist plan.

ANTI-SEMITISM

Anti-Semitism is another tactic to divert attention from the Rothschild's plan for world tyranny.

Cherep-Spiritovitch concludes:

"According to Bismarck, the awful Civil War in America was fomented by a Jewish Conspiracy, and Abraham Lincoln the hero and national saint of the United States was killed by the same Hidden Hand which killed six Romanov Czars, ten kings and scores of Ministers only to easier bleed their nations." (181)

He is not talking about Jews in general but only those who advance the Rothschild Illuminati agenda. His book makes an appeal to righteous Jews, and recognizes that many non-Jews have sold out.

"The Jews should bring to bay the 'Satanists' who corrupt the countries in which they have found asylum," the Preface says: "the Gentiles should render every Judas who accepts the bribes of the Jews."

Bankers and their agents (B'nai Brith etc.) deflect this challenge by conflating the Rothschilds with all Jews. Thus they transform a political, cultural and economic issue into a racial one that can be dismissed as 'prejudice.'

The bankers' Satanic Conspiracy is the source of anti-Semitism. The sooner more Jews oppose it; the sooner anti-Semitism will disappear.

CONCLUSION

A "right wing crackpot" such as Cherep-Spiritovich is anyone who favors individual freedom and self-reliance, family, nation, race, and God. The ostensible ideals of our society are the things that the Illuminati need to destroy.

The ruling classes have been hoodwinked to believe they are building a Brave New World. In fact they are accomplices in the mental, spiritual and possibly physical enslavement of humanity.

England's Jewish Aristocracy

Did you know that Simon Cowell, the acerbic judge on American Idol, is half-Jewish?

British Jews keep a low profile but they are extremely influential. Similarly, it is hardly known that the British aristocracy largely is half-Jewish too, and that, in the words of L.G. Pine, Editor of *"Burke's Peerage,"* "the Jews have made themselves so closely connected with the British peerage that the two classes are unlikely to suffer loss which is not mutual." (219)

This is confirmed by British social critic Hilaire Belloc who described the British Empire as a partnership between Jewish finance and the British aristocracy. (Under the aegis of Freemasonry, this is the Illuminati.)

"After Waterloo [1815] London became the money market and the clearing house of the world. The interests of the Jew as a financial dealer and the interests of this great commercial polity approximated more and more. One may say that by the last third of the nineteenth century, they had become virtually identical." (*The Jews,* 1922)

My thesis is that the British Empire was a Masonic Jewish proxy, and that British & American imperialism derived its mojo from the perverse desire of Cabalist bankers to own and control everything. The Illuminati bankers (i.e. the "Crown") colonized England & the US as well as the world. The "Jewish Conspiracy" was the British Empire now repackaged as the New World Order. Of course, now it encompasses everyone with a stake in "globalism."

In this article, I will regale you with Pine's amusing account of "Jewish infiltration into the aristocracy." ("The Anglo Jewish Peerage" in *"Tales of the British Aristocracy,"* 1956, pp. 217-223.)

Pine is outspoken in a way few people are today. He says that for every Rothschild or Disraeli, there were "10 cases of Jewish connection which are now forgotten. The reason is that in many cases, Jewish origin is concealed." (218)

The marriage of Jewish finance and British aristocracy took place literally. Spendthrift gentry married the daughters of rich Jews. Pine is scornful of the British aristocracy: "A man is not usually thought the more of, because he has married a woman for her money...An ancient estate is likely to be sold unless some large sums are found. The sums are found from marriage with a Jewish heiress..."

An outstanding example is the marriage of the 5th Earl of Roseberry who married the only daughter and heiress of Baron Mayer de Rothschild and later became Prime Minister.

"She stayed in the Jewish religion but her children were educated as Christians...The alliances between Jewish ladies and British lords are mostly of this type, the wife providing large sums...while the aristocrat has the title and ancient estate. The children are able to look back upon a varied bag of ancestors."

Pine obviously does not approve of these parvenus: "There can be no question that the British Peerage is now very much diluted with Jewish blood and has many connections among its most ancient and august families with those who only a few generations ago were inhabitants of the Ghetto."

But he opines that England's enfeebled elite may need this protection from the "forces of revolution":

"The power of money is very great and as almost every liberal newspaper is under Jewish influence it follows that the forces of revolution when directed against the peers are likely to meet with as determined an opposition from the Jewish kinfolk of the aristocracy..."

L.G. Pine needn't worry about the "forces of revolution" since they were created by Jewish finance to concentrate power and wealth in its own hands. This will find its apogee in the New World Order.

The "Jewish Conspiracy" may indeed be the British Empire, and the "Jews" may in fact be the Masonic British aristocracy who regard themselves as Jews, and often are. They consider themselves one of the lost tribes of Israel, the real "Chosen People." The word "Brit" apparently derives from the Hebrew for "pact" or "covenant" (i.e. the Jewish Covenant with God.) Members of the British royal family are circumcised by a Jewish mohel.

The Dreyfus Affair Was A Rothschild Psy-Op

In 1894, a French artillery captain, Alfred Dreyfus, was falsely accused of passing secrets to the Germans. A Jew, Dreyfus seemed to confirm the belief that Jews, led by Baron Edmund de Rothschild, constituted a fifth column and undermined French independence and culture.

Dreyfus was publicly stripped of his commission and given a life sentence at Devil's Island where he was put in leg irons. Throughout his trial and imprisonment, Dreyfus professed his innocence.

The Dreyfus Affair was an elaborate psy-op designed to discredit opponents of the Rothschilds. The real spy, Ferdinand Esterhazy, was actually in the pay of Baron Edmund de Rothschild.

They deliberately implicated Dreyfus so that when he was finally vindicated, conservative and nationalist forces would be humiliated and discredited.

In 1895, the truth was leaked to the new Intelligence Chief Georges Picquart. The spy was actually Esterhazy, who was not a Jew. Nevertheless the army incriminated itself further. Its prestige at stake, it buried the new information and forged new evidence against Dreyfus. Picquart was exiled to a remote location.

The army was a bastion of national pride. Anti-Semitism, i.e. resistance to Jewish domination, flourished. There was a strong prejudice against Dreyfus. Rothschild used this to outwit them.

For ten years France was destabilized as the nationalists (army, landowners and church) faced off against the Dreyfus family, liberals and socialists demanding justice. Governments fell, anti-Semitic rioters roamed the streets, duels were fought, and the whole world watched in dismay.

Emile Zola, a Rothschild protege and Freemason, wrote the famous "J'Accuse" exposing the army cover-up. Celebrities signed petitions demanding justice for the innocent Jewish artillery captain.

Eventually Esterhazy was fired, escaped to England and, in 1899, admitted he was the spy. Nevertheless the government and army dug itself an even deeper hole, ignoring the evidence and prosecuting Dreyfus' defenders.

Eventually, the government changed and after numerous trials and appeals, partial reality was finally recognized.

Dreyfus was exonerated in 1906 and made "Chevalier of the Legion of Honor" in the same courtyard where he had been disgraced. French patriotism and Catholicism were discredited. All history books relate a comforting morality play where the innocent Jew is finally vindicated. Dreyfus was innocent but Rothschild certainly was not.

WHAT ARE THE CHANCES?

The man guilty of the treason blamed on Dreyfus, Major Ferdinand Esterhazy, was a schoolmate of Baron Edmund de Rothschild, and became his lifelong agent.

In July 1894, Esterhazy, a translator with the French General Staff, approached the German Military Attache in Paris, Von Schwartzkoppen, saying that financial duress compelled him to sell military secrets.

In fact, Esterhazy had just received a large sum from Edmund de Rothschild in June 1894. It was only one of many payments. (Herbert Lottman, *"The French Rothschilds The Great Banking Dynasty Through Two Turbulent Centuries,"* 1995, pp. 115-117)

There are many other indications that the whole "Dreyfus Affair" was orchestrated. At the beginning, news of Captain Dreyfus' guilt was leaked to the anti-Semitic newspaper *La Libre Parole.* The publisher Edouard Drumont took the bait and began a vitriolic campaign against the Jewish officer. In fact, Esterhazy was also a friend of Drumont.

It is possible that Drumont was also financed by the Rothschilds. The *Protocols of Zion* acknowledge funding anti-Semitic publications. It also says anti-Semitism is useful in controlling "our lesser brethren."

This may explain why anti-Semites blame all Jews instead of focusing on the Rothschilds and their Sabbatean/Masonic confreres. Similarly, socialists never mention the Rothschilds when attacking capitalism.

In Jan 1898, Emile Zola published his *"J'Accuse"* in the newspaper *L'Aurore* edited by Freemason and future Prime Minister Georges Clemenceau.

Zola was charged with libel and sentenced to a year in jail and fined 3000 francs. In 1902, Zola died "accidentally" in his home, poisoned by carbon monoxide. Did he learn something he should not have?

Decades after Zola's "accidental" death, a Paris roofer confessed on his deathbed to closing the flu on Zola's chimney on purpose. The roofer said he did it for "political reasons." (Frederick Brown, *"Zola: A Life."*)

In the *Protocols of the Elders of Zion*, the author refers to their ability to make the murders of Masons who become an obstacle look natural. (*Protocol* 15)

On Feb. 16, 1899, the President of the Republic, Felix Faure, died suddenly in his office. He had just met with an exponent of Dreyfus' cause and argued. There was speculation he was poisoned. Faure was succeeded by Emile Loubert, a supporter of Dreyfus. The Rothschild press made up a story that Faure died while having sex, and this is repeated in Wikipedia.

SIGNIFICANCE

Edmund de Rothschild (1845-1934) was the man who financed the Zionist colonization of Palestine. Like the holocaust, the Dreyfus Affair told assimilated Jews they would be never accepted and must have their own country. It motivated the Hungarian-Jewish journalist Theodor Herzl, the founder of Zionism.

According to Wikipedia, "The anti-Semitism and injustice revealed in France by the conviction of Alfred Dreyfus had a radicalizing effect on Herzl, demonstrating to him that Jews, despite the Enlightenment and Jewish assimilation, could never hope for fair treatment in European society."

This is another example of how the Rothschilds secretly incite anti-Semitism in order to dupe Jews into advancing their demented scheme for world government. The same principle guided the Jewish holocaust where millions of innocent Jews were sacrificed.

Sponsoring Hitler was just a few levels of duplicity above sponsoring Esterhazy. In both cases, the "anti-Semites" fell into the trap.

Thus, Jews who only want to assimilate act as agents and human shields for the Rothschild's satanic agenda. The same Jews, of course, will be blamed.

CONCLUSION

The Dreyfus Affair is yet another example of how historical events are manufactured by the Rothschilds. Looking backward, we have: 9-11; the Kennedy Assassination; the Cold War; Vietnam War; Korean War; Hiroshima; Second World War, the Jewish holocaust; Pearl Harbor and so on...

Obviously the Rothschilds' mass media helps them put over their subterfuges. Another example of their duplicity is the phony banker's coup of 1933, which was used to give their pawn FDR credibility. (See my *"Illuminati"*) Social movements and ideologies are also contrived to advance the New World Order: sexual liberation, women's liberation, the civil rights movement, gay rights, feminism, diversity, multiculturalism.

We can apply these lessons today by looking at current events in terms of how they advance World Government.

(I am indebted to Carol White, *"The New Dark Ages Conspiracy"* (1980) pp. 45-48 for alerting me to the Rothschild-Esterhazy connection.)

Illuminati Bankers
Instigated World War One

When we left off, we were exploring the proposition that the New World Order is the British Empire repackaged, and this empire was literally a marriage of effete British aristocracy and virile (or virulent) Jewish finance.

Webster Tarpley is a gifted historian who generally eschews mention of Jewish bankers in favor of euphemisms like "Venetians." Therefore it is unusual for him to state bluntly that King Edward VII was in the pay of the Rothschilds and was responsible for World War One.

Edward VII didn't become king until 1901 when he was 60 years old. As Prince of Wales, he was estranged from his mother, kept on an allowance and deeply in debt. He allowed a "series of Jewish bankers to manage his personal finances." These included Baron von Hirsch and Sir Ernest Cassell.

"Edward also cultivated the Rothschild and Sassoon families. In short, Edward's personal household finance agency was identical with the leading lights of turn-of-the-century Zionism." ("King Edward VII: Evil Demiurge of the Triple Entente & WW1.")

Tarpley is equally forthright in stating that "Edward VII, far more than any other single human being, was the author of the First World War...the most destructive single event in the history of Western civilization" which opened the door to Communism, Fascism, the Great Depression and World War Two.

Tarpley falls into the trap of establishment historians by attributing great events to single personalities. These personalities are invariably puppets of the people who pay their bills.

Tarpley goes into some detail about how King Edward and his Foreign Secretary Sir Edward Grey, the son of Edward's horse master, engineered World War One. As in World War Two, it was "Appeasement."

Essentially, they deceived Germany into believing that England would remain neutral. To prevent the war, all they had to do was clarify this point. Germany would have backed down and reined in Austria.

In August 1914, Kaiser Wilhelm realized he had been fooled: "England, Russia and France have agreed among themselves ... to take the Austro-Serbian conflict as an excuse for waging a war of extermination against us...That is the real naked situation slowly & cleverly set going by Edward VII...The net has been suddenly thrown over our heads, and England sneeringly reaps the most brilliant success of her persistently prosecuted anti-German world policy against which we have proved ourselves helpless, while she twists the noose of our political and economic destruction out of our fidelity to Austria, as we squirm isolated in the net."

BACKGROUND

"England's" animosity against Germany was part of an agenda to use a catastrophic war to undermine Western civilization, and advance the Judeo-Masonic New World Order. Three empires disappeared in that inferno while Communism and Zionism rose like the phoenix.

The decadent British aristocracy is totally complicit in the cabalistic bankers' plan to degrade and enslave mankind. Who are these "aristocrats?" Greg Hallett makes some astonishing, some might say ridiculous, claims. I present them here without judgement, to be proven or discredited as evidence emerges.

Edward VII was the mentally deficient product of the marriage between Queen Victoria and her first cousin Albert. He was the oldest male of her nine children. He married in 1863 and had five legitimate children between 1864 and 1869. His eldest son, Clarence, was mentally deranged and the prime suspect in the Jack the Ripper murders.

Edward VII routinely and openly cheated on his wife. He had dozens of mistresses, some as young as age 14. One of these was the Jewish-born Lady Randolph Jennie Jerome Churchill. Hallett believes Edward VII was Winston Churchill's real father.

Hallett claims that Queen Victoria had children with Lionel de Rothschild and that two of Edward's sisters, Helena and Beatrice, were Rothschilds. He claims the British Royal family is "a biological, financial and moral subset of the Rothschild international bankers."

"Interbreeding amongst the British royal family over generations has created concubines, illegitimate children and agents of war. The British Royal family are then shamed by these events and then manipulated into any activity their owners require...This gave [the Rothschilds] consummate power over the British Royal family, and any others they interbred with, which was all the royal families of Europe..." ("Breeding Concubines" in *Stalin's British Training,* 2007, pp. 1-38.)

CONCLUSION

These claims seem far fetched yet it is plain to see that something is wrong with the Royals. It is widely acknowledged that Edward VII was dissolute. If Hallet's claim that "the British Royal family are a subset of the Rothschild family and are utilized as part of the Rothschild business as a money-making venture to create war," it would explain King Edward VII's role in starting World War One.

The reports of homosexuality, drugs, pederasty, promiscuity, occultism in the history of the British aristocracy are consistent with what we know about the Illuminati. They are depraved yet somehow able to subvert mankind without serious resistance.

What a tawdry tale is modern history! Instead of grasping greatness within reach, the human race is paralysed by a morbid spell.

Was The "Spanish Flu" Epidemic Man-made?

In 1948, Heinrich Mueller, the former head of the Gestapo, told his CIA Interrogator that the most devastating plague in human history was man-made.

He was referring to the influenza pandemic of 1918-1919 that infected 20% of the world's population and killed between 60 and 100 million people. This is roughly three times as many as were killed and wounded in World War One, and is comparable to WWII losses, yet this modern plague has slipped down the memory hole.

Mueller said the flu started as a US army bacteriological warfare weapon that somehow infected US army ranks at Camp Riley, KS in March 1918, and spread around the world.

He says that it "got out of control" but we cannot discount the horrible possibility that the "Spanish Flu" was a deliberate elite depopulation measure that could be used again. Researchers have found connections between it and the "Bird Flu."

There was nothing "Spanish" about this flu. According to *Wikipedia*: "In the U.S., about 28% of the population suffered, and 500,000 to 675,000 died. In Britain 200,000 died; in France more than 400,000. Entire villages perished in Alaska and southern Africa. In Australia an estimated 10,000 people died and in the Fiji Islands, 14% of the population died during only two weeks, and in Western Samoa 22%. An estimated 17 million died in India, about 5% of India's population at the time. In the Indian Army, almost 22% of troops who caught the disease died of it."

"...Another unusual feature of this pandemic was that it mostly killed young adults, with 99% of pandemic influenza deaths occurring in people under 65 and more than half in young adults 20 to 40 years old. This is unusual since influenza is normally most deadly to the very young (under age 2) and the very old (over age 70.) "

MUELLER'S SOURCE

At a 1944 Nazi bacteriological warfare conference in Berlin, General Walter Schreiber, Chief of the Medical Corps of the German Army, told Mueller that he had spent two months in the US in 1927 conferring with his counterparts. They told him that the "so-called double blow virus" (i.e. Spanish Flu) was developed and used during the 1914 war.

"But," according to Mueller, "it got out of control and instead of killing the Germans who had surrendered by then, it turned back on you, and nearly everybody else."

(*"Gestapo Chief: The 1948 CIA Interrogation of Heinrich Mueller,"* Vol. 2 by Gregory Douglas, p. 106) The Armistice took place Aug. 11, 1918.

The interrogator, James Kronthal, the CIA Bern Station Chief asked Mueller to explain "double blow virus." It reminds me of AIDS.

Mueller: "I am not a doctor, you understand, but the 'double-blow' referred to a virus, or actually a pair of them that worked like a prize fighter. The first blow attacked the immune system and made the victim susceptible, fatally so, to the second blow which was a form of pneumonia...[Schreiber told me] a British scientist actually developed it...Now you see why such things are insanity. These things can alter themselves and what starts out as a limited thing can change into something really terrible."

The subject of the Spanish Flu arose in the context of a discussion of typhus. The Nazis deliberately introduced typhus into Russian POW camps and, along with starvation, killed about three million men. The typhus spread to Auschwitz and other concentration camps with Russian and Polish POWS.

In the context of the Cold War, Mueller says: "If Stalin invades Europe...a little disease here and there would wipe out Stalin's hoards and leave everything intact. Besides, a small bottle of germs is so much cheaper than an atom bomb, isn't it? Why you could hold more soldiers in your hand than Stalin could possibly command and you don't have to feed them clothes them or supply them with munitions. On the other hand, the threat of war...does wonders... for the economy." (108)

Is Mueller credible? In my opinion he is. Gregory Douglas apparently is a pseudonym for his nephew with whom he left his papers. Normally a hoax would not run to thousands of pages. The interrogation is 800 pages. The memoirs are 250 pages. Mueller's microfilmed archive apparently covers 850,000 pages. Finally, the material I have read is incredibly well informed, consistent and full of plausible revelations .

CONCLUSION

The "Elite" cult has made no secret of its desire to decrease the world population.

It's possible that World War One was a disappointment to the Elite in terms of the numbers killed.

The Spanish Flu killed three times as many people as the war. Whether the "Spanish Flu" was deliberate or not, we cannot say. But apparently the US Army has a record of experimenting with drugs/chemicals/bacteria on unwary soldiers. Did such an experiment get "out of control" ?

Recently we have had the Swine Flu. Are they harbingers of something more deadly? Hopefully they are not, but we should be mindful of the shocking precedent set by the 1918 Influenza Pandemic.

The British Agent at Hitler's Ear

The name "Baron William de Ropp" isn't well known. There is no photo available, no *Wikipedia* entry. Yet he was a British agent who befriended Hitler and may have been his handler.

Hitler's "daring" diplomatic & military coups, which astounded the world, were based on advanced knowledge of British intentions provided by de Ropp.

That's not Baron de Ropp in the picture. That's Ernst ("Putzi") Hanfstaengl, another Allied agent at the heart of Hitler's entourage. Both men add credence to the argument that the Illuminati created Hitler to foment world war. More about Putzi later.

According to Ladislas Farago, William de Ropp was "one of the most mysterious and influential clandestine operators" of the era. Born in Lithuania in 1877, educated in Germany, he moved to England in 1910. After serving the British in World War One, he moved to Berlin and contacted fellow Balt, Nazi theoretician Alfred Rosenberg who introduced him to Hitler.

Farago: "A close personal relationship developed between the Fuhrer and de Ropp. Hitler, using him as his confidential consultant about British affairs, outlined to him frankly his grandiose plans...a trust no other foreigner enjoyed to this extent." (*"The Game of the Foxes,"* p.88)

De Ropp worked closely with Rosenberg, who headed the Nazi Party Foreign Office. The Nazis considered him their agent in England where he organized support among a powerful segment of the British elite known as the "Cliveden Set." He organized visits of high officials and exchanges of information. In this congenial atmosphere, the Luftwaffe naively opened its secrets to the British. This was part of a larger Illuminati plan ("Appeasement") to make Hitler think England would support his conquest of Communist Russia.

In *"King Pawn or Black Knight,"* (1995) Gwynne Thomas writes: "The Nazi leader took an instant liking to him, particularly when he discovered that de Ropp had powerful connections among English society and was well informed about much of what was happening in London. De Ropp not only enjoyed [Hitler's] confidence but became his spokesman in dealings with the many important British people Hitler wished to influence...there is strong evidence that de Ropp was instrumental in raising funds in the City of London to finance several of the Nazi election campaigns which ensured that by the end of 1933 the Nazi party was totally established and in control." (p.25)

Hitler has a British agent funding, advising and representing him. At what point was Hitler a "British" agent himself?

A FINE LINE

After the Illuminati put Hitler in power, they kept him there by sabotaging German opposition.

On May 4, 1938, Ludwig Beck, Chief of the German General Staff, called for the overthrow of Hitler, warning that the country was headed for disaster.

On May 10, 1938, Prime Minister Chamberlain held a news conference at Cliveden House stating that Britain was seeking a pact with Germany and Italy, and favored the breaking up of Czechoslovakia. As a result of this British acquiescence, the German army dropped its resistance to Hitler's war plans.

In 1939, De Ropp spelled out the British stand in the event of a German attack on Poland.

"Rosenberg was told the British would fight a defensive 'war', that is to say, would take no action in defence of Poland or in retaliation for Germany's attack on that country. In particular, there would be no aerial bombardment of German territory- and the Germans agreed to reciprocate, a decision which held throughout the 'phony war' period."

"This 'deal' struck between de Ropp and Rosenberg would leave open the possibility of quickly ending the war because, de Ropp said, 'neither the British Empire nor Germany would wish to risk their future for the sake of a state which had ceased to exist'. "

Thus, by double crossing the Poles, the British-based Illuminati succeeded in giving the Nazis a common border with Stalin. It was only a matter of time before war would break out between them.

The task now was to entrap Hitler in a two-front war by provoking an attack on the West. Possibly, Baron de Ropp assured him that the British and French would roll over again.

After the war began, De Ropp moved his base of operations to neutral Switzerland but, according to Farago, "several times during the war he was summoned to Hitler for consultations." (89)

Remember, William de Ropp was a British agent. The question remains, was Hitler a conscious British (i.e. Illuminati) agent himself? The Illuminati sponsor misguided people whose natural goals are in line with the Illuminati agenda and manipulate them. But Hitler was no fool. It is quite possible Hitler was a conscious agent and de Ropp was his handler.

In the LaRouche-sponsored book, *"The New Dark Ages Conspiracy: Britain's Plot to Destroy Civilization"* (1980), Carol White writes: "The truth about Hitler is that he was not only created by the British and British-allied networks, but that the British government led by Winston Churchill continued to use Hitler throughout the war. If this fact was not clearly understood by the allied forces, it was strongly suspected in Germany itself." (p.126)

HANFSTAENGL

"Putzi" Hanfstaengl (1887-1975) is another mysterious character who identified himself as an American agent in his memoirs, *"Hitler: The Missing Years"* (1957.) He may have an Illuminati background, possibly a Jewish mother, a "Heine." He hobnobbed with FDR and other members of the elite at Harvard and later in NYC where he ran his father's art business.

He moved to Germany in the 1920's and was introduced to Hitler by the American Military attache in Berlin, Truman Smith.

Smith asked him to "keep an eye on Hitler." Hanfstaengl became a part of Hitler's inner circle often soothing the Fuhrer with his piano playing. More materially, Hanfstaengl financed the expansion of the Nazi newspaper into a daily. He composed the Nazi marching songs, based on Harvard football anthems. He hid Hitler after the failed Beer Hall Putsch and his pretty wife prevented the distraught Fuhrer from committing suicide. Hanfstaengel was Hitler's Foreign Press Chief from 1933-1937. Again, this man was an American agent.

Finally, Truman Smith deserves a mention. Although a member of the State Dept. he helped organize Nazi support in the US. He organized Charles Lindbergh's tours of Luftwaffe facilities. Later, in Washington, he organized political and military opposition to US participation in World War Two. (Farago, pp. 556-557)

Essentially, Hanfstaengl and Smith played roles parallel to that of Baron de Ropp. They deceived Hitler (and Germans in general) into believing they had the support of the British American establishment (i.e. Illuminati) in their confrontation with Russia.

The Illuminati back both sides in every war, and can easily control the outcome by withdrawing support from one side at a key juncture.

Martin Bormann was Rothschild Agent — Damning Evidence

The second most powerful man in Nazi Germany, Martin Bormann, was a "Soviet" (i.e. Illuminati British) agent who ensured the destruction of both Germany and European Jewry.

Thus, he advanced two of the Illuminati's main goals: integrate Germany into a world govern-

John Ainsworth-Davis (Center) Rescued Martin Bormann

ment by annihilating its national, cultural and racial pretensions, and establish Israel as the Masonic bankers' world capital by threatening European Jews with extinction.

When I first presented this case in 2007, in an article "Bormann Ran Hitler for the Illuminati," (available online or in my book "Illuminati") a reader suggested "OPJB" (1996) Lieut. Commander John Ainsworth-Davis' account of how he and Ian Fleming led a 150-man team that rescued Martin Bormann from war-torn Berlin on May 1, 1945 using river kayaks.

According to this book, Bormann lived under an assumed identity in England until 1956 before dying in Paraguay in 1959.

The title of the book stands for "Operation James Bond." Ian Fleming took the name of the author of *"A Field Guide to the Birds of the West Indies"* for the Bormann rescue and later gave it to the hero of his spy series modelled on Ainsworth-Davis, who now uses the name, Christopher Creighton.

Talk about the hiding in plain sight! The evidence that the man responsible for the holocaust was a British agent has been on bookshelves since 1996. The book includes a 1963 letter from Ian Fleming confirming that he and Creighton led the Bormann rescue. It also includes a photograph of a 1954 letter from Winston Churchill giving Creighton permission to tell this story after Churchill's death, "omitting of course those matters which you know can never be revealed."

According to Creighton, Martin Bormann was actually sitting in a private visitor's gallery at the Nuremberg Trial when he was condemned to death in absentia! (p. 243)

The fig leaf covering this rescue was that Bormann would help the Allies retrieve Nazi wartime plunder and return it to its rightful owners. If you believe that, I have some swampland in Florida... Bormann had been an Illuminati British agent all along and was largely responsible for the Nazi defeat. In fact, World War Two was a monstrous Rothschild fraud on Germans, Jews and the human race. The plunder ended up in Illuminati hands and was used to enslave humanity.

REAL "JAMES BOND" WAS AN ILLUMINATI MASS MURDERER

The real James Bond helped kill thousands of people, mostly British allies. He was haunted by the ghosts of "perfectly loyal and innocent people who had been caught up in our operations..." (79)

He was just "following orders" which made no sense from a patriotic p.o.v. "We were not acting from patriotism or high moral principles. We were not doing this for England or Uncle Sam. As usual, we were doing what we had been told to do: we were carrying out our orders." (170)

For example, Creighton tipped the Nazis off to the exact time and location of the 1942 Dieppe raid which cost 3000 Canadians their lives. He was told that the British wanted to test Nazi defences. The real reasons: Convince Stalin it was too early for a second front, and build up Creighton's credibility when it came time for the Normandy Invasion.

In 1944, he told the Germans the invasion was coming in Normandy. This time the betrayer was betrayed. The Nazis were informed Creighton was a British agent so naturally they assumed this information was wrong.

Creighton also talks about "Operation Tiger" in April 1944, a training exercise at Slapton Sands, Dorset that was rudely interrupted by eight German torpedo boats. The toll: over 800 US servicemen drowned. (Gestapo Chief Heinrich Muller wrote that the Nazis were tipped off by a German spy.) The fiasco was kept secret to protect D-Day morale. Creighton says survivors were interned or killed by a sea mine in order to keep the debacle secret. (p. 25) In spite of the fact that the Dorset shoreline resembled Normandy, the Nazis apparently failed to draw the logical conclusion.

Agents who stumbled on the "true secrets of World War Two" (i.e. the fact that the Nazis were infiltrated and run by the "English") were often betrayed and met death in action. This happened to Creighton's girlfriend, Patricia Falkiner. Morton confessed that Falkiner was his ward: "He had done his utmost to keep Patricia out of operations... only when she had stumbled on the most vital secrets at Bletchley that he had been forced to deploy her..." (p.85)

Creighton also made sure Pearl Harbor, another example of Illuminati chicanery, was kept secret. On Nov. 28, 1941, a Dutch submarine, the K-XVII, intercepted the Japanese Fleet en route to Pearl Harbor and alerted British naval HQ.

In order to maintain the illusion that Pearl Harbor was a surprise, the submarine and its crew were destroyed. Creighton "wiped out the entire ship's company with two tiny cylinders of cyanide inserted into their oxygen supply, and a box of high explosives disguised as whiskey...the war had turned me into a fiend and mass murderer..." (p.81)

"M SECTION" (For Morton) A PEDOPHILE PARADISE?

Officially Desmond Morton was Winston Churchill's "adviser." In fact, he was in charge of a top secret Illuminati organization dedicated to advancing world government dictatorship through skulduggery. It was funded by the "Crown" i.e. the Rothschild's Bank of England.

It answered only to Churchill who, of course, answered only to Victor Rothschild. The Director of the Bank of England, Montagu Norman, recommended Ian Fleming to Naval Intelligence. Fleming was 15 years older than Creighton.

"M SECTION" had the resources of the Royal Navy and Marines at its disposal and was responsible for rescuing Martin Bormann, and possibly Hitler as well.

Morton never married and there are rumors he and Churchill had an homosexual attachment. He accused Churchill of having homosexual feelings for FDR. (*"Winston Churchill,"* by Chris Wrigley, p. 268)

Top agents and commandos like Creighton were chosen from men and women in their late teens who were personally known to the Illuminati. Creighton was only 21 years old in 1945. Often the youths were orphans or separated from their parents. For example, Creighton's parents were divorced but Louis Mountbatten and Desmond Morton were family friends. Morton took Creighton under his wing and became his "uncle." In a moment of crisis, "I hugged him as I had hugged him so often in the past." (85)

Creighton speaks of his service in Section M in sinister terms: "ghastly years of betrayal and horror into which I had been forced." (78) He speaks of the "Svengali-like influence and control that Morton had exercised over me since my early childhood."

At age 15, Creighton had an apparition of a "Black Angel" who possessed him as an "Angel of Death."

"I awoke in the middle of the night, soaked in sweat and there he was, standing at the foot of my bed. ...I could not move. With a feeling of utter degradation and terror I realized I was powerless to stop him possessing me — as he would often do in the weeks, months and years that followed." Sound like Creighton was the victim of a pedophile?

That Black Angel was probably Morton. Creighton directly continues: "Looking back I can see how completely I was in Morton's grip throughout most of the war. From 1940-1945, I was his puppet, manipulated by him and executing his orders." (18)

The final endurance test for "both boys and girls was 12 strokes of the cane administered by a Marine Commando Sergeant across their bare buttocks in front of their class." (69)

It's possible that like some MI-5 and MI-6 agents today, Section M agents may have been mind controlled sex slaves.

PAWNS IN THEIR GAME

Morton's MO was "deception and double-dealing," says Creighton. It is amazing he's alive to tell the story. Perhaps it's because he accepted the spin that Bormann was saved in order to restore Nazi plunder to its rightful owners.

Like Creighton, we are all pawns in their game. For example, Otto Gunther, Bormann's double, was a POW found in Canada. Bormann's records were altered to fit Gunther so when his dead body was found, people believed he was Hitler's Deputy.

The commandos accompanying Bormann on his escape had no idea of his identity. Many were Jewish "freedom fighters." What an irony!

Great nations, England, the United States, Germany, France are all Illuminati pawns. What good is democracy when the Illuminati Order owns the politicians and controls information?

Think of the millions who died in World War Two, all to destroy and degrade mankind so the Illuminati inbreeds can own and control everything. They are still dividing us, so we will never unite against them.

Did Hitler Betray Rudolf Hess (and Germany)?

According to former Nazi officials, Rudolf Hess was following Hitler's orders when he flew to Scotland in May 1941 with an offer to reverse Nazi victories in Western Europe in exchange for peace and a free hand in the East.

When Churchill rejected this offer, Hitler pretended that Hess was insane and acted on his own initiative.

Around 1980, Frank Brandenburg spoke to Hess' wife Ilse, as well as many other Nazis who made a convincing case that Hess's mission was in fact authorized by the Fuhrer.

"My husband would not have acted without the Fuhrer's consent," Mrs. Hess said. "My husband was totally loyal to the Fuhrer." (263-264)

Nevertheless, the Powers That Be have succeeded in portraying Hess as a lunatic rather than an idealistic peacemaker.

They have managed to bury Brandenburg's book. *"Quest: Searching for the Truth of Germany's Nazi Past"* was published in 1990 by Presidio, a tiny publisher of military books, in Novato CA. In 2002, Presidio was bought by Random House which is owned by Bertelsmann. You can bet Bertelsmann is controlled by the Illuminati.

Louis Kilzer's *"Hitler's Traitor,"* which outed Martin Bormann as an Illuminati agent, was also published by Presidio. Both books were hardly reviewed and are now out of print.

Mrs. Hess's conviction was confirmed by Hitler's personal pilot Hans Baur who said Hess had been given secret map codes in Hitler's possession. (260) Hess' closest associate Ernst Wilhelm Bohle said he translated Hitler's offer into English. (271-2)

SS General Karl Wolff said Hitler's outrage was a "show." Wolff was at a meeting with Hitler at the Berghof when the news of Hess's flight to England was brought to him. "The Fuhrer threw a terrible temper tantrum...he put on quite a show...the Fuhrer was an accomplished actor when he wanted to be..." (246)

More telling is the fact that Hitler punished many of Hess's minor associates but not his family nor Boehle. When you think about it, Hess would never have tried to usurp peace-making powers from Hitler nor left his family as hostages.

SIGNIFICANCE

If Hitler authorized Hess' flight May 10, 1941 to visit the Duke of Hamilton, there are two possible interpretations.

The first is that Hitler genuinely wanted peace with England before attacking Russia 12 days later. To send the Deputy Fuhrer of the Third Reich on such a mission, Hitler must have had reasonable assurances of its success.

We know from other sources that Hess, Hitler and Churchill and the Duke of Hamilton all belonged to a homosexual occult group — the Thule Society in Germany and the Order of the Golden Dawn in England — both branches of the Illuminati. Did the English branch lead the Germans to think it was doing England's bidding by attacking Bolshevik Russia? In other words, was Hitler double-crossed and tricked into a two-front war?

If this is true, it suggests the Illuminati run their pawns at arm's length, tricking and manipulating them, as opposed to using them as conscious agents. Barack Obama should take note.

CONSCIOUS AGENT

But there is a second interpretation. I suspect Hitler, being "an accomplished actor," was like Bormann, a conscious Illuminati agent. He knew the Rothschilds (i.e. Illuminati Freemasons) ran both England and the USSR. He was probably a Rothschild himself, albeit illegitimate. There was no way England would make peace and thereby hang Stalin out to dry. I suspect Hitler deliberately led Germany into a trap when he attacked Russia. Lebensraum? Germany already ruled all of Europe.

No, Hitler's loyalties were to the Fourth Reich, the New World Order. That's why he disowned Hess. He could have made public his generous peace offer and painted Churchill as a war-monger. He could have sued in the Court of Public Opinion for the release of a peacemaker.

Instead, Hitler protected Churchill and double crossed Hess. Apparently, Hitler needed to get rid of Hess. Probably, Hess knew too much and stood in the way of Bormann's advancement to second place in the Nazi hierarchy.

There are additional indications in this book that Hitler was an agent. The Russians who supposedly found Hitler's body never believed Hitler was dead. They tortured his pilot Hans Baur for eight years to reveal where he took Hitler. (49)

In the bunker, Hitler instructed one of his secretaries, Christa Schroeder, to burn secret correspondence in three safes at different locations. They were the records of his "personal intelligence network" a "far flung network of informers, advisers and confidants... powerful and knowledgeable men...Big Business. Scientists. Many important industrialists...the Fuhrer could not have built and reached the level of his power without the help, conscious or not, of such people, could he?' " (103-105)

Hitler blocked development of nuclear weapons, calling it a "Jew science."

SS General Werner Best, who ran Denmark in an enlightened fashion, told Brandenburg that he was in contact with anti-Communist leaders in Ukraine in 1939. Had

Hitler promised them a degree of autonomy, they could have brought two million soldiers to the Nazi cause. (195)

OTHER REVELATIONS

Quest author Frank Brandenburg was only 20-years- old in 1978 when he decided to look up high ranking Nazis in West Germany. His youth gained him access. These Nazis trusted him and tried to recruit him to their cause. They were in desperate need of young blood.

Gen. Karl Wolff helped by giving Brandenburg his SS ring and told him that a code word for gaining trust was the name of Hitler's third German Shepherd dog, "Muck."

It seems that Hess was not the last high ranking Nazi Hitler eliminated.

Reinhard Heydrich's wife Lina said that her husband was recovering from the assassination attempt when Hitler had his own medical staff take charge. Four days later Heydrich was dead. Lina was convinced Hitler and Himmler feared her husband. SS General Wilhelm Hottl said Heydrich had made the mistake of telling Walter Schellenberg that he thought the Fuhrer "was insane and had to be replaced." (151)

Possibly, the British dispatched the two Czech agents to kill Heydrich for this reason. They had to protect their agent, Adolf Hitler. Heydrich was the only Nazi leader assassinated by the Allies.

As for Bormann, Brandenburg spoke to dozens of high ranking Nazis and almost all implied that Bormann escaped. Moreover, Bormann led a powerful Nazi movement that intended to regain ascendancy. This movement is part of the Illuminati.

Medard Klapper, a member of Hitler's personal bodyguard, told Brandenburg he met Bormann in Spain in 1982. The post war Nazi movement was called Mariborsol (from Martin Bormann & sun) and was headquartered in Madrid. It was financed by investments on a world scale, "real estate, manufacturing plants. All kinds of profitable investments and business ventures, controlled by our people..." (291)

CONCLUSION

Rudolf Hess' story is a tragic one. He was locked away in Spandau prison until his suicide (his son says murder) in 1987. He was allowed four letters from family and one visit from his wife a month. But they were never alone. "I was never able to touch my husband," Ilse Hess said.

What was his crime? He was incarcerated in 1941 before the holocaust began. He served a man who was *Time's Man of the Year* in 1938.

No, his crime was knowing about the Illuminati, and the extent of "British" collaboration in the rise of Hitler. His crime was not knowing that his beloved Fuhrer was setting him and Germany up for annihilation.

Were Illuminati Jews Responsible for the Holocaust?

In 1988, Gunther Plaut, a prominent Canadian Rabbi, published a book implying Frankist Jews were responsible for the holocaust. The idea was endorsed by no less an authority than Elie Wiesel.

"The Man Who Would be Messiah" is a novelized biography of Jacob Frank (1726-1791) who led a satanic heresy against orthodox Judaism. He claimed to be the Messiah and reincarnation of another satanic impostor, Shabbetai Zvi (1626-1676.) Their aim was to destroy the social order (nation, family, race, religion, property) and turn Torah morality on its head.

What had been prohibited would be allowed: adultery, incest, pedophilia. (This is the occult origin of our "sexual liberation.") Inspired by the Cabala, they practiced "holiness through sin." Good would come through the annihilation of Western civilization and the triumph of Evil.

The Rothschilds were Sabbatean-Frankists. This satanic movement gave birth to the Illuminati, Communism and the NWO. It controls the world today. But ironically, while many Illuminati pretend to be Jews, they actually wish to destroy Jews who earlier had excommunicated and vilified them. Thus, there is an unrecognized schism in the Jewish people, where heretics have exterminated the mainstream and taken control of the remnant through Zionism. Yet, due to the anti-Semitism the Illuminati Jews cause and organize, Jews mistakenly cling to their villainous leadership.

The Nazi hierarchy was probably of Frankist origin. We'll look at this evidence later. But first we'll examine what Rabbi Plaut, who was President of the Canadian Jewish Congress, said about their holocaust plan.

THE MAN WHO WOULD BE MESSIAH

The Frankists cover their tracks. Biographies of Jacob Frank are out of print and very expensive. Nevertheless Gunther Plaut researched Frank thoroughly and presented a perceptive and complex portrait of Frank as a conscious con-artist who sought power for its own sake. According to Plaut, Frank regarded Jews as a barrier to the "new order." He puts these words in Frank's mouth:

"Yes, the Jews. Someone will come and discover that he can't upset the old values without destroying the people who really believe in them and, what's worse, practise them. And when he's convinced that the Jews stand in his way he'll find ways to kill them all. Destroy them, exterminate them like vermin." (141)

In his Foreword, Elie Wiesel says Plaut "offers an interpretation of another personage [i.e. Hitler] who on a different level allied himself with the Evil one to destroy our people." (13)

Plaut has Frank say, "the Jews should be killed because they believe in traditional morality and thereby perpetuate the status quo in the world." (151)

But Frank's satanic hatred of God naturally extended to all religions: "I have come to bring revolution into the world. Muslims, Catholics, Russian or Greek Orthodox, Jews — I've come to liberate people from their enslavement to law, and I start with religion. Deceiving their priests and acolytes is a benefit to mankind, you understand." (151)

Jacob Frank

THE NAZIS

Frankists achieved power by pretending to subscribe to every religion and ideology, and by intermarriage with generational Satanists. Behind the scenes, they advanced their kinsmen and manipulated events. Thus, they gained covert control of government and the economy.

They are recognized by the fact that they pretend to be Christians or Jews or Muslims etc. A typical example is John Kerry who pretended he was an Irish Catholic, when in fact his father was a Frankist Jew (who worked for the CIA) and his mother a Forbes. Barack Obama's mother may have been a Frankist/Illuminati Jewess. Another example is the English Rothschilds who marry non-Jews yet pretend to be Jews. They are all Illuminati Satanists.

The Frankists waged war against Jews by denouncing the Talmud and accusing orthodox Jews of ritually sacrificing Christian children. Frankists were responsible for numerous pogroms. Is it possible that Hitler's psychotic hatred against Jews was due to his Frankist background? His grandfather is believed to be Jewish. (A Jew, Frankenberger, paid child support.)

In the book, *"Adolf Hitler: Founder of Israel,"* (1974) author Heineke Kardel quotes German Jew Dietrich Bronder:

"Of Jewish descent, or being related to Jewish families were: the Leader and Reichschancelor Adolf Hitler; his representatives the Reichsminister Rudolf Hess; the Reichsmarshall Hermann Goering; the Reichsleader of the NSDAP Gregor Strasser, Dr. Josef Goebbels, Alfred Rosenberg, Hans Frank, Heinrich Himmler; the Reichsminister von Ribbentrop (who pledged close friendship with the famous Zionist Chaim Weizmann, the first head of the State of Israel who died in 1952); von Keudell; field commanders

Globocnik (the Jewish destructor); Jordan and Wilhelm Hube; the great SS-Leaders Reinhard Heydrich, Erich von dem Bach-Zelewski and von Keudell II, who also were active in the destruction of Jews. (All of them were members of the secret Thule Order/Society.) " (Bronder, *"Before Hitler Came,"* 1964)

Moreover, Churchill, FDR and Stalin were also Illuminati or Frankist Jews. So you can see how the Second World War could have been contrived partly to fulfill Frank's goal of exterminating the Jewish people.

Frankists may explain the presence of 150,000 part-Jewish soldiers in the German army. http://www.kansaspress.ku.edu/righit.html

CONCLUSION

By blaming "the Jews" for the NWO, patriots are falling into an Illuminati trap. Patriot and Jews alike need a new paradigm. The Jewish people, and indeed all religions and nations, are led by Frankist (Illuminati) Satanists, their lackeys and dupes.

Whatever we think of European Jewry, like Germans, Poles and Russians, they had a highly developed civilization. The goal of both revolution and war is to destroy Western civilization. Thus the Frankists (Illuminati) took charge of both sides and incited war for its own sake. In the process, they exterminated civilized Jews who had traditionally opposed them.

We remain in denial until we recognize that culture and politics are controlled by Satanists bent on destroying Western civilization. We can't see it because we "see through the spectacles they set astride our nose."

Did A Nazi Jew Design the Holocaust?

Ironically, the only member of the Nazi hierarchy who met the Aryan ideal was probably part-Jewish. More ironic still, Reinhard Heydrich (Chief of Gestapo and SD) is considered the architect of the "Final Solution," the plan to exterminate European Jewry.

Recently, I argued that a heretical Jewish Satanic cult, the Sabbatean Frankists, have plotted to exterminate the Jewish people since the 18th century. The hallmark of this cult is that they intermarry and impersonate members of other nations, ideologies and religions, including Judaism. Heydrich's background fits this profile.

The Sabbatean-Frankists are the progenitors of the Illuminati, responsible for Communism, Fascism, Zionism, Socialism, Liberalism, Neo Conservatism and the NWO.

As my readers know, my hypothesis is that the Second World War was a hoax, and that the leaders of all sides were Illuminati (Freemason) Sabbatean Frankist Jews. The object was to destroy Western civilization by eradicating natural leadership, and degrading and demoralizing the population. The goal is world government secretly directed by this satanic cult. In other words, FDR, Churchill, Hitler and Stalin may have been in cahoots. Heydrich may have been assassinated in 1942 because he knew too much and posed a threat.

THE JEWISH BLOND BEAST

The issue of Heydrich's Jewishness centres on his grandfather. Was his father, Bruno Heydrich, the scion of his mother's first or second husband? Defenders of Heydrich's Aryan purity (like Edouard Calic) say Ernestine Linder's first husband, Karl Julius Reinhard was Bruno's father. But the consensus is that her second husband Robert Suess, a Jew, was in fact Bruno Reinhard's father.

Blond Beast

Bruno Reinhard was a Wagnerian opera singer, composer and conductor who wanted to be accepted as a non-Jew. He married his professor's daughter, a real Aryan, and opened a music school in Halle with 120 students. But he could not overcome the suspicion that he was Jewish. The fact that he was a Freemason supports the view he was a Frankist.

Brian Rigg, author of *"Hitler's Jewish Soldiers"* writes: "When Heydrich was a child in Halle, neighborhood children made fun of him, calling him "Isi" (Izzy), short for Isidor, a name with a Jewish connotation. This nickname upset Heydrich. When he served in the navy, many of his comrades believed he was Jewish. Some called him the "blond Moses." Others who lived in Halle have claimed that everybody believed that his father, the musician Bruno Heydrich, was a Jew. Half-Jew Alice Schaper, nee Rohr, who took piano lessons from Bruno, claimed, "We all knew he was Jewish. ...He looked just like a typical Jew." In town, Bruno was called Isidor Suess behind his back. With such rumors going around, it was not surprising that [Reinhard] Heydrich felt continually burdened by these allegations, especially when he served as an SS general."

The Illuminati created both Communism and Nazism in order to destroy Russia and Germany. One purported to be about class war; the other about race war but both had war in common. Hitler cared nothing about racial purity. His own grandfather was Jewish.

"Throughout Hitler's political career, he made several exemptions from his ideology," Brian Rigg writes. "Hitler granted thousands of Mischlinge (partial Jews) exemptions from the provisions of his racial laws."

HEYDRICH THE MISCHLINGE

Heydrich (1904-1942) was one such exemption. Heinrich Himmler was Heydrich's boss. He told his doctor, Felix Kersten, that Heydrich was part-Jewish and that Hitler knew this. Hitler said his "non-Aryan origins were extremely useful; for he would be eternally grateful to us that we had kept him and not expelled him and would obey blindly. This was in fact the case." (*"The Kersten Memoirs,"* 1957, p 97.)

Heydrich was doubly ruthless to prove his loyalty. Heydrich accepted tasks "which no one else would care to do."

Himmler went on: Heydrich "was convinced the Jewish elements in his blood were damnable; he hated the blood which had played him so false. The Fuhrer could really have picked no better man than Heydrich for the campaign against the Jews. For them he was without mercy or pity." (99)

Joachim Fest writes that Abwehr Chief Wilhelm Canaris was able to resist Heydrich by obtaining "documents proving his adversary's Jewish antecedents..." (*"The Face of the Third Reich,"* p. 105)

Heydrich was in charge of the Einsatzgruppen units, trucks which followed the Wehrmacht and gassed Jews. He set up the system of concentration camps and planned the "Final Solution" at the Wannsee Conference in Jan. 1942.

Though he died at age 38, Heydrich's list of other "accomplishments" is formidable. Calic credits him with the Reichstag Fire (1933) and the "Night of the Long Knives" (1934) . Fest credits him for fabricating evidence that led to the purge of the USSR army in 1937-39, and traditional generals in the Wehrmacht. He paved the way for the Anschluss and the piecemeal incorporation of Czechoslovakia. He organized the anti-Semitic pogrom known as "Crystal Night."

But I suspect he posed a threat to Hitler and Himmler. And just as Churchill helped Hitler get rid of Hess (making room for Bormann), the British PM and Freemason also disposed of Heydrich. The British sent Czech agents to ambush Heydrich and Hitler's doctors finished him off.

The story of Reinhard Heydrich is another reminder that things are not what they seem. The architect of the "Final Solution" had Jewish blood and may have been Sabbatean Frankist Illuminati. The adversaries in World War Two were all part of this satanic cult. The object, to enslave humanity in a world government dedicated to Lucifer.

Stalin's Complicity in "Operation Barbarossa"

Stalin's inaction despite fore-knowledge of "Operation Barbarossa," Hitler's 1941 invasion of Russia, is one of the great mysteries of World War Two.

Like the improbable Dunkirk, where Hitler allowed the evacuation of 335,000 Allied soldiers, the explanation lies in the collusion of the wartime leaders: Hitler, Churchill, FDR and Stalin.

Hitler & Stalin: Illuminati Twins

The Illuminati bankers use war to advance a satanic world government agenda. The wartime leaders belonged to the Illuminati Order and were chosen to impose another calamity upon the human race. Their puzzling behavior can be explained by a desire to prolong the war.

According to author David Murphy, Stalin had precise intelligence regarding Barbarossa yet "rejected it and refused to permit his military to take necessary actions to respond lest they 'provoke' the Germans." (*"What Stalin Knew: The Enigma of Barbarossa,"* 2005, p.xix)

FOREKNOWLEDGE

Russian intelligence had thoroughly penetrated Nazi ranks. There were hundreds of accurate reports as early as August 1940 pointing to the future Nazi invasion. One of the most definitive came from spy Victor Sorge, a journalist on intimate terms with the German ambassador in Japan.

On May 5, 1941, Sorge sent Moscow a microfilm of a telegram from Foreign Minister Ribbentrop saying, "Germany will begin a war against the USSR in the middle of June 1941." Ten days later, Sorge reported the exact date, dawn, June 22. (87)

For his reward, Stalin castigated Sorge as "a little shit," a pimp and war profiteer. After Sorge's arrest, the Japanese proposed a prisoner exchange with Russia. Stalin declined and let the gifted spy die.

On April 17, 1941, "Starshina" an agent in Luftwaffe Intelligence reported that bombing targets had been selected and the occupation authority organized. (100) On April 18, a Nazi NCO deserted with the exact hour of the Nazi attack: 4 a.m. June 22. The next day Churchill also warned Stalin of the Nazi plan. (262)

How could Stalin ignore all these warnings when the Nazis had nine Armies consisting of 150 Divisions, 4,500,000 soldiers and 650,000 vehicles amassed in his border?

Are we supposed to believe that Stalin, a ruthless criminal, accepted Hitler's "word of honor" that this troop concentration was intended for England, and was being kept out of bomber range? (258)

Stalin's refusal to permit a mobilization or take countermeasures contributed to the loss of 20 million Russian lives.

He didn't just leave his country naked in 1941. Stalin had been undermining USSR defences for at least five years.

THE REAL TRAITOR

In 1937, Stalin purged the Red Army, murdering Marshall Mikhail N. Tukhachevsky and decimating the officer corps. Murphy writes: "Thousands of officers with combat experience and higher education were executed, sent to the Gulag or discharged from the service. These actions ...continued right up to the early days of the German invasion." (xvi)

Significantly, the pretext for executing thousands of patriotic Russian officers was "treasonous" letters forged by Reinhard Heydrich, Deputy Chief of the Gestapo, another example of Illuminati collusion.

The real enemy was the cream of Russian manhood, patriots and nationalists who were educated and posed a threat to the fanatics in power.

For a year prior to the invasion, Stalin allowed the Luftwaffe to make hundreds of reconnaissance flights over western Russia, forbidding his air force from interfering. Why on earth would he do that?

In addition, Nazi Germany received millions of tons of raw material from Russia in return for armaments. This is from *Wikipedia*:

"Germany received one million tons of cereals, half a million tons of wheat, 900,000 tons of oil, 100,000 tons of cotton, 500,000 tons of phosphates and considerable amounts of other vital raw materials, along with the transit of one million tons of soybeans from Manchuria. These and other supplies were being transported through Soviet and occupied Polish territories. The Soviets were to receive a naval cruiser, the plans to the battleship Bismarck, heavy naval guns, other naval gear and thirty of Germany's latest warplanes, including the Me-109 and Me-110 fighters and Ju-88 bomber. The Soviets would also receive oil and electric equipment, locomotives, turbines, generators, diesel engines, ships, machine tools and samples of Germany artillery, tanks, explosives, chemical-warfare equipment and other items."

Trainloads of iron ore passed from Russia to Nazi occupied Poland on the night of the invasion. *Wikipedia* concludes, "The imports of Soviet raw materials into Germany over the duration of the countries' economic relationship proved vital to Barbarossa."

Once under way, Hitler and Stalin took command of their respective armies making disastrous decisions that may have been deliberate.

For example, by the end of July 1941, Army Group Center was poised to take Moscow, only 200 km. away. But Hitler insisted that critical panzer units be diverted to the Ukraine. It wasn't until Oct. 2 that the offensive against Moscow was resumed, and by then the weather had turned. (233)

Similarly, during this diversion against Kiev, Stalin refused to allow his troops to withdraw to a defensive position. The battle ended Sept. 26 with the destruction of five Soviet armies, the capture of 665,000 men and an enormous amount of equipment. (233)

CONCLUSION

Communism and Fascism were evil twins, conceived in the same Illuminati womb, made from interchangeable parts, practically mirror images. Both were fronts for monopoly capital, the same monopoly capital.

Judging from their actions, both Hitler and Stalin were determined to extend the war and make it as costly as possible.

No, the real war was between the Illuminati and the human race. The Illuminati bankers are a relatively small group. They divide and conquer, so humanity will degrade and destroy itself. They do this by putting their pawns in power and using the mass media to conjure the illusion of a genuine conflict.

Was the Polish Holocaust Also a Hoax?

Hardly a week goes by without attempts by Internet die-hards to debunk the Jewish holocaust as a "holo-hoax."

At the same time, no one questions that three million non-Jewish Poles were killed by the Nazis. The Jews were below Poles in the scale of "untermenschen" (sub-humans.) Poles received about 650 calories per day in rations compared to 450 for Jews.

A Polish priest, Father Piotr Sosnowski, before his execution, near Gdynia, late 1939

Do the die-hards expect us to believe the Nazis would exterminate Poles and somehow spare Jews?

Poland was a Catholic country and came in for especially brutal treatment from the Nazis Illuminati Satanists.

In a speech August 22,1939, Hitler said his aim is to "kill without pity or mercy all men, women and children of Polish descent or language. Only in this way can we obtain the living space we need…:" (Gumkowski, *"Poland Under Nazi Occupation,"* p. 59)

In *"Forgotten Survivors: Polish Christians Remember the German Occupation"* (2004), Richard Lukas writes:

"The Germans killed their Polish victims in a variety of ways—shooting, gassing, hanging, torture, hard labor, lethal injections, beatings and starvation. The first victims of the gas chambers at Auschwitz were Poles and Russian POWs. The Nazi determination to obliterate the Polish intelligentsia resulted in wiping out 45% of Polish physicians and dentists, 40% of professors, 57% of attorneys, 30% of technicians, and a majority of leading journalists." (p. 5)

From the first days of occupation, the Nazis began a systematic campaign to exterminate Poles. Polish POW's were slaughtered; statues and cultural sites razed and 200,000 Polish children with Aryan characteristics sent to Germany for "Germanization."

LARGER CONTEXT

The Jewish holocaust took place in the context of "Generalplan Ost" ("General Plan East") the planned genocide of over 50 million Slavs, 75 % of the population of Nazi-occupied Poland, Ukraine and Russia. The Nazis intended to "Germanize" a few of the remaining 25%, and keep the rest as agricultural serfs who wouldn't even learn to read.

The Nazis managed to kill 20 million Russians including 7 million civilians by a variety of means. Three million Russian POWs died from bullets, deliberate typhus infection and starvation.

I deplore the persecution of those who question the details of the Jewish holocaust. Nothing casts more doubt on the holocaust than these attempts to control thought and speech.

In my view, the die-hard's real objection is to the political exploitation of the holocaust by Zionists and the undeserved status, and immunity from criticism it gives them. They would be wiser to address this issue directly rather than pretend the Jewish holocaust didn't take place.

They could neutralize its propaganda value by drawing attention to the pattern of Nazi-Zionist collaboration and by talking about the Jewish role in Stalinist mass-murder. (See online, Steve Plocker, "Stalin's Jews.")

MORE CONTEXT

The treatment of Jews in Nazi-occupied Europe depended on the Nazi relationship to host nations and allies. For example, the 5,000 Danish Jews were mostly unscathed because the Nazis wanted good relations with the Nordic Danes, and access to their farm produce. Unlike the Poles, who had 3.3 million Jews, the Danes were very protective of their Jews.

Nazi persecution was held in check as long as Hitler desired peace with England, or good relations with Russia. However the invasion of Russia June 22, 1941 signalled the beginning of a genocidal death-struggle. In this war zone, Slavs and Jews who were unfit for slave labor, (i.e. roughly 80% of the total) were marked for extermination.

In the Nazi mind, all Jews represented the Bolshevik peril. "German National Socialism and Jewish Bolshevism could not coexist," German soldiers were told. "This is a war of extinction." There is simply no way Jews could escape the fate of Russians and Poles. By July 1942, the first extermination camps, Belzec, Sobibor and Treblinka were opened.

FOOD

During the winter of 1940-41, there were food shortages and public grumbling in Germany. The Nazis realized the food was the key to public support.

According to historians Deborah Dwork and Jan van Pelt, the Nazis calculated that "tens of millions of Russians would have to die in order to safeguard German meat rations. German food would not go east to the invading army; rather [2.5 million] German soldiers would be fed at the expense of the local population." (*"Holocaust: A History"* p 265.)

The Nazis "looked to the east to become the breadbasket of New Europe...a true granary [characterized by] low density of settlement...prosperous farms and attractive small towns." They envisaged "the deportation of 41 to 51 million people which included 80-85% of all Poles...It was tacitly understood that they would be killed." (266)

Goring remarked to Italian Foreign Minister Ciano in Dec. 1941: "This year between 20 and 30 million persons will die in Russia of hunger. Perhaps it is well that it should be so, for certain nations must be decimated." (190)

At the same time, the Allies subjected the German civilian population to a murderous bombing campaign. In July 1943, 50,000 people died in a Hamburg fire storm called "Operation Gomorra." 800,000 fled the city in the aftermath.

World War Two was a time of unparalleled savagery and ethnic cleansing. I will not attempt a complete inventory here. It's simply implausible that the Jews, who were vilified as official Nazi policy, would evade the pattern of genocide.

I am all for determining the facts but, in historical context, denying the Jewish holocaust makes no sense and discredits its advocates.

Katyn: The Story of Heroism Hollywood Won't Tell

"Defiance," yet another movie about Jewish victimhood and heroism opened in 1800 US theatres in 2008.

This story of Jewish partisans fighting Nazis adds to a growing holocaust film genre that includes "Sophie's Choice," "Shindler's List" and "The Pianist."

But one incredible Jewish story of genocide continues to elude Hollywood. This is the execution of 20,000 Polish Officer POW's, (devout Roman Catholics who represented much of the Polish elite), by the Bolshevik Jewish-led NKVD in the Katyn forest in 1940.

Why has Hollywood ignored this story? My opinion is that, with six degrees of separation, Hollywood (and indeed America) is ultimately run by the spiritual descendants of these murderers.

Thus we are brainwashed to ignore genocide that doesn't fit the Nazi-Jew paradigm. Movies are essential to this programming. Part of an ongoing psychological war on the Christian European majority, we are made to identify with minorities. If we object, we are counted as Nazis.

Andrej Wajda, 82, Poland's most celebrated film director, lost his father at Katyn. In 2008, Wajda made a movie about this massacre and its effect on the victims' families. Financed by Polish TV, the film, "Katyn," was a major artistic and commercial success in Poland. It was nominated for an Oscar for Best Foreign Film in 2008, but has not found wide distribution outside Poland.

It didn't win the Oscar. The award went to a Jewish holocaust movie, "The Counterfeiters," a "true story" from Germany. It described the moral dilemma faced by a Jewish master-counterfeiter forced to forge British and US currency. ("Should I sabotage this process?") I saw this movie. It is an enjoyable piece of propaganda which helps the audience identify with Jews. In real life, I doubt if the hero had any such moral qualms. Even in the film, he filled his own pockets.

KATYN

I haven't seen the movie but I did stumble across information that illustrates why this is the stuff of which epics are made, if the Illuminati didn't control culture.

First, some background from *Wikipedia*: "Since Poland's conscription system required every non exempt university graduate to become a reserve officer, the Soviets were able to round up much of the Polish intelligentsia. Those who died at Katyn included an admiral, two generals, 24 colonels, 79 lieutenant colonels, 258 majors, 654 captains, 17 naval captains, 3,420 NCOs, seven chaplains, three landowners, a prince, 43 officials, 85 privates, and 131 refugees. Also among the dead were 20 university professors; 300 physicians; several hundred lawyers, engineers, and teachers; and more than 100 writers and journalists as well as about 200 pilots. In all, the NKVD executed almost half the Polish officer corps."

In 1945, Maurice Shainberg was the Assistant to KGB Col. Grigory Zaitzev who was the Commandant of the main Katyn work camp. In his book, *"Breaking from the KGB,"* (1986) Shainberg, a Polish Jew, tells how he discovered Zaitzev's Katyn diary in the safe. Shainberg had misgivings about Communism and identified with his fellow Poles. He took great personal risks to copy sections of the diary. The Zaitzev Diary was dynamite because the Soviets always claimed the Nazis had committed the war crime.

The diary appears authentic except for one major discrepancy. Zaitzev pretends the slaughter was necessitated by lack of transport to remove the prisoners in advance of the Nazi onslaught in June 1941. In fact, Stalin and Beria gave the order to murder the Poles in early March and the executions took place in April and May 1940. Only 4250 were actually shot in Katyn forest. The remainder were executed in prisons elsewhere. Many were taken out in barges on the White Sea and drowned.

Otherwise, the diary describes how the Soviets tried to indoctrinate and intimidate the Poles into betraying their culture and their country (as the Western-elite has done today), by forming a puppet class in a future Soviet-dominated Poland. The Poles refused and that is the reason they were slaughtered.

THE ZAITZEV DIARY

When Zaitzev got his assignment, he was warned that the Poles were all "educated religious fanatics" always singing patriotic songs and hymns with their chaplain. Zaitzev was confident he could teach them to "pray to a new God."

The prisoners worked cutting trees from 6 a.m. to 6 p.m. In the evening they boycotted the indoctrination sessions. They had no desire to assist in building the future Soviet Poland.

One officer explained: "As a Pole I know my nation. None of us have the desire to dictate to other people, and we don't want other people to dictate to us. We are neither a Fascist or a Communist nation, but a devoutly Catholic one."

Once during a speech, the Polish Army Chaplain Jozwiak lifted up the crucifix he wore and began to chant a prayer. The prisoners followed suit. That night, Jozwiak was taken to the Interrogation Chamber.

"The use of electrical currents on Father Jozwiak's eyes and body didn't help. Nor was the Chinese method successful, where the prisoner was stripped from the waist down and forced to sit over an open cage of starving rats. We couldn't allow the priest to go back to the other prisoners in the condition he was left in, so we finished him off." (Shainberg, p. 165)

The NKVD thought the priest's example would have a sobering effect on the POW's but instead they curtailed their work. The NKVD retaliated by decreasing rations which made the prisoners too weak to work. When the NKVD started shooting prisoners who didn't work; the others turned on the guards with their axes and 192 Poles were shot.

Now the Poles were more defiant than ever. When a collaborator lectured to them, they began to chant a prayer: "We Polish soldiers and prisoners of the Soviets have been brought here to foreign lands to die. We beg of you, Mother of God, to take care of our nation...Save us from German and Soviet imprisonment. We are offering ourselves as a sacrifice for the independence of our fatherland..."

Of course this is the kind of self sacrifice and patriotism that our masters don't want us to see.

"Our task was impossible," Zaitzev wrote. "People who have never met these Poles will not understand how difficult it was to change their attitude toward us. No beating or abuse would make them stop their singing. They are a hard and proud people. Every day they get physically weaker but their anger and hatred increased."

Polish historian Krzystztof Siwek tells me that Poland has declared April 13 a National Day of Remembrance of the Katyn martyrs. "A joint Polish-Russian commission was formed to develop an official position of both sides. Most of controversies remain un-resolved. Russians fear that admitting fully to the crime against humanity would allow the victims' families to demand compensations and other penalties as in the case of Germany."

MOVIES AS PROPAGANDA

The Illuminati bankers established the USSR as a precursor to the New World Order. The execution of the Polish elite was necessary to the long term plan. The Nazis, also an Illuminati Jewish creation, treated Polish and other national elites in a similar fashion.

Culture is a function of money and the Illuminati control credit. Thus our culture maintains a conspiracy of silence about the gradual subversion of Western civilization by its own traitorous elite.

We will undermine every collective force except our own, say the *Protocols of Zion*. They undermine European Christian heterosexual norms in the name of "Diversity."

Thus, the 2009 Oscar Nominees included Clint Eastwood's "Gran Torino," about a redneck who learns to love Asian immigrants kids. Oscar winner "Slumdog Millionaire" was about Bombay street kids. Sean Penn's "Milk" was about a crusader for "homo-sexual rights." In "The Reader," a German youth had an affair with a women twice his age, who turned out to have been a concentration camp guard. The affair ruined his life but was presented in positive terms. It relies on the mawkish device that he sent audio tapes to her in prison, just as he had read to her during their fling.

"Revolutionary Road" offered a negative view of marriage and family in the 1950's. "Doubt" was about homosexuality in the Catholic Church. French Best Foreign Language nominee "The Class" was about immigrant youths and how loveable they are. And on it goes, movies are propaganda for the Illuminati agenda.

When the movie is about white Americans, as in "Benjamin Button," no collective identity can be upheld, no universals revealed. Life must be literally turned upside down, in this case reversed from old to young, before it has any interest for the screenwriter, Eric Roth. This diverting but ultimately vacuous movie is a triumph of make-up. It has nothing important to say to Americans at this critical moment.

So there should be no surprise that a film about Christian martyrs and patriots coming from an anachronism like a proud Christian nation will be quietly swept under the carpet by Hollywood.

Heaven forbid the sheep figure out the same fate may await them.

Postscript:

The Katyn Massacre was repeated April 10, 2010 when about 95 high Polish officials, including the President of Poland, and the head of Security Service and the National Bank, were supposedly killed in a plane crash on their way to commemorate the 70th Anniversary of Katyn. A Polish videographer, who was later murdered, managed to film the crash scene and reveal that there were no bodies and no baggage. The plane came in a tree level so it is highly unlikely there would be no survivors. However, the Russians showed great foresight by not sending any ambulances.

This is what may have happened: Artificial fog enveloped the Smolensk airport and the plane was diverted to another airport where the passengers were removed and assassinated. Then a dummy airplane made to look like the Presidential plane staged a deliberate crash. The video, which is online, suggests the pilots were finished off. Gunfire and the words "Change of Plans" are heard. Later, the passengers' bodies were burned and returned to Poland.

The heirs of the Katyn murderers are probably still in charge of Russia. They are Satanists willing to perform any abomination to eliminate patriotic opposition to Luciferian world tyranny.

Trauma Brainwashing – Hiroshima and the Cold War

In 1945, a half million Japanese civilians were slaughtered or maimed when the US dropped two atomic bombs on Japan. These war crimes were committed to threaten the West with annihilation and thereby justify the needless expenditure of trillions of dollars in the Cold War.

There must always be an external enemy so people don't realize they are being fleeced by the bankers who appoint the leaders, control the media and create the money.

With World War Two winding down, the bankers needed a "Cold War." In May of 1945, Secretary of State Edward Stettinius Jr., called a meeting in San Francisco. The Japanese were already privately suing for peace. The atomic bomb would not be ready for several more months.

 "We have already lost Germany," Stettinius, a Yale *Skull and Bones* alumnus said. "If Japan bows out, we will not have a live population on which to test the bomb. Our entire postwar program depends on terrifying the world with the atomic bomb."

"To accomplish that goal," said John Foster Dulles, "you will need a very good tally. I should say a million." "Yes," replied Stettinius, "we are hoping for a million tally in Japan. But if they surrender, we won't have anything."

"Then you have to keep them in the war until the bomb is ready," said John Foster Dulles. "That is no problem. Unconditional surrender."

"They won't agree to that," said Stettinius. "They are sworn to protect the Emperor."

"Exactly," said John Foster Dulles. "Keep Japan in the war another three months, and we can use the bomb on their cities; we will end this war with the naked fear of all the peoples of the world, who will then bow to our will."

My source here is Eustace Mullin's excellent online essay, "The Secret History of the Atomic Bomb." Mullins, who died in 2010, was one of a handful of courageous historians the bankers don't own.

According to Mullins, President Truman, whose only real job before Senator had been Masonic organizer in Missouri, did not make the fatal decision alone. A committee led by James F. Byrnes, Bernard Baruch's puppet, instructed him. Baruch was the Rothschild's principal agent in the USA and a Presidential "adviser" spanning the era from Woodrow Wilson to JFK.

Baruch, who was chairman of the Atomic Energy Commission, spearheaded the "Manhattan Project." He chose life-long Communist Robert Oppenheimer to be Research Director. It was very much the bankers' bomb.

On August 6, 1945, an uranium bomb 3-235, 20 kilotons yield, was exploded 1850 feet in the air above Hiroshima for maximum explosive effect. It devastated four square miles, and killed 140,000 of the 255,000 inhabitants.

Mullins quotes a Japanese doctor: "My eyes were ready to overflow with tears. I spoke to myself and bit my lip so that I would not cry. If I had cried, I would have lost my courage to keep standing and working, treating dying victims of Hiroshima."

When the Air Force dropped the atomic bomb on Nagasaki, the principal target was a Catholic church: "The roof and masonry of the Catholic cathedral fell on the kneeling worshippers. All of them died."

Back in the United States, the news of the bombing of Hiroshima was greeted with a mixture of relief, pride, joy, shock and sadness.

Oppenheimer's colleague remembers the shouts of joy: "Hiroshima has been destroyed! Many of my friends were rushing to the telephone to book tables at the La Fonda Hotel in Santa Fe in order to celebrate. Oppenheimer walked around like a prize-fighter, clasping his hands together above his head as he came to the podium."

The bankers serve a diabolical power whose goal is to thwart and enslave humanity. The Cold War served to brutalize a whole generation.

Mullins writes: "In the United States, the schools held daily bomb drills, with the children hiding under their desks. No one told them that thousands of schools children in Hiroshima had been incinerated in their classrooms; the desks offered no protection against nuclear weapons. The moral effect on the children was devastating. If they were to be vaporized in the next ten seconds, there seemed little reason to study, marry and have children, or prepare for a steady job. This demoralization through the nuclear weapons program is the undisclosed reason for the decline in public morality."

We hear a lot about holocaust denial, but the gratuitous bombing of civilians in Japan and Germany reached holocaust scale both in brutality and malice. The Japanese were forbidden from commemorating the atomic bombings. Compared to Auschwitz, we hear very little of Hamburg, Dresden, Hiroshima and Nagasaki.

"Soviet" Agents Designed IMF, World Bank & United Nations

We usually think of the New World Order as something coming in the future. In fact, a veiled Masonic Jewish banker dictatorship has existed for some time.

This is world conquest executed by deception, infiltration and subversion. They took over the levers of power while maintaining the facade of democracy and freedom. They did this by duping Jews and Masons, and the population in general with Liberalism, Socialism, Zionism and Communism.

("Far back in ancient times we were the first to cry among the masses of the people the words "Liberty, Equality, Fraternity," words many times repeated since these days by stupid poll-parrots who, from all sides around, flew down upon these baits and with them carried away the well-being of the world..." *Protocols of the Elders of Zion,* 1-25:)

The Illuminati formalizes its tyranny by, for example, using the phony "war on terror" as a pretext to suspend civil liberties and build a police state. Notice, no one has asked Barack Obama to withdraw the "Patriot Act." The real target is the American people.

DE FACTO TYRANNY

Recently, I was reminded of this de facto tyranny when I read that the major institutions of the post-war world were created by "Soviet spies," i.e. men working directly for the Illuminati (Masonic) Jewish bankers. The most prominent was Harry Dexter White, a founder (and Director) of the IMF, as well as the World Bank.

As Assistant to the Secretary of the Treasury, Henry Morgenthau, also a Soviet agent, White (originally "Weit") delivered the printing plates for US occupation currency in Germany to the Soviets, costing the US $50 billion. FDR's administration was rife with Soviet spies, mostly Jews, protected by FDR himself. This included spies in the Manhattan Project who delivered the plans for the atomic bomb to Russia.

There was nothing "Russian" about the USSR. It was an Illuminati (Masonic) Jewish state. So were/are England, the United States and most of Europe.

If White helped found the IMF and World Bank, Alger Hiss, a Colonel in the Soviet GPU, helped design the United Nations and served as its first acting Secretary General. A revival of the League of Nations, the UN is the main mechanism of Masonic Jewish world government.

I say "Masonic Jewish" because most Jews aren't Masons and most Masons aren't Jews. But Freemasonry is a secret society based on Judaism. The essence of a secret society is that the membership is manipulated to fulfill a hidden agenda, in this case world domination.

White and Hiss could have been dupes, believing in "changing the world." But think about it folks. The architects of the IMF, World Bank and United Nations were both "Soviet" agents, traitors, proof that the covert Illuminati takeover was complete in the 1930s or earlier.

(My source for White and Hiss' spying is the CIA Interrogation of Gestapo Chief Heinrich Muller, who intercepted Soviet cables from Washington to Moscow. *"Gestapo Chief,"* Vol III Edited by Gregory Douglas pp. 162-173. This was later confirmed by the testimony of Soviet defector Elizabeth Bentley and the release of the VENONA material by US Army Signal Intelligence.)

SABBATEANS

Although Hiss wasn't a Jew, he was a protege of Felix Frankfurter, a Supreme Court judge and Sabbatean Jew. The Sabbateans were a 17th Century Jewish heresy, a satanic cult that gave birth to the Illuminati.

Numbering over a million, they included powerful bankers like the Rothschilds. When their leader Sabbatai Zvi pretended to convert to Islam (under duress from the Sultan), the Sabbateans imitated him by infiltrating other nationalities and religions. This is the origin of Jewish assimilation (the "Haskalah"), all the more effective because most Jews were sincere. Thus, the Rothschilds instituted Nazism to reclaim them as their pawns.

The hard-core Sabbateans were Cabalists determined to be their own God/Messiah and make the world worship them. They advanced this program by recruiting, under the rubric of Freemasonry, non-Jewish elites willing to betray their country. Communism and Zionism are both Masonic movements and Illuminati instruments.

Frankfurter was an "adviser" to both Woodrow Wilson and FDR. "Advisers" or "brain trusts" were the handlers, intermediaries between the Illuminati bankers and the politicians who are front men. Another Jewish "Soviet" agent was LBJ's handler, Abe Fortas, a Supreme Court judge who resigned in a bribery scandal.

Financed by the central banking cartel, the Illuminati Order control intelligence agencies and most organizations and corporations of significance. But they operate at arm's length. FDR and Stalin both wanted Vice President Henry Wallace, another Soviet agent, to succeed to the Presidency.

But Truman was installed instead, probably because the Illuminati wanted a Cold War. Like all wars, the Cold War was a hoax designed to further concentrate power and profit in the hands of the Illuminati bankers. The Illuminati always require an external enemy to distract attention from themselves, the enemy within.

THE SECRET SOCIETY MODEL

The whole world is now structured like a Cabalistic secret society. The vast majority of people are duped into thinking they are free and pursuing laudable goals. Only the "adepts" understand that the true purpose of all social trends, movements and world events is to condition the masses to serve the Masonic banker world tyranny.

In a famous statement at the June 1991 Bilderberg Conference, David Rockefeller thanked the media for advancing a "supranational sovereignty of an intellectual elite and world bankers, which is surely preferable to the national auto determination practised in past centuries. "

Of course, the "intellectual elite" is really a fig leaf to cover banker tyranny. More accurately "intellectual whores," they sugar coat the world government agenda in spurious platitudes. As I have said, the bankers want to translate their economic monopoly into a total political, cultural, spiritual and mental monopoly. "Hate" laws enforce this monopoly on thought itself.

We live in a colonized, totalitarian society masquerading as a free society. That should be obvious by the way they murdered Americans with impunity. They assassinated JFK, killed sailors on the USS Liberty and later thousands of Americans on 9-11.

We live in a totalitarian society trying to take off its mask in a way that makes tyranny appear normal, natural and necessary, so the masses will passively accept further degradation and servitude.

The Profumo Affair
Exposed Masonic Control

A fan of the 1989 movie Scandal, I recently bought Christine Keeler's memoir *"The Truth At Last"* (2001) at a used book store.

Keeler's memoir puts the scandal which helped topple Harold Macmillan's government in 1963 in the context of the Illuminati conspiracy.

Keeler's mentor Stephen Ward was a Russian agent, part of a ring that included royal art curator Sir Anthony Blunt and Sir Roger Hollis, head of MI-5 (1956-1965.) In her presence, they conspired to give British Defence secrets to the USSR. She told the police and Lord Denning but it was suppressed.

This is confirmation that Communism was a creation of British Freemasonry which in turn is an instrument of the Rothschild banking empire.

The British establishment is rotten with traitors if that word has any meaning when treason is the norm. Our view of the world as warring nation-states does not reflect reality.

History and current events are theatre. A tightly-knit satanic sex cult subtly controls all states and pits them against each other in a profitable and diverting Punch-and-Judy show. The nearly accomplished goal: world government tyranny.

Left-Right distinctions are meaningless. Keeler witnessed the "Communist" Stephen Ward meeting with "Fascist" leader Oswald Mosley. (99)

The only real distinction is between men who serve God and those who serve the devil, and between the dupes and the damned.

STEPHEN WARD

Stephen Ward was prosecuted for being a pimp and Keeler for prostitution but this did not reflect reality. Ward (an Osteopath who "committed suicide" while on trial) was a spy master who used the innocent Keeler to get information from important men.

John Profumo, 48, married and a father, was the Minister of War, and touted to become Prime Minister. Yet, he betrayed this great private and public responsibility by having a schoolboy affair with a nineteen-year-old girl. Keeler describes him as simply unable to control his lust.

Ward made his subordinate Soviet Naval Attache Ivanov seduce Keeler in order to compromise Profumo. Stephen Ward's job was to undermine the Conservative government to make way for Harold Wilson's Labor Party. Most likely the "Profumo Affair" was staged.

It wouldn't surprise me if Ward 's suicide was faked and he was whisked off to a Russian dacha, to join his colleagues Kim Philby and Donald MacLean. Or, he was murdered.

In Oct. 1962, Keeler overheard Ward tell Eugene Ivanov, his Soviet contact: "a man like John Kennedy will not be allowed to stay in such an important position of power in the world, I can assure you of that." (146)

PARTY GIRL

Christine Keeler was a beautiful teenager who mostly gave it away in return for admission to the fast lane. She slept with everyone from Ringo Starr to George Peppard to the captain and officers of the ocean liner *New Amsterdam*. "I had sex with captain and officers because I could, because I had the power to make them want me." (137)

Keeler & Profumo from "Scandal"

She became a symbol for sexual "liberation" (or depravity) in the early 1960's, a siren like Marilyn Monroe. But what was presented to the public as a relaxation of sexual repression was just getting the camel's nose under the tent.

The Masonic elite were/are into every form of sexual depravity and have inducted society as-a-whole into what is in fact a pagan sex cult. It's one thing not to be a prude; another to have sex shoved in your face constantly.

At Cliveden, the seat of the Astor family and a centre of British power, Keeler reports finding in the wood "a witch circle, the real thing, about ten feet in diameter." (30)

Keeler describes orgies:

"Stephen knew all the Masonic handshakes and he said that at some of the parties, the girls would just wear Masonic aprons. They would be flicked up and down like a sporran, he would laugh. Some of the women...were heavily into sadistic sex and there were 'black magic' parties which were really just an excuse for group sex sessions. There would be phallic totem poles around which all these women would bow and scrape ." (39-40)

The curdled "cream" of British politics, business, culture and law participated in this scene. The Duke of Edinburgh (husband of Queen Elizabeth) was known to have affairs and had at least one illegitimate child. (41)

"Some of these people seemed insatiable," Keeler said. "They could go at it for ages and come and come and come. And after all of that, it was casual chat about government policy on this and that. That's civilization for you. I suppose the Romans started it." (43)

"It was always a posh crowd who would arrive in chauffeur driven Bentleys or Rolls Royces. It seemed to me that having money dictated that you had group sex as often as you possibly could." (45)

Perhaps sex addiction and a lack of what Mathew Arnold called "high seriousness" are prerequisites for our political leaders. After all, they must represent the interests of the Masonic central banking cartel, and in case they forget, must be easily blackmailed.

Mankind will remain a perennial underachiever so long as we are secretly governed by these Satanists and their minions.

Che! The West's Fatal Embrace of Communism

Americans can't expect to avoid destruction as long as they embrace Communism in all its myriad disguises.

Symptomatic of the problem is a new four-hour 17 min biopic of Soviet Comintern agent and terrorist Che Guevara. Rather than make movies about genuine American heroes, Hollywood is celebrating people dedicated to the demise of Western civilization.

Benicio Del Toro in Steven Soderbergh's "Che"

Movie critic Mick LaSalle of the *San Francisco Chronicle* cannot understand why Director Steven Soderbergh made the movie:

"If Soderbergh made as idol-worshiping an epic about George Washington or Abraham Lincoln - actual heroes with tangible, positive legacies - people would gag at the naive treatment. Instead of making the case for Guevara as a hero, Soderbergh just assumes we all agree. The movie is the Communist guerrilla version of the Stations of the Cross, in which we see Guevara at various stages, enduring various hardships. The invitation is not to think but to admire, and maybe to worship."

This is not the first time Hollywood has presented this ruthless killer as a saint. In 1969, Omar Sharif played "the most controversial rebel of our time" with Jack Palance as Castro. Then, there was "The Motorcycle Diaries" in 2004 and at least a half-dozen made-for-TV films.

Communists always portray their demented drive for world domination in terms of serving the poor. Surprisingly, many suckers swallow this bait. But, why do these dupes include the US corporate media establishment?

WHY THE MEDIA (AND EDUCATION) SOFT-PEDAL COMMUNISM

The US mass media (and most corporations) are controlled by the central banking cartel, i.e. the Rothschilds, Warburgs, Rockefellers etc. These are the same people who sponsored Communism.

The guiding principle behind world events is their plan to translate their monopoly over government credit into a government monopoly of power, business, culture and religion, i.e. Communism.

These bankers use a Hegelian dialectic to achieve their end. They created both capitalism and Communism as thesis and antithesis. Their aim is a synthesis, combining the political and cultural tyranny of Communism with the appearance of capitalist free markets. China may be the end model for the New World Order.

In 1953, Ford Foundation President, H. Rowan Gaither told Congressional Investigator Norman Dodd that his instructions were to use "our grant-making power so to alter our life in the United States that we can be comfortably merged with the Soviet Union."

This is why the Communist Party term "political correctness" has become part of our lexicon. Why the elite media and foundations promote feminism, homosexuality, pornography and promiscuity to destabilize society.

Why they sponsor "diversity" to undermine American identity. Why the education system is devoted to Leftist indoctrination; and conservatives have been driven out. Why the culture industries are dedicated to sex, violence, alienation, deviance and the occult. We'll never know what we have missed in terms of cultural works that boost our sense of who we are and where we should be going.

Eustace Mullins told this story: Early in his career, a New York publisher (who are all banker controlled) told his agent that it's too bad Mullins had decided to go against them. Look at the success they arranged for such "high school" talents as Hemingway, Steinbeck and Faulkner. Unfortunately, Mullins would be consigned to the wilderness.

Rupert Murdoch, whose media operations are subsidized by the Rothschilds, said in early 2009, "We are in the midst of a phase of history in which nations will be redefined and their futures fundamentally altered."

Such anecdotes confirm that we are being dispossessed and prepared for servitude. Our culture and most of our assumptions about the world, are controlled by the central bankers.

GUEVARA, CASTRO AND THE CUBAN REVOLUTION

Fidel Castro came to power in Cuba with the covert help of New World Orderlies in the US State Dept. and mass media. They cut off arm sales to Batista while at the same time allowing Castro to be supplied, partly by Russian submarines. This told the Cuban military which way the wind was blowing and they quietly defected.

This is the conclusion of Nataniel Weyl in *Red Star Over Cuba* (1962, p.152) Weyl was a Communist in the 1930's who knew the top leaders of the Cuban Communist Party. He actually worked for the central bankers at one time, as Latin American research chief for the Federal Reserve System. He is one of many Jews who recognized Communism as a dangerous ruse and devoted his life to exposing Comintern subversion in Latin America.

Both Ernesto Guevera and Fidel Castro were trained as Soviet agents as teenagers. Guevara, an Argentine, was liaison between the Soviet espionage network and the Castro forces who masqueraded as an indigenous force. In fact, they were largely bankrolled and supplied by the Soviet Union.

"Fidel's secret weapon was money—-incredible millions of dollars, with which he bought "victories." He bought entire regiments from Batista's officers and, on one occasion, purchased for $650,000 cash an entire armored train, with tanks, guns, ammunition, jeeps and 500 men." (p.141)

"The [Castro] Cuban forces themselves never won a military victory," US Ambassador Earl Smith later testified. The basic reason for the defeat of Batista's army was that covert US intervention shattered their morale. (152)

Rothschild-dominated Freemasonry was also a factor. Communism is a Masonic order, and both Castro and Guevara were Masons. (Other Freemasons include Stalin, Trotsky, Lenin and most US Presidents incl. Barack Obama.) Freemasonry is big in Cuba: there is a 15-story Grand Lodge of Cuba HQ in Havana.

GUEVARA-MASS KILLER

According to Humberto Fantova's *"Che! Hollywood's Favorite Tyrant,"* Guevara was complicit in the execution of 10,000 Cubans after the revolution: He was "a blood-thirsty executioner, a military bumbler, a coward, and a hypocrite...it's no exaggeration to state that Che... was the godfather of modern terrorism. And yet Che's followers naively swallow Castro's historical revisionism. They are classic 'useful idiots,' the name Stalin gave to foolish Westerners who parroted his lies..."

Nat Hentoff met Che at the United Nations and asked "this idealist" — "Can you conceive — however far into the future — a time when there will be free elections in Cuba?"

"Not waiting for his interpreter, Guevara broke into laughter at my naively ignorant question. He made it clear that I had no understanding of a true people's revolution, firmly guided by Maximum Leader Castro."

If the Cuban Communists were sponsored by the central bankers, how do we account for the CIA's covert Bay of Pigs invasion? This failure was probably designed to enhance Castro's image and reinforce the Hegelian dialectic. If the US could go to Vietnam "for the sake of democracy," it certainty could have invaded Cuba openly. The debacle opened the door for the missile crisis and the assassination of Kennedy, both part of the agenda.

How do we account for the CIA's killing of Guevara? He had served his purpose and was worth more dead than alive. His image is plastered all over Cuba.

CONCLUSION

The Rothschilds and Rockefellers must be laughing up their sleeves at the young rebels who treat Che Guevera as a symbol of social justice and equality. In fact, Communism is the mirror image of Western imperialism, benefiting the same people.

Communism is devoted to the concentration of all wealth in the hands of the central bankers. In theory, the wealth is "public" but in fact, the bankers and their henchmen own and control the State.

Guevara helped establish a Communist regime that may be a harbinger for Obama's America. Yes, the people are all equal — dirt poor. Yes, they get free education and health care but education is indoctrination and people cannot toil for nothing if they are sick. Their MD's get $20 a month. The people are paid in platitudes.

Essentially, you have a prosperous island (oil, sugar, nickel, tobacco, coffee) with a large labor force that works for a pittance. All the wealth seems to flow to the Communist nomenclature and their sponsors. Secret police are everywhere and no one can say a word against the regime.

Herberto Padillo, a poet who was tortured for "deviationism" said after his escape: "I have lived in frightening laboratories for social experimentation, spaces walled by test tubes, where the same experiment always ended with the same result: tyranny. I have learned something of the value of freedom." (*"And the Russians Stayed,"* Carbonell, p. 295)

This is where we are heading when we tolerate a government full of New World Orderlies (Communists) and mass media that venerate their ruthless agents.

In broad historical context, the wealth and privileges enjoyed by the masses in the West have been the exception, not the rule. We may be gradually reverting to the norm.

Taliban Still Working for the CIA?

As President Obama decided to send more troops to Afghanistan, there was mounting evidence the Taliban is supported by the CIA. If correct, the Afghan war is a charade with a hidden agenda.

First, we have many reports that unmarked helicopters are ferrying the Taliban to targets, and relieving them when cornered. (Google: IWPR "Helicopter Rumours Refuse to Die.")

"Just when the police and army managed to surround the Taliban in a village of Qala-e-Zaal district, we saw helicopters land with support teams," an Afghan soldier said. "They managed to rescue their friends from our encirclement, and even to inflict defeat on the Afghan National Army."

This story, in one form or another, is being repeated throughout northern Afghanistan. Dozens of people claim to have seen Taliban fighters disembark from foreign helicopters in several provinces.

"I saw the helicopters with my own eyes," said Sayed Rafiq from Baghlan-e-Markazi.

"They landed near the foothills and offloaded dozens of Taliban with turbans, and wrapped in patus (a blanket-type shawl.)"

"Our fight against the Taliban is nonsense," said the first soldier. "Our foreigner 'friends' are friendlier to the opposition."

CIA AIR BASES IN PAKISTAN

Last February, there were reports of CIA airbases within Pakistan used for drones. If this is true, Pakistanis are being attacked by drones based in their own country. Obviously, the Taliban helicopters could also come from these CIA bases.

In May, Pakistani President Asif Ali Zardari, told NBC News that the CIA and the (U.S.-Funded) Pakistani ISI intelligence service "has created the Taliban." Zardari said that the CIA and the ISI are still supporting the Taliban.

On Oct 29, 2009, Hillary Clinton infuriated Pakistani officials by saying she found it "hard to believe" the ISI didn't know where Al Qaeda leaders were hiding. Her role is to maintain the fiction that Al Qaeda and the Taliban are not CIA creations. (CBS News.com)

Just the day before, (Oct. 18) four American citizens were caught photographing sensitive buildings in Islamabad. All four were dressed in traditional Afghan outfits and were found to be in possession of illegal weapons and explosives.

Their vehicles contained 2 M-16A1 rifles, 2 handguns and 2 hand-grenades. The police held the American citizens in custody for an hour before the Interior Ministry interfered and had them released without charge even as preliminary investigation was being carried out.

The CIA could be involved in the recent "Taliban" attacks on Pakistani institutions. Who knows? In some cases, the Afghan "Taliban" could be CIA mercenaries.

In Feb. 2008, the British were caught planning a training camp for the Taliban in Southern Afghanistan supposedly to make them "change sides." Karzai expelled two top British "diplomats." (Independent.co.uk)

THE HIDDEN AGENDA

All wars are charades. This is true of the world wars, the Cold War, Korea, Vietnam, 9-11 and the current war on terror. The human race is caught in a hologram controlled by the Illuminati Rothschild central bankers.

I'm not an expert on the politics of the Asian subcontinent. But it appears that the Afghanistan war should be seen in a larger regional context. Zbigniew Brzezinski advocated a "global-zone of percolating violence," that included Central Asia, Turkey, southern Russia, and the western borders of China. It also included the entire Middle East, the Persian Gulf (Iran), Afghanistan and Pakistan.

The plan to destabilize this vast area was outlined in Brzezinski's book, *"The Grand Chessboard"* (1997) . Ostensibly, the purpose was to prevent Russia from becoming an imperial power again. But that doesn't make sense.

What do these countries have in common? They are Muslim. Islam is the last redoubt of faith in God. The Illuminati are Satanists. Put two and two together.

The Afghan war has some immediate "benefits" to the bankers: perpetual war, arms spending, drugs, pipelines etc. But it is part of a larger "war of civilizations" designed to pit Christians against Muslims, and degrade and destroy Islam. Look for it to expand and go on forever.

Latest! "Taliban Using New US Ammo"
http://www.presstv.com/detail.aspx?id=110932&ionid=351020403

US Army Pays Taliban for Security
http://www.guardian.co.uk/world/2009/nov/13/us-trucks-security-taliban

On a related note, citing current and former U.S. officials, *The New York Times* reported Oct. 28, 2009 that the brother of Afghan President Hamid Karzai has been getting regular payments from the Central Intelligence Agency.

"Ahmed Wali Karzai is a suspected player in Afghanistan's opium trade and has been paid by the CIA over the past eight years for services that included helping to recruit an Afghan paramilitary force that operates at the CIA's direction in and around the southern city of Kandahar," the newspaper reported.

And lest we forget — from *The New Yorker,* (21/1/02)

November 14-25, 2001: US Secretly Authorizes Airlift of Pakistani and Taliban Fighters

At the request of the Pakistani government, the US secretly allows rescue flights into the besieged Taliban stronghold of Kunduz, in Northern Afghanistan, to save Pakistanis fighting for the Taliban (and against US forces) and bring them back to Pakistan.